FROM HISTORICITY
TO FICTIONALITY

The Chinese Poetics
of Narrative

From Historicity to Fictionality

THE CHINESE POETICS
OF NARRATIVE

Sheldon Hsiao-peng Lu

Stanford University Press
Stanford, California

Stanford University Press
Stanford, California
© 1994 by the Board of Trustees
of the Leland Stanford Junior University

Printed in the United States of America

CIP data appear at the end of the book

Stanford University Press publications are
distributed exclusively by Stanford University
Press within the United States, Canada, and
Mexico; they are distributed exclusively by
Cambridge University Press throughout the
rest of the world.

*Dedicated to my mother, Lin Peidan,
and to the memory of my father, Lu Zhi*

ACKNOWLEDGMENTS

This study was first conceived and written from spring 1989 to summer 1990 as my doctoral dissertation in comparative literature at Indiana University. Since then, I have worked on parts of the project intermittently when circumstances allowed. The weight of my initial textual analysis was on T'ang fiction. In summer 1992, I wrote what is now Chapter 6, "From Historicity to Verisimilitude: The Emergence of a Poetics of Fiction in China," which focuses on materials from late imperial China. Consequently, the scope and orientation were changed. Further revisions, cuts, and additions were made after I established contact with Stanford University Press.

As this manuscript goes to press, I take the opportunity to express my gratitude to the people who have offered me help and guidance at the various stages of my education, my career, and the writing of this book.

Thanks are due my teachers at Indiana University: David Bleich, Matei Calinescu, Y. J. Chih, Claus Clüver, Eugene Eoyang, Clifford Flanigan, Irving Lo, Thomas Sebeok, Lynn Struve, and many others. Some provided direct guidance when I began working on the monograph, and all transmitted knowledge to me, gave me emotional support, and played a major role in my intellectual development. I am especially indebted to Eugene Eoyang, who directed my graduate studies and encouraged my scholarly inquiries.

I thank Andrew H. Plaks of Princeton University for reading early drafts of the manuscript, for his kind encouragement, and his invaluable criticisms of my work. I thank Cecile Chu-chin Sun, Cho-yun Hsu, Anthony C. Yu, and Zhang Longxi for reading the manuscript and offering helpful comments. I thank John R. Ziemer of Stanford University Press for his interest in my work, for his meticulous copyediting of the manuscript, which saved me from numerous embarrassing errors, and for his many insightful suggestions for revision. I am grateful to Han Jining at Indiana University, whose expertise in computer science helped me solve many editing problems in the writing process.

I am profoundly indebted to Feng Lan for her support in completing this book. In moments of stress and despair, she comforted me and urged me to keep working and not waste precious time. I owe a debt of gratitude to my uncle C. C. Lin of the University of Wisconsin at Madison. He was responsible for my education in America, and he has supported my pursuit of literary studies. Last but not least, it is to my mother, Lin Peidan, that I owe my love of antiquity, the classical Chinese language, and classical Chinese literature. She was my first teacher, and to her I dedicate my first book.

S.H.-P.L.

Contents

FROM HISTORICITY
TO FICTIONALITY

*The Chinese Poetics
of Narrative*

Introduction

A seventh-century Chinese catalogue of books lists the titles of
817 historical works. These diverse "histories" are classified
into thirteen categories in the following order: (1) 67 official histories (*cheng-shih*); (2) 34 ancient histories (*ku-shih*); (3) 72 miscellaneous histories (*tsa-shih*); (4) 27 histories of hegemonies (*pa-
shih*); (5) 44 daily records of emperors' activities (*ch'i-chü chu*); (6)
25 records of past events (*chiu-shih p'ien*); (7) 27 books on official
titles and government offices (*chih-kuan p'ien*); (8) 59 books on
ritual (*i-chu p'ien*); (9) 35 books on laws and penalties (*hsing-fa
p'ien*); (10) 217 miscellaneous biographies (*tsa-chuan*); (11) 139
geographies (*ti-li chih chi*); (12) 41 genealogies (*tieh-hsi p'ien*); and
(13) 30 bibliographies (*pu-lu p'ien*) (Wei et al., 953–96).

Modern scholars interested in studying the nature and variety
of Chinese narrative writings may be perplexed by this catalogue
of "histories."[1] One may wonder about the rationales behind this
enigmatic system of classification and the range of historical discourse in China. What are the criteria for differentiating and cate-
gorizing historical texts? Where, for example, is the line drawn to
separate "official histories" and "miscellaneous histories" and are
all works outside "official histories" "miscellaneous histories"?
Apparently not, for other kinds of histories beyond the seeming
dichotomy of official/miscellaneous are also listed. If subject matter is a crucial criterion for the Chinese bibliographers, what then
of the categories "ancient histories" and "records of past events,"
which seem to imply a treatment of historical events as historical
events outside any particular category? Is there any connection
between "miscellaneous histories" and "miscellaneous biographies"? Why indeed are ritual books, geographical works, legal

documents, books of official titles, genealogies, and bibliographies all considered historical writings?

The catalogue of histories from the "Ching-chi chih" (Bibliographic treatise) of the *Sui-shu* (History of the Sui) serves to remind us of the scope and complexity of the Chinese narrative tradition. The modern scholar has to wrestle with the peculiar terminologies and characteristics of a long and diverse tradition of narrative writing. The purpose of the present investigation is precisely to describe the features and assumptions of what might be called the traditional Chinese "poetics of narrative."[2] Such an inquiry implies the tracing of the persistent and major conventions and strategies of reading and interpreting narrative works, historical or fictional, in pre-modern China. This study attempts a theoretical reconstruction of how the Chinese have historically read and thought about narrative and raises questions regarding Chinese assumptions and conceptions of the nature and characteristics of narrative.[3]

One of the most remarkable developments in Western literary studies in the past several decades has been the explosion of interest in "narrative theory" or the study of narrative in general. This twentieth-century Western poetics of narrative grows out of the unique philosophical and literary background of the West, beginning with the comments of Plato and Aristotle.

In the Chinese literary tradition, however, the generic category of narrative is conspicuously absent from critical discussions. As is evident from the list of histories given above, Chinese critics, bibliographers, and historians have observed their own systems of literary classification. Many examples of what could be taken as narratives have been treated, not without good reason, as types of "histories" or varieties of "philosophical discourse" in China.

Because of these differences in approach, the first two chapters of this study are devoted to the clarification of some important terms. How are terms such as "narrative," "history," and "fiction" defined, used, and conceptualized in the West? What is the Chinese approach to them or their approximate equivalents? What are the presuppositions and expectations of traditional Chinese critics and scholars when they discuss these terms and concepts? Are there deep-seated ideological, epistemological, and aesthetic underpinnings to their solutions to these issues?

The Western tradition may provide a good backdrop to better

understand the Chinese counterpart. My hope is in part to discover the rules of "discursive regularity" that govern the definition, classification, genesis, and reading of narrative discourse. The divergences and similarities in the "order of narrative discourse" embedded in the literary traditions of China and the West point to differences in their conceptions of what constitutes the unity of discourse and to differences in their mechanisms for controlling the formation, spread, and reception of various discourses. A better sense of the Chinese appreciation of the problem will surely contribute to a more general, cross-cultural, and comparative poetics of narrative.

In defining and "rectifying" key names and terms, my overall purpose is to trace important phases in the development and evolution of the Chinese poetics of narrative. Ideas and assumptions about narrative appear, change, and develop in a critical history over two thousand years old. I will attempt to give a diachronic account of the emergence of and important changes in Chinese conventions of reading narrative works from the earliest times down to the Ming and Ch'ing. More specifically, what will be described in Chapters 2 through 6 is the evolution from a history-centered "narrative theory" to a fiction-centered poetics—the change from "historicity" to "fictionality," so to speak.

It is a gradual change over a long period of time from an emphasis on historical authenticity and factual accuracy to the toleration and recognition of invention and fabrication in the production and reception of narrative texts. Until quite late in the Chinese tradition, most literary theorists adopted a "historical" approach to narrative. Notions and theories of narrative were essentially based on the model of historical narratives. More often than not, fictional narratives were theorized and judged in accordance with the standards of historical narratives. Historical interpretation remained the predominant mode of reading narrative works. Narrative was history, and fiction was unofficial, defective history. At this stage, the Chinese poetics of narrative was the "poetics of historiography" despite the existence and popularity of countless fictional narratives. Historiography taught one the goals, norms, and methods of composing narrative. An independent poetics of fiction did not appear until late imperial China.

The idea of narration is as common in China as it is in the West.

"Narrative," however, rarely appears as a generic category in Chinese literary systems and genre studies. For most of Chinese history, historical writing remains the predominant narrative genre. Chinese "literary" anthologies may contain such narrative or quasi-narrative genres as the elegy, the epitaph, the "career account" (*hsing-chuang*), and the fictional biography, but never examples of works in historical genres.[4]

For a glimpse of the range of narratives, one must turn to the Chinese bibliographer-historians concerned with the types and varieties of historical and quasi-historical writings. They had their own procedures for organizing writings and establishing the unity of discourse based on an institutional conception of writing. Literary works were conceived as social institutions that recorded and reported events and fulfilled representational as well as moral-didactic purposes. Official history in the form of dynastic history was indisputably the master narrative discourse; other narrative genres appeared minor in comparison. Chinese historiography developed a system of representation that privileged a faithful, straightforward recording and a reproduction of external reality in compliance with the sanctioned, official worldview. In certain respects, historical writings provided the prototypes, plots, themes, and characters used and transformed by "fictional" writings. The study of narrative in the Chinese case sometimes takes the shape of the enumeration and classification of types of historical and quasi-historical discourses.

It has been pointed out[5] that the prevailing historical mentality may have prevented Chinese "fiction" or "fictional narrative" from receiving the kind of favorable reception seen in some other cultures, such as India. Although popular attitudes toward fiction began to change after the arrival of Buddhism in China, the official position on fiction remained essentially the same. *Hsiao-shuo*, the approximate equivalent of "fiction" in Chinese, was regarded as a political force, a mode of discourse, and ideological persuasion.[6]

In philosophers' discussions and the bibliographies of literature compiled by historians, the meaning of *hsiao-shuo* ranged from "gossip" to "petty occupation" to "minor discourse" to "heterodoxy." It was considered either a form of writing beneath the dignity of the literati or as a discourse potentially subversive of orthodox views. At best, *hsiao-shuo* might serve as "unofficial history," "deficient history," or "supplemental history," whose sources, records, and accounts were unreliable from the standpoint of the rationalistic, empirical, and historical mind.

Throughout Chinese history, great efforts were made to control fictional discourse by suppression (censorship) or disavowal (denigration and trivialization). In the historians' catalogues and classifications, fiction was relegated to the margins of discourse and downgraded to the lower ranks of writing. The difference between history and fiction was no longer solely the dichotomy of fact and invention, actuality and probability, or literal truth and imaginative truth. The line separating them was, to a large extent, between canonical and non-canonical texts, between officially sanctioned discourse and non-official discourse, between orthodoxy and heterodoxy.

I will argue that there is a single continuous tradition of historical interpretation in the reading of Chinese narrative, both historical and fictional, and that this tradition still exists. The Chinese historical approach is but another major way of establishing the unity of discourse. I will further argue that within the Chinese historical approach are two further polarities: historical interpretation and the "poetics of historiography." Both are strategies to assimilate, recuperate, and naturalize narrative discourse. Of the two, historical interpretation is the more important in the Chinese tradition. Confucian historical hermeneutics first emerged from the exegesis of the *Ch'un-ch'iu* (Spring and autumn annals), the chronicles of the state of Lu, traditionally attributed to Confucius and thought to contain his judgments on historical events. It became the dominant tradition of historical interpretation and was applied to the reading of all forms of narrative. It supplied interpretive procedures that allowed one to impose sense, meaning, and order on texts. The task of reading was to go beyond the surface manifestations of the text to its deeper significance. Interpretation moved from the manifest level of the seemingly impartial, objective record to the hidden moral, ideological, and political pattern. In reading one uncovered the meaning of history from the records of contingent, meaningless events. This Confucian hermeneutics was frequently carried over to the analysis of Chinese "novels" by Ming and Ch'ing critics of *hsiao-shuo*.

Given the underlying moral-historical vision in Chinese historical discourse, practicing historians opted for direct, straightforward recording to remain faithful to events. The descriptive realism of official historiography produces an atmosphere of verisimilitude or, better still, a "reality effect." Official dynastic histories incorporate significant portions of "unprocessed" primary materials, historical data, and original documents. Readers of such histories are left with an impression of the authenticity of the historical materials and the factuality of the recorded events. Official historiography is made to appear to be a record and transcription of the real. The historians believed that the morals of human relations were somehow grounded in the very transparency of historical discourse. They treated language as though it stands for, is identical with, and is equivalent to the world. Such historiography naturalizes the arbitrariness of the sign and posits an identity between the "signifier" and the "signified." What has been said about European realist writing may also serve as an apt criticism of aspects of traditional Chinese historiography.

> The identity between signifier and signified which is established in realist writing is the precondition of its ability to represent a *vraisemblable*, an accepted natural view of the world. It does not mean that all writing is absolutely transparent, but rather that the narration, the dominant discourse, is able to establish itself as Truth. The narration does not appear to be the voice of an author; its source appears to be a true reality which speaks. (Coward and Ellis, 49)

But what is backgrounded in historiography is an intricate and ideologically motivated system of organizing historical materials that conforms to specific views of human beings and reality. The effects of *vraisemblance* do not succeed in concealing the entrenched structure of legitimation and the establishment of subjects. Historiography is far from being the natural discourse it might seem at first; rather, it is nothing less than an ideology, "a system (with its own logic and rigor) of representations (images, myths, ideas or concepts . . .) endowed with a historical existence and role within a given society" (Althusser, *For Marx*, 231).

Could the system of historical representation, historical hermeneutics, and the historian's conception of literary discourse also apply to "unofficial histories" and "defective histories"? The T'ang and Sung periods produced a large quantity of fictional narratives.

The short story (fictional biography, *ch'uan-ch'i*) especially flourished. However, the understanding of the nature of fictional discourse did not fundamentally change. The strategies and conventions of reading narratives remained basically the same as those in previous times. Historical interpretation persisted to a large degree in the reading of fiction in this period.

A noticeable generic intersection between history and fiction at this point is the Chinese biography, a literary form first established in official historiography. It later becomes an important genre of fiction. The historical biography was readily understood within a familiar horizon of generic, literary, and ideological expectations. The question is whether such a horizon or a set of norms was also operative in the reading of the fictional biography, for a preconditioned horizon of expectations must be available to orient the reader's understanding and reception.

My reconstruction of the horizons of expectations in the T'ang suggests that there were two major modes of reading the fictional biography: historical and allegorical. The historical and allegorical modes are nothing more than conventions of interpreting and making familiar fictional texts. The historical mode reads fiction as history. It applies the criteria of historical writing to fictional writing. A fictional unofficial biography becomes acceptable if it appears so sufficiently real and "historical" that it is believed to be history by readers. Fiction writers often take pains to imitate the rhetoric of the historian and to adopt narrative devices that evoke an aura of historicity and factuality in a biography.

When the historical mode of reading is no longer applicable, one moves to the allegorical mode. In this mode, the events depicted are not regarded as literally true and historically real. The stories are read as signifying a didactic message beyond the literal level of the text. They are true, useful, and edifying on moral and philosophical levels.

Stories that can be interpreted neither historically nor allegorically become inexplicable, "fantastic." The "fantastic" was not really a mode of reading among the literati but a term that we can use to describe, in retrospect, the nature of some fictional texts at this time. The fictional biography appears to have resisted being appropriated by Confucian historical hermeneutics and caused a "horizonal change" in generic expectations.

The T'ang fictional biography often describes the transgression of identities and prescribed roles, mixes the natural and the supernatural, and depicts the individual in crisis, at the threshold of two orders of reality. The stories suspend the ordinary spatio-temporal continuum, question the validity of historical rationality, and introduce alternative versions of reality beyond the conventionally real. They mix different social voices, various religious systems, and time schemes. (In contrast, characters of diverse beliefs and professions in a historical narrative are all pre-arranged and narrated from a unified, all-encompassing, and totalizing Confucian conception of history and society.) Fictional scenes become parodies of the "imaginary identifications" of the subjects in official historical discourse.

Unlike historical biography, fictional biography delegitimizes and decenters the subject. The reader, along with the characters, experiences a sense of ideological indeterminacy and cultural disorientation. At the level of discourse itself, there occurs an asymmetry and disjunction between the signifier and the signified. The signifying process disturbs the fixity of the sign and the stability of the position of the subject. And at the interpretive level, an incongruence opens between the dominant Confucian historical mode of literary interpretation and the new horizons opened by the rise of fiction. Fictional discourse makes apparent both the limitation of the historical paradigm of reading narrative discourse and the dissolution of the Confucian subject/character.

One may say that the discourse of Chinese fiction coordinates a conjunction of varied ideological positions. Confucian orthodoxy, the authority of the Classics, historical discourse, and the heterodoxies (Taoism and Buddhism) all make their own claims in the heteroglossia of the text. The representation of the subject as a homogeneous, self-contained being is seriously challenged in such a multi-voiced discourse. What one sees in the fictional biography is not the integration of the Confucian protagonist into an organic society but his step-by-step decomposition amid competing ideologies. A T'ang character may—Proteus-like—assume the "identity" of human / insect / governor / Taoist recluse; the character doubles, triples, and multiplies itself, and experiences many metamorphoses. The subject is unable to come to terms with itself because of the shifting and multiple frames of reference in the world.

Beset by diverse ideological persuasions, the characters in T'ang tales are unable to arrive at a homogeneous, centered self. The dialogic juxtaposition of clashing ideologies in the text generates an unmasking of ideologies and initiates a retreat from ideology itself. But to say that the T'ang tale, like all works of art, is inextricably linked to ideology is not the same as reducing it to ideology. It is a truism that the literary structure "reflects and refracts the reflections and refractions of other ideological spheres (ethics, epistemology, political doctrines, religion, etc.)" (Bakhtin and Medvedev, 16–17). We should, however, allow some latitude for a relationship of disjunction and difference as well as one of conjunction and identity between official ideology and fictional discourse. One still needs to address the specific components of the T'ang tale that are critical of the official ideology. In the fictional biography, there is a retreat, an internal distanciation, from the very ideology from which it emerges, that is, from the ideology of historiography. In one of his dialectic formulations of the problem, Althusser writes: "What art makes us *see*, and therefore gives to us in the form of '*seeing*,' '*perceiving*' and '*feeling*' (which is not the form of *knowing*), is the *ideology* from which it is born, in which it bathes, from which it detaches itself as art, and to which it alludes" (Althusser, *Lenin and Philosophy*, 222). Although inescapably bound to the dominant ideology of the official biography, the fictional biography attempts to detach itself from and expose that very ideology. The reader is permitted an inside view of the ideological underpinnings of the biographical form in the experience of reading fiction.

A story's disengagement from the Confucian ideals of eminent civic service as expounded in historiography must nevertheless be expressed in the very form of historiographical discourse, the biography. By achieving self-reflexivity, the text makes the historical mode of representation the object of representation in fiction. A story raises to a conscious level the problems and dilemmas of the historical representation of human beings. As suggested by the felicitous title of one specific T'ang tale, "Biography of the Governor of the South Branch" ("Nan-k'o t'ai-shou chuan"), the fictional biography constitutes an inter-generic parody as well as a self-parody of the standard tale of the Confucian official. This tale uses historical discourse to present a deluding, "farcical," and imaginary representation of the subject's real condition of existence. Fiction parodies the direct word, the monologic voice, and the one-dimensional image of life as presented in historical discourse. By exaggerating certain generic features of historical representation, it points to its generic conventionality and reveals the absurd aspects of the biographical form. An internal bipolarization in the mode of representation/signification occurs within the biographical form itself. The fictional biography signifies that which is otherwise excluded by the very system of signification. It stretches the biographical form to its limits, explodes its narrow framework, restructures its system of signification, and consequently enlarges the extent of the signifiable.

The dominance of the historical approach to narrative discourse inhibited the appearance of a theory of fiction. The emergence and flourishing of a poetics of fiction in the Ming and Ch'ing result from a long, slow, but inevitable process of "dehistoricization." Up to the Ming, Chinese theorists of narrative had been most concerned with issues of historicity in narrative. With the widespread popularity of vernacular fiction in the last two dynasties of Chinese history, critics finally came to terms with the nature and characteristics of fiction, that is, with "fictionality." People began to recognize short stories and novels as fictional products rather than defective, unofficial forms of history. Critics acknowledged the fictionality of *hsiao-shuo* without attaching pejorative connotations to it. Eminent critics such as Li Chih, Yeh Chou, Chin Sheng-t'an, Mao Tsung-kang, Chang Chu-p'o, and Chih-yen Chai noted and studied the formal, aesthetic features of popular novels. Their commentaries on the major novels represent the full flourishing of Chinese poetics of fiction.

As critics moved away from the norms and criteria of historiography and formulated a set of terms to discuss fictive narrative works, a new conception of the true and the real in narrative discourse emerged. Earlier, in historiography, the real had meant what actually happened. Truth required that historical writing be based on real events. Only what really happened was worth recording. Whatever did not happen was untrue and had to be relegated to the domains of gossip and fabrication. In the new poetics of fiction, however, events did not have to be historically verifiable. "Verisimilitude" replaced "historicity" as the criterion of truthfulness. A truthful narrative is not necessarily based on historical events; rather, it is one that succeeds in creating a vivid and lifelike world of its own. Theorists advanced several justifications for this type of fiction. First, the literary game is itself sufficient raison d'être. Second, good fiction can penetrate the nature and feelings (*ch'ing*) of human beings in ways other types of writings cannot. Finally, the reader is able to discover the uttermost principles (*li*) of life in fiction just as in the Confucian classics and historical writings.

By this stage, the Chinese poetics of narrative has moved from being centered on *shih* (historicity) to being centered on *ch'ing* and *li*; that is, it has moved away from a historiography based on authentic historical events to an aesthetics that focuses on the depiction of realistic human emotions and truthful principles. Narrative is no longer restricted solely to the function of being a "factual record" (*shih-lu*) or "credible history" (*hsin-shih*). Its existence is justified because it conjures up a world that is lifelike, credible, and, "verisimilar" (some of the most frequently used Chinese terms are *pi-chen* [lit., closing in on the real], *hsiao-hsiang* [resembling the image], and *ch'uan-shen* [transmitting the spirit]).

At this point, in terms of the study of cross-cultural poetics, one may note a parallel between the flourishing of a poetics of fiction in Ming China and a similar trend in the West during the Renaissance. The rediscovery of Aristotle's *Poetics* led to a new justification for writing fiction and poetry and the appearance of "defenses" of and "apologies" for fictive writings that cleared poets of the charges of fabrication and lying. The standards of verisimilitude, *vraisemblance*, the "probable," and the "credible" replaced strict fidelity to history.

A comparative poetics of narrative in China and the West, the persistent patterns in the Chinese poetics of narrative, its important moments of change, and the long and steady evolution from history to fiction—these are the issues to which I now turn.

1

Rectifying the Terms, I

"NARRATIVE," "HISTORY," AND "FICTION" IN THE WEST

Idols of the Theatre, or of Systems, are many, and
there can be and perhaps will be yet many more.
—Bacon, *The New Organon*, 90

At the beginning of the "Introduction to the Structural Analysis of Narratives," Roland Barthes posited the universality of narrative in all cultures of the world: "Narrative is present in every age, in every place, in every society; it begins with the very history of mankind and there nowhere is nor has been a people without narrative. . . . Narrative is international, transhistorical, transcultural: it is simply there, like life itself" (*Image—Music—Text*, 79). Whatever the truth of this statement, the category of narrative itself is far from universal. In looking beyond the Western literary tradition, one immediately notices the conventionality and arbitrariness of the category of narrative—a concept defined in the specific contexts of Western thinking but extended, by Western scholars and scholars trained in the West, to the analysis of literary works in other parts of the world.

One of the most perplexing dilemmas in cross-cultural literary studies is the absence of any ancient literary system centered on narrative. Earl Miner, a scholar of Japanese and comparative literature, claims that the majority of the world's critical systems originated in a definition of literature out of lyric. The Greek system was unique in beginning with the concept of mimesis and in making drama the center of literary theory. "What seems to defy explanation is the absence of a critical system defined from narrative" (Miner, 353).

In the Chinese literary tradition, there is a profusion of writings that would be called "narratives" from a Western viewpoint. Modern Chinese scholars themselves do not hesitate and sometimes prefer to use the Western notion of narrative in dealing with ancient Chinese literature. But until modern times, the Chinese did not have a generic concept equivalent to the Western notion of narrative. They had their own systems for classifying literature. Since the T'ang dynasty, the majority of bibliographers had divided writings into four categories, each with numerous subdivisions. What might be labeled narratives today had been variously and overlappingly grouped under one of the four major categories: "classics" (*ching*), "historical writings" (*shih*), "philosophical writings" (*tzu*), and "belles lettres" (*chi*). Narrative was hardly to be found as an organizing generic principle in this framework. The Chinese had an increasingly acute awareness of dozens of types of histories and numerous genres of "fiction" (*hsiao-shuo*), but they rarely imagined calling them narratives.

For the present study, however, it seems unnecessary to prove or deny the existence of narrative from an essentialist perspective by invoking Western or Chinese authorities. My focus is rather on the contexts and pragmatics of the use and non-use of literary terms. It is more fruitful to probe the question of how generic labels have imposed unity and regularity on discourses. As some have argued, generic conventions "are essentially possibilities of meaning, ways of naturalizing the text and giving it a place in the world which our culture defines" (Culler, *Structuralist Poetics*, 137). Genres or literary types are "institutional imperatives which both coerce and are in turn coerced by the writer" (Wellek and Warren, 226). To assign a corpus of writings to one class of things rather than another is to put it in order, to bring it within perspective, to regulate it, to control it. It is these processes of assimilation, naturalization, and institutionalization that are of interest here.

In imperial China, the definition and classification of modes of discourses were almost exclusively the tasks of historian-bibliographers. Their job was to sort out the vast, heterogeneous output of writings, devise a system of classification, enumerate the possible types, and ensure that every type found a place in the order of discourse. As for texts that appeared unfamiliar and heterodoxical in terms of accepted cultural norms, it was essential that the bibliographer reduce their otherness and eliminate their contingency, or marginalize and trivialize them, through the mechanisms of categorization and classification. The tendency was to delimit the different types of writings by institutional, functional, discursive, and ideological means. The question often centered on how a certain kind of writing might gain a proper social function. The classification of literary types sometimes became a classification of their ideological effects and social utility.

There was also a heightened awareness of literature as an institution. However devious and subversive a discourse might be at the beginning, once it is institutionalized and becomes part of a state apparatus, it is circumscribed, defined, delimited, naturalized, and adopted to the service of the state. For instance, to define a literary genre such as *hsiao-shuo* (fiction) by tracing its roots to the ancient imperial institution of *pai-kuan* (Office of Fiction) is equivalent to setting its generic, social, and political boundaries. To various extents and in different ways, China and the West alike have invented procedures for ordering the formation and proliferation of discourses.

The following analysis is concerned with what Michel Foucault called "discursive formations" and the mechanisms of discursive regularities in the field of literary criticism. In Foucault's words,

> We must grasp the statement in the exact specificity of its occurrence; determine its conditions of existence, fix its limits, establish its correlations with other statements that may be connected with it, and show what other forms of statement it excludes. . . . We must show why it could not be other than it was, in what respect it is exclusive of any other, how it assumes, in the midst of others and in relation to them, a place that no other could occupy. (*Archaeology of Knowledge*, 25)

These are issues of terminologies, names, concepts, and discourses. To paraphrase Confucius, the "rectification of names" has the highest practical, ideological, and political significance.

In this chapter, I review some representative, prevailing, and historically important Western approaches to "narrative," "history," and "fiction." In the next chapter, I discuss the Chinese counterparts. My review of the Western tradition is by no means meant to be exhaustive. My desire is to emphasize those Western ideas that, in providing interesting parallels and sharp contrasts to the Chinese counterparts, help provide a vantage point for the analysis of related issues in the Chinese tradition. I hope that the result will highlight the distinctive Western and Chinese solutions to the problem of defining the varieties of discourses. And more important, the effort of delimiting the nature and range of types and kinds of literary and non-literary discourses may expose the inadequacy and capriciousness of the usual definitions and categories.

The Idea of Narrative in the West

Although one of the most widely used terms in contemporary Western literary criticism, "narrative" is also one of the most loosely defined. For a long period of time following the Renaissance, people could comfortably discuss the nature and characteristics of narrative in the context of a largely Aristotelian literary theory. Recent criticism has questioned the Aristotelian tradition on various grounds. There also exist great disparities between theories of narrative and actual literary practice. Any attempt to achieve generic precision with regard to narrative immediately runs into the kind of impasse confronted by genre theory in general. A clear definition of what constitutes narrative raises more problems than it solves. Often, the setting forth of generic boundaries leads to the destruction of those boundaries and to the further separation of writings.

A classic attempt at defining "narrative" is Northrop Frye's "Theory of Genres" in *Anatomy of Criticism*. Frye speaks of the "radical of presentation," and for him, "the basis of generic criticism in any case is rhetorical, in the sense that the genre is determined by the conditions established between the poet and his public" (247). Similarly, in *The Nature of Narrative*, Robert Scholes and Robert Kellogg adopt the rhetorical approach to defining narrative. Literary works may be classified as narrative if they are distinguished by two characteristics: "For writing to be narrative no more and no less than a teller and a tale are required" (4).

In *Narrative Discourse*, Gérard Genette pays more attention to the nuances of the term *narrative* and finds that narrative (*récit*) has been variously used in at least three meanings. The first "has *narrative* refer to the narrative statement, the oral or written discourse that undertakes to tell of an event or a series of events" (25). A second meaning "has *narrative* refer to the succession of events, real or fictitious, that are the subjects of this discourse, and to their several relations of linking, opposition, repetition, etc." (25). "A third meaning, apparently the oldest, has *narrative* refer once more to an event: not, however, the event that is recounted, but the event that consists of someone recounting something: the act of narrating taken in itself" (26). The three meanings of narrative are narrative discourse, story (*histoire*), and the act of narrating (*narration*). Narrative in the sense of narrative discourse remains the principal object of study. Yet the analysis of narrative is for Genette a study of the relationships of the three senses of narrative: "a study of the relationships between narrative and story, between narrative and narrating, and (to the extent that they are inscribed in the narrative discourse) between story and narrating" (29).

Modern theorists trace the idea of narrative to Plato and Aristotle, who defined narrative discourse in relation to drama and possibly lyric within the framework of a mimetic theory of literature. In Book III of the *Republic*, Plato distinguishes three ways in which storytellers and poets relate things. They employ either simple narrative (diegesis) or imitation (mimesis) or both (240). The difference between diegesis and mimesis is the difference between narrative and drama. Since art is imitation, drama—as the most imitative mode of art—thus defines the essence of art. Narrative, which mixes direct and indirect discourse, is impure, imperfect imitation and hence a lesser art in comparison to drama. The "pure imitator of virtue" is preferable to the mixed style (244). Although the mixed style is "charming" and "by far the most popular with children and their attendants, and with the masses," "such a style is unsuitable to our State, in which human nature is not twofold or manifold, for one man plays one part only" (244). Plato is especially concerned with the social function of literature. The mixed style of narrative, as opposed to the pure style of drama, appears most attractive to the people and is thus the most pernicious and dangerous to the state.

Aristotle follows Plato in defining art as mimesis, even though he endorses the value of art in the representation of reality. He speaks of "three factors by which the imitative arts are differentiated: their media, the objects they represent, and their manner of representation." As for the manner of representation, "it may be done partly by narration and partly by the assumption of a character other than one's own, which is Homer's way; or by speaking in one's own person without any such change; or by representing the characters as performing all the actions dramatically" (34). Later in the West, these three manners of representation came to be understood as the three "universal" modes of literature: narrative, lyric, and drama. Whatever the answer to the question of whether a "triad" of literary modes is implied in Plato and Aristotle, there seems to be a clear difference between epic (narrative) representation and dramatic representation. The distinguishing hallmark of narrative is the presence of both the voice of the poet and the voice of the characters.

The tendency to define kinds of literature according to the manner of representation or presentation, as first established by Plato and Aristotle, is visible in a great many studies of narrative and genres. Beneath the seeming innocence and transparency of the Aristotelian categories, however, exist fundamental presuppositions about human experience and the nature of knowledge. The definition and characterization of the literary kinds are accompanied by an evaluation and hierarchization of their relative merits. Aristotle declares tragedy (drama) superior to epic (narrative), and although he spells out the differences between the two, he asserts that a narrative plot should be constructed in the same way as a dramatic plot. Narratives "should centre upon a single action, whole and complete, and having a beginning, a middle, and an end . . . like a single complete organism" (Aristotle, 65–66). "Except for noting the consequences of its mode of presentation, Aristotle does not entertain the possibility that a narrative plot, or narratives generally, might be constructed on principles independent of the model of tragedy, principles inherent in narrative as such" (Leitch, 5). In Aristotle's opinion, their multiplication of plots and episodes, their inordinate length, their mixing of modes of presentation make most narrative poems inferior to tragedies. Homer is an exception because, ironically, he is the least narrative and the most dramatic of epic poets. Homer spoke "as little as possible in his own person" and came close to "impersonal representation" (Aristotle, 67–68). The presupposition seems to be that the storyteller should speak as little as possible and allow the story to tell itself— just as a drama does.

Following the rediscovery of Aristotle's *Poetics* in the Renaissance, the distinctness of narrative as a major mode of representation became an important issue. The formal characteristics of narrative were often contrasted to those of drama, and theorists disagreed over which was the superior mode of imitation. One of the clearest formulations of the differences between the two is Lodovico Castelvetro's commentary on the *Poetics*.

The dramatic manner, which, as we said, employs things where the original had things, and words in direct discourse where the original had words, is different from the narrative, first, in that it uses words and things instead of the original words and things, while narrative uses words alone in the place of things and indirect discourse in the place of direct discourse. . . . [The] dramatic method cannot represent places very far apart, while the narrative method joins together places that are widely separated. . . . [The] narrative method joins together diverse times, something the dramatic method cannot do. In addition, there is between them the difference that the narrative method tells things that are visible and invisible, audible and non-audible, and the dramatic represents only things that are visible and audible. (309)

Narrative and drama are here defined as fundamentally different modes of representation. Each has its characteristics, strengths, and disadvantages. The nature of the "narrative method" can be understood in its difference from the "dramatic method."

Francis Bacon was one of the first to use the English word "narrative" to designate a major mode of literature. In *The Advancement of Learning*, Bacon divides "Poesy" into three kinds: *narrative, representative,* and *allusive* or *parabolical.*

The *Narrative* is a mere imitation of history . . . ; choosing for its subject commonly wars and love, rarely [matters of] state, and sometimes pleasure or mirth. *Representative* is as a visible history; and is an image of actions as if they were present, as history is of actions in nature as they are (that is) past. *Allusive* or *Parabolical* is a *Narrative* applied only to express some special purpose or conceit. (83)

In the Latin version of the work, *De Argumentis*, the three divisions of poesy are *narrative, dramatic,* and *parabolical.* "Narrative Poesy is a mere imitation of History, such as might pass for real, only that it commonly exaggerates things beyond probability. Dramatic Poesy is as History made visible; for it represents actions as if they were present, whereas History represents them as past" (440). With Bacon, "narrative" is distinguished from "history" and "philosophy" as belonging to "poesy" and appealing to the "imagination." Within poesy itself, narrative is one of the three major modes.

The triadic division of literature was also observed by the German Romantics, for whom the three irreducible, universal modes of literature were epic (narrative), drama, and lyric. In the words of Goethe, these are the permanent *Naturformen der Dichtung*. Although this triadic division is suspect today, it is invariably observed in literature curricula and the examination system in the universities.

The narrative method and dramatic method imply different ways of writing. Modern American criticism of fiction has maintained a distinction between diegesis ("telling") and mimesis ("showing"). For such critics as Henry James and Percy Lubbock, showing, rather than telling, is the superior mode of fictional presentation. It is demanded of the writer of fiction that the narrator efface his or her existence as completely as possible so that the characters may speak for themselves in the manner of dramatic characters. Although the Chicago neo-Aristotelian critics such as Wayne Booth may be critical of Lubbock's idea of objective, "dramatic" narration, they too adopt a rhetorical approach to fiction by making the question of the author's point of view the central issue in their theory of fiction. (The Western, Aristotelian formula of narrative as drama has been so pervasive that Western or Western-trained critics have censured traditional Chinese fiction for failing to measure up to Western narrative standards, singling out such "defects" as episodic construction, the absence of a consistent point of view, and loose plots.)[1]

Twentieth-century narrative theories feature plot prominently, though in changed forms and under various names, as the form-shaping, organizing principle in storytelling. The Russian formalists distinguish between *fabula* ("fable"), the basic story stuff or chain of events, and *sjuzet* ("plot"), the actual ordering and expression of the story. The structuralist distinction between *histoire* (story) and *discours* (discourse) is another formulation of the dichotomy between the content of the story and the communication of the content. Seymour Chatman points out that there is nothing new in all this; these categories are already found in the *Poetics* in the Aristotelian distinction between *logos* and *mythos*. "For Aristotle, the imitation of actions in the real world, *praxis*, was seen as forming an argument, *logos*, from which were selected (and possibly rearranged) the units that formed the plot, *mythos*" (19).

The features and limitations of the kind of narrative theory outlined above are not difficult to see. It is based, directly or indirectly, on a mimetic view of literature and its formal requirements derive from the drama. The values of unity, coherence, integration, and "imitativeness" (objectivity) are preferred for certain cognitive, epistemological, and aesthetic ends. Especially in the period of Neoclassicism with the positing of the "three unities," drama became the valorized mode of writing, and dramatic representation the paradigm for other modes of representation. The Aristotelian legacy reduced the function and domain of literature to representational literature under the formula *mimesis* is *poiesis*. A large corpus of literature is excluded from Aristotle's poetics for not being representational. One thinks of the lyric and didactic poets: Pindar, Sappho, Hesiod, Archilochos, and so forth. Such a poetics would also exclude, one assumes, such modes of Latin literature as elegies, satires, moral and philosophical reflections, theoretical treatises, essays, letters, and journals. What all these poets and literary modes have in common, as Genette points out, is that "their work does not consist in imitation, by narrative or theatrical representation, of an action, real, or pretended, external to the person and speech of the poet, but simply a discourse spoken by him directly and in his own name" (*Figures of Literary Discourse*, 137). A vast domain of literary discourse is neglected in a mimetic theory of literature.

The rhetorical and mimetic approaches to literary genres have been criticized for their formal demarcations of drama, narrative, and lyric. Generic "universals" and hierarchies are now seen as untenable.[2] For Alastair Fowler, the mistakes "stem from a single misconception of the category of the representational 'modes.'" The "representational mode, in fact, is only one of many elements in a work or a genre. Moreover, it is usual for several representational modes to combine or alternate or mix within a single work. ... Mixture is the rule rather than the exception" (236–37).

The problem lies not only in the formal description of the various modes of discourse, but even more important in the ideological assessment of them. Aristotelian poetics simply valorizes one specific mode of discourse. Its task is to ensure discursive unity and to prevent heterogeneity. It establishes closure, boundaries, and limits around and above narrative discourse. It promotes a unified image of human actions and perpetuates a "monologic" conception of social reality. In rebellion against the theory and practice of such a poetics, Bertolt Brecht developed what he called the non-Aristotelian "epic theater," replacing the old unities with loosely constructed plots, deliberate digressions, and multiple episodes for political, ideological, and aesthetic reasons.

One of the most trenchant critiques of the legacy of Aristotelian narrative theory is found in the work of M. M. Bakhtin. Bakhtin's point of departure is also a rhetorical one in that he distinguishes narrative, drama, and lyric, but his evaluation reverses previous positions. He celebrates "novelistic discourse" because it breaks up the separation of genres and levels of presentation. Novelistic discourse constitutes a dialogic, open-ended, and multi-voiced world. He criticizes the monologic genres of drama and lyric poetry because of their purity and one-dimensionality. "Drama is by its very nature alien to genuine polyphony; drama may be multi-leveled, but it can not contain *multiple worlds*; it permits only one, and not several, systems of measurement" (*Problems of Dostoevsky's Poetics*, 34). Bakhtin regroups literary discourses into two kinds: on one side a centralizing, centripetal, and authoritative force in language and literature is at work; on the other, a decentering, centrifugal, and subversive force. The Western critical tradition has on the whole been determined to guarantee unity, homogeneity, and ready-made truths and to smooth out the rough edges of the subversive, carnivalistic, and critical elements in literary and ideological discourse. In the following sweeping statement, Bakhtin criticizes what he considers the unifying and self-limiting conceptions of language and literature:

Aristotelian poetics, the poetics of Augustine, the poetics of the medieval church, of the "one language of truth," the Cartesian poetics of neoclassicism, the abstract grammatical universalism of Leibniz (the idea of a "universal grammar"), Humboldt's insistence on the concrete—all these, whatever their differences in nuance, give expression to the same centripetal forces in sociolinguistic and ideological life; they serve one and the same project of centralizing and unifying the European languages. The victory of one reigning language (dialect) over the others, the supplanting of languages, their enslavement, the process of illuminating them with the True Word, the incorporation of barbarians and lower social strata into a unitary language of culture and truth, the canonization of ideological systems, philology with its methods of studying and tracing dead languages, languages that were by that very fact "unities," Indo-European linguistics with its focus of attention, directed away from language plurality to a single proto-language—all this determined the content and power of the category of "unitary language" in linguistic and stylistic thought, and determined its creative, style-shaping role in the majority of the poetic genres that coalesced in the channel formed by those same centripetal forces of verbal-ideological life. (*Dialogic Imagination*, 271)

In Bakhtin's view, the high literary genres and "official" languages of epic, tragedy, poetry, and drama present finished images of life and valorize monologic, absolute truths detached from the diversity of contemporary reality. He sees a polyglot linguistic consciousness and stratified literary images in low, "unofficial" literary discourse: varieties of Latin literature, comedy, satire, and the novel. These genres are never pure "direct discourses" but incorporate multiple generic conventions and compositional styles. There exist in these open forms of literary discourse images of images, representations of representations, parodies, and relative visions of the world, "for any and every straightforward genre, any and every direct discourse—epic, tragic, lyric, philosophical—may and indeed must itself become the object of representation, the object of a parodic travestying 'mimicry'" (*Dialogic Imagination*, 55). In the end, the multi-layered reality and the polyphony of social voices embedded in the marginalized low genres contest and challenge the discursive unities and official ideologies of the high canonical genres. Here, Western "narrative theory" becomes an anti-theory that refuses to enclose narrative discourse or "novelistic discourse" within a generic boundary.

Interrelations of History and Fiction in the West

In the *Theory of Literature*, René Wellek and Austin Warren point to a "popular view, disseminated by pedagogues, that the reading of non-fiction was instructive and meritorious, that of fiction, harmful or at best self-indulgent." In comparison to history and philosophy, "imaginative literature is 'fiction,' a lie" (212–13). This suspicion of imaginative writing, fiction, or *Dichtung* in German usage is a long-standing and deeply rooted one in the West. In the following, I first consider some of the philosophical, institutional, and ideological reasons for this view of fiction. I then discuss an opposing, Aristotelian critical tradition that rehabilitates the usefulness of fiction.

The prejudice against fiction began as early as Plato. In the mimetic view of literature, fiction is an inaccurate, deceptive, and socially subversive representation of reality twice removed from the Forms. In the *Sophist*, Plato distinguished two kinds of imitation: the "icastic" (the "making of likenesses") and the "fantastic" (the "making of appearances"). In the first kind of imitation, "a likeness of anything is made by producing a copy which is executed according to the proportions of the original, similar in length and breadth and depth, each thing receiving also its appropriate colour" (384). In the second kind of imitation, sculptors and painters do not reproduce the proportions of the original but distort them so that they look real from a distance.

> In works either of sculpture or of painting, which are of any magnitude, there is a certain degree of deception; for if artists were to give the true proportions of their fair models, the upper part, which is farther off, would appear to be out of proportion in comparison with the lower, which is nearer; and so they give up the truth in their images and make only the proportions which appear to be beautiful, disregarding the real ones.   (384–85)

"Fantastic" imitation is an art of deception. It does not recreate a true likeness to the original but a semblance and an illusion of the original. It is a distortion of the real but appears in the guise of the real. For Plato, the sophists practice exactly this art of appearance-making and lying. They are the deliberate counterfeiters of the

truth and producers of misleading images. Imitation is thus associated with sophistry and deceit right from the beginning of the
Western philosophical tradition.

Saint Augustine's statement in *On Christian Doctrine* that "human institutions are imperfect reflections of natural institutions or
are similar to them" (62) is an expression of the Platonic prejudice
against imitation and invention. Human institutions are useful insofar as they lead to the worship of God; they are deceptive and
dangerous to the extent that they create fictions, superstitions, false
images, and idols. Augustine advises particular caution in regard
to imaginative writing and verisimilitude in works of art.

When pictures or statues are concerned, or other similar imitative works,
especially when executed by skilled artists, no one errs when he sees the
likeness, so that he recognizes what things are represented. And all things
of this class are to be counted among the superfluous institutions of men
except when it is important to know concerning one of them why, where,
when, and by whose authority it is made. Then there are thousands of
imagined fables and falsehoods by whose lies men are delighted, which are
human institutions.   (61–62)

If not put to good use, art becomes a "superfluous" institution
disseminating fictions, fables, and falsehoods. Human beings are
quite susceptible to the charms of these fabrications and misrepresentations. Art is a subversive human institution if not properly
guided.[3]

In his *Novum Organon* (New science), Francis Bacon introduced his famous "four classes of Idols which beset men's minds"
(76). The Idols of the Tribe, the Idols of the Cave, the Idols of the
Market-place, and the Idols of the Theatre are false notions that
infect the human understanding. They are like a "false mirror,
which, receiving rays irregularly, distorts and discolours the nature
of things" (*New Organon*, 77). For Bacon, the Idols of the Market-
place are the most pernicious and the most deeply rooted in people's minds. These idols are formed by human intercourse and
association. "For it is by discourse that men associate, and words
are imposed according to the apprehension of the vulgar. And
therefore the ill and unfit choice of words wonderfully obstructs
the understanding" (78). This class of idols arises from the inherent

nature of language. The existing structure of language, with its ill-defined and confusing words, names, and terms, imposes itself upon the human mind and causes misunderstanding.

> But the *Idols of the Market-place* are the most troublesome of all: idols which have crept into the understanding through the alliances of words and names. For men believe that their reason governs words; but it is also true that words react on the understanding. . . . Now words, being commonly framed and applied according to the capacity of the vulgar, follow those lines of division which are most obvious to the vulgar understanding. And whenever an understanding of greater acuteness or a more diligent observation would alter those lines to suit the true divisions of nature, words stand in the way and resist change.   (86–87)

For Bacon, "words" shape thought and language is a mold in which the human mind is inescapably cast. Bacon distinguishes two categories of Idols of the Market-place:

> The idols imposed by words on the understanding are of two kinds. They are either names of things which do not exist (for as there are things left unnamed through lack of observation, so likewise are there names which result from fantastic suppositions and to which nothing in reality corresponds), or they are names of things which exist, but yet confused and ill-defined, and hastily and irregularly derived from realities.   (87)

The "fantastic suppositions," nonexistent entities, and the "confused and ill-defined" names are to be discarded in the new science. The non-correspondence of names and reality and the cross-signification of words are a source of confusion and error. These idols can be said to be, to borrow the title of a work by the seventeenth-century English essayist Thomas Browne, a *pseudodoxia epidemica*, a catalogue of human error and superstition that tells us something about human waywardness, fantasies, weaknesses, and wish-fulfillment.

It was also the opinion of John Locke that the task of philosophical investigation is to do away with "obscure," "confused," "fantastical," "inadequate," and "false" ideas and to get rid of the "imperfections" and "abuses" of words. In *An Essay Concerning Human Understanding*, Locke defined *fantastical* or *chimerical* ideas as those that "have no foundation in nature, nor have any conformity with that reality of being to which they are tacitly referred, as to their archetypes" (181). "*Inadequate ideas* are such which are but a partial or incomplete representation of those archetypes to which they are referred" (183). These fantastical and inadequate ideas hinder efforts to arrive at a true understanding of the nature of things. What is needed is nothing less than a "rectification of names." Ideas should be "clear," "distinct, "real," "adequate," and "true." Locke makes the "doctrine of signs" or logic one of the three divisions of science along with natural philosophy and ethics. The business of the "doctrine of signs" is to "consider the nature of signs the mind makes use of for the understanding of things, or conveying its knowledge to others" (385). The purpose is to ensure that words and ideas are accurate rather than "fantastical" representations of things.

The strength of the Platonic tradition of denigrating fiction is indicated by Renaissance critics' perceived need to defend fiction and write apologies for it under the aegis of Aristotle's *Poetics*. Writers such as Boccaccio, Scaliger, Sidney, and Mazzoni argued that poetry is not frivolous and poets are not liars. Aristotle's discussion of the relationship between history and poetry became a source of inspiration for the defenders of imaginative writing. Francis Bacon, for example, divided learning into three parts: history, poesy, and philosophy. He defined poesy as *feigned history*, which could be in either prose or verse. Bacon makes the following distinctions between true history and feigned history:

Therefore, because the acts or events of *true history* have not that magnitude that satisfieth the mind of man, *poesy* feigneth acts and events greater and more heroical: because *true history* propoundeth the successes and issues of actions not so agreeable to the merits of virtue and vice, therefore poesy feigns them more just in retribution, and more according to revealed providence: because true history representeth actions and events more ordinary, and less interchanged, therefore poesy endueth them with more rareness, and more unexpected and alternative variations: so as it appeareth that poesy serveth and conferreth to magnanimity, morality, and to delectation. And therefore it was ever thought to have some participation of divineness, because it doth raise and erect the mind, by submitting the shows of things to the desires of the mind; whereas reason doth buckle and bow the mind into the nature of things. (*Advancement of Learning*, 82–83)

Bacon here affirms the value of poesy vis-à-vis history. "Feigned history" is able to lift acts and events from the narrow scope of "true history" to moral and aesthetic levels more satisfying to the mind. Poetry is more agreeable and more "according to revealed providence" than the ordinary facts of history can be. It is even more ennobling and edifying than reason, which "doth buckle and bow the mind to the nature of things." The Aristotelian idea that poetry is philosophically higher than history seems to be the warrant for this discussion.

Bacon's celebration of "feigned history" is matched only by his own enthusiasm for a true history of nature in all its aspects. In *Preparative Towards a Natural and Experimental History*, Bacon catalogues 130 kinds of natural histories. In *The Advancement of Learning*, he calls for a history of marvels, "a substantial and severe collection of the *heteroclites* or *irregulars* of *nature*, well examined and described" (70). From this history, Bacon would not altogether exclude the "superstitious narrations of sorceries, witchcrafts, dreams, divinations, and the like, where there is an assurance and clear evidence of the fact" (71). Bacon's unusual openness to the "instances of exception to general kinds" in his inquisition of truth is certainly not a de facto acceptance of popular "superstitious narrations." In his overall scientific and philosophical project, the investigation of marvels and irregularities leads to the clearing away of those fictions and idols that obstruct the true understanding of nature.

Bacon's "true history" and "feigned history" can be seen as analogues to "historical narrative" and "fictional narrative" in the poetics of narrative. Today in the West, it is customary to speak of historical narrative and fictional narrative as two subdivisions of narrative. As we will see, the relationship between historiography and fiction is extremely meaningful and even fundamental in the study of the Chinese "narrative" tradition. The opposition between historical and fictional discourse may, however, not be an important issue in pre-modern times in the West. According to Lionel Gossman, "For a long time the relationship of history to literature was not notably problematic. *History was a branch of literature.* It was not until the meaning of the word literature, or the institution of literature itself began to change, toward the end of the eighteenth century, that history came to appear as something distinct from literature" (23). True as the observation might be, it requires a closer examination of the specific meanings of history and historical discourse in order to clarify the question. The relationship between history and fiction or between history and literature has been a complicated one. The terms of differentiation and criteria of truth have not always been the same and may differ from those of our present analytic framework.

The ancient Greek word *histor* was used either to refer to someone known for an ability to distinguish which of two conflicting accounts was correct, or, used as an adjective, to attribute that capacity to someone.[4] The verb *historein* seems to have been derived from *histor*. It indicates the activity characteristic of the *histor*, the activity of finding out or inquiring into the correct account. The noun *historia* indicates an inquiry into a matter. After Herodotus published his account of the Persian Wars under the title *Historiai* (Histories), *historia* came increasingly to indicate the results of inquiring and written accounts of events. The Greek word *historia*, and its Latin transliteration *historia*, meant primarily an informational account and was considered a literary genre with its rules and styles, canons of greatness, and political, professional, or moral utility. Hence, history had the sense of *story*. History also came to have the meaning of *the past*. Before Saint Augustine, history was neither a philosophical problem nor a category of reality. "The ancients' theory of history was limited largely to questions of technique and presentation" (Unger, 63).

History was understood as a branch of literature and rhetoric, and the criteria of accuracy and truth were maintained. History was distinguished from fable and taken to be a true, informational account of events. Thucydides, whose work has been regarded as the beginning of Western "scientific" historiography, adopted the principle of authenticating evidence and made a clear distinction between a truthful and a false account. In explaining his principles for writing the *History of the Peloponnesian War*, Thucydides stated:

And with regard to my factual reporting of the events of the war I have made it a principle not to write down the first story that came my way, and not even to be guided by my own impressions; either I was present myself at the events which I have described or else I heard of them from eyewitnesses whose reports I have checked with as much thoroughness as possible. Not that even so the truth was easy to discover: different eyewitnesses give different accounts of the same events, speaking out of partiality for one side or the other or else from imperfect memories.   (48)

Thucydides intended to tell the truth about the past by adopting a rigorous procedure for sifting sources and evidence. Yet at the same time he was not unaware of the inevitability of fabrication. Immediately after informing the reader of the unreliability of the accounts of poets and chroniclers and the reasonable accuracy of his own history, he makes a qualification about his own writing:

In writing history, I have made use of set speeches some of which were delivered just before and others during the war. I have found it difficult to remember the precise words used in the speeches which I listened to myself and my various informants have experienced the same difficulty; so my method has been, while keeping as closely as possible to the general sense of the words that were actually used, to make the speakers say what, in my opinion, was called for by each situation.   (47)

   In attributing invented words to historical personages, the historiographer is using the techniques of fictional writing. In commenting on a passage from Tacitus' *Annals* in *Mimesis*, Erich Auerbach pointed out that ancient historiography is first and foremost ethical and rhetorical rather than "historical." The historian creates grandiloquent fictitious speeches as products of a specific stylistic and rhetorical tradition. Despite its descriptive clarity and dramatic impact, ancient historiography "does not see forces, it sees vices and virtues, successes and mistakes. Its formulation of problems is not concerned with historical developments either intellectual or material, but with ethical judgments" (38). Auerbach's historicist notions notwithstanding, Greek and Roman historiography pertains to ethics and myth at a deeper level. As twentieth-century critics have repeatedly pointed out, even in the work of Thucydides, the most rational and scientific-minded historian in the ancient Western world, there exists an underlying "mythic" structure. His history does not differ from tragedy in attributing the cause of Athens's decline to the repetition of a pattern of human behavior, to the fatal quality of pride or hubris.[5]

   In other examples of ancient historiography, the entwinement of history and myth is even more obvious. Livy sets as his task the writing of a national history of Rome from its earliest days. At the beginning of his *History of Rome from Its Foundation*, Livy reflects on the difficulty of separating fact from fiction in early Roman history:

Events before Rome was born or thought of have come to us in old tales with more of the charm of poetry than of a sound historical record, and such traditions I propose neither to affirm nor refute. There is no reason, I feel, to object when antiquity draws no hard line between the human and the supernatural: it adds dignity to the past, and, if any nation deserves the privilege of claiming a divine ancestry, that nation is our own; and so great is the glory won by the Roman people in their wars that, when they declare that Mars himself was their first parent and father of the man who founded their city, all the nations of the world might well allow the claim as readily as they accept Rome's imperial dominion.   (17–18)

Here myth legitimates the history of Rome and Rome's dominion over the rest of the world, and national history performs an ideological function. The irony in the passage is that Livy argues it is better at times for the historian not to draw a line between truth and fiction about the remote past but to accept myth as historically real. Here another notion of history emerges, a notion that applies as well to Biblical histories and many medieval narratives. What is considered history may or may not involve the validation of sources and evidence or the process of critical inquiry. History is often that which is *believed* to be true. Myths and legends, and outright forgeries, were appropriated in ancient and medieval history and utilized to legitimize politics grounded in the authority of the past.[6]

The interweaving of history and fiction in ancient and medieval historiography does not mean that the two were not distinguished. Rather, it implies different conceptions of truth, history, and fiction. In her essay "On the Representation of History and Fiction in the Middle Ages," a reception study that follows the lead of Hans Robert Jauss,[7] Suzanne Fleischman asserts that the medieval chroniclers and storytellers did maintain a separation between history and fiction.

There was a concept of history which was distinct from fiction, and which was linked to a particular criterion of truth. But historical truth did not imply, as it does for us, the authenticity of facts and events. . . . Were we to compile a medieval dictionary, history would no doubt have to be redefined as "familiar," "legendary," "what was held to be true." . . . For the Middle Ages and even well beyond, historical truth was anything that belonged to a widely accepted tradition.   (305)

After the rediscovery of Aristotle's *Poetics* in the Renaissance, critical discussions of the interrelations of history and fiction took a new turn. Aristotle's speculations on the philosophical differences between historical writing and poetic writing became the source of reference for many subsequent theories. In Aristotle's opinion, poetry is more philosophical and higher than history since it deals with universal truths, with things that should happen, rather than with particular facts, with things that actually happen. History and fictional writing are antithetical. History is characterized by seriality, parataxis, contingency, and sequentiality, whereas poetry is a unified, coherent whole organized by a central plot. History, which is concerned with a period rather than a single complete action, is not intelligible in the same way that a dramatic plot is. In Aristotle's mimetic theory of art, the central term is plot.

The plot of a play, being the representation of an action, must present it as a unified whole; and its various incidents must be so arranged that if any one of them is differently placed or taken away the effect of wholeness will be seriously disrupted. For if the presence or absence of something makes no apparent difference, it is no real part of the whole.   (43)

The Renaissance defense of poetry against Plato's charge that poetry is lying was launched under the authority of Aristotle's *Poetics*. An echo of Aristotle's view of the relation between history and poetry can even be found in Cervantes's *Don Quixote*. In Chapter 3, Part II, of the novel, Sansón Carrasco tells Don Quixote that poetry is philosophically higher than history. Accompanying this defense of poetry was a growing recognition of the importance of fictionality and verisimilitude in narrative texts. As Michael McKeon shows, the claim to historicity was gradually displaced by the criterion of verisimilitude, or in the French scene, *vraisemblance*. Aristotelian "probability" superseded factuality. "In seventeenth-century prose narrative, verisimilitude and the claim to historicity are incompatible and competitive expressions of the [early modern historicist] revolution. Verisimilitude will prevail, but only

in the long run and only as the reformulated doctrine of 'realism' "
(53).

Eighteenth-century historians and theorists of history were much concerned with narrative and epic qualities and with the question of different points of view in the composition of history. Historians like Voltaire and Gibbon were interested as much in composing a coherent work of literature with data provided by history as in writing a history.[8] Voltaire thus explains his method of writing history: "My aim has been to make a great picture of events that are worthy of being painted, and to keep the reader's eyes trained on the leading characters. History, like tragedy, requires an exposition, a central action, and a denouement. . . . In short, I have tried to move my reader, even in history" (quoted in Canary and Kozichi, 13). Voltaire here seems to follow Aristotle's observation on history and epic and transfer the techniques of epic composition to the writing of history.

One may have doubts about Aristotle's views on the relationship between historical writing and fictional (poetic) writing. One may also disagree with him as to the presence or absence of fictive elements in historical representation. In fact, many contemporary critics have turned Aristotle's theory upside down in arguing for the indispensable persistence of poetic modes of configuring events in historical writing. But although they may differ from and even reverse Aristotle's judgment at this point, they are only reasserting the ever-present authority of Aristotle in insisting on the significance of fictional ways of envisioning reality even in historiography. For these critics, history would be meaningless without fictional components. History must be read along the lines of fiction in order to be understood. This view does not imply that the historiographers are allowed to insert imaginary events in historical narrative. The point is that fictional narrative may provide a conceptual model for understanding sequences of historical events. In order to make sense of history, one needs to read it as having the unity of a story (or, better still, a play) with a pattern of beginning, development, crisis, climax, peripeteia, and denouement.

Some modern historical criticism has attempted to reduce the distinction between fiction and history and to illustrate the conceptual significance of the former for understanding the latter. Historical understanding is seen as analogous to following a story or having followed a story. For W. B. Gallie, history is a species of the genus story. Historical research is incomplete if it only investigates the particular facts, dates, and miscellaneous events. It cannot stop at the questions of "when" and "what," but must inquire about the "how" and "why" as well. Understanding historical processes requires a mode of comprehension that is operative in the reading of fiction. In the words of Louis O. Mink, "the features which enable a story to flow and us to follow, then, are the clues to the nature of historical understanding. A historical narrative does not demonstrate the necessity of events but makes them intelligible by unfolding the story which connects their significance. History does not as such differ from fiction, therefore, insofar as it essentially depends on and develops our skill and subtlety in following stories" (111). For Mink, the comprehension of history is basically a "configurational mode," a "grasping together" of relations in a single act. Just as in reading a story, the understanding of a historical narrative is a bringing together of things separate in time, place, or kind into a unity of successive temporal moments.

Plot, or emplotment, is elevated to a central principle in Hayden White's poetics of nineteenth-century Western historiography. In *Metahistory*, White argues that historical narrative is prefigured on the basis of aesthetic, poetic, and tropological structures. Historical modes of consciousness are determined at a deep level by poetic figures: metaphor, metonymy, synecdoche, and irony. The creation of a historical narrative is an act of storytelling, and interpretation in history is in part the identification of the kind of story or the sort of plot the historian is telling. Along with explanation by argument and explanation by ideological implication, explanation by emplotment is one of the three ways of giving meaning to a set of otherwise meaningless historical events. White defines explanation by emplotment as "providing the 'meaning' of a story by identifying the *kind of story* that has been told" (7). "Emplotment is the way by which a sequence of events fashioned into a story is gradually revealed to be a story of a particular kind" (7). The historian may narrate his story by employing specific plot structures, such as tragedy, comedy, romance, and irony, thus producing different types of historical understanding. White sets out to demonstrate how the masters of nineteenth-century Western historiography, Michelet, Ranke, Tocqueville, and Burckhardt, and the philosophers of history, Hegel, Marx, Nietzsche, and Croce, have resorted to these metahistorical strategies in explaining the drama of human history and thus proved to be tragedians, comedians, romance writers, and ironists.

At first glance, White seems to be contradicting Aristotle on the issue of the cognitive potentiality of historical narrative. He dismisses Aristotle's low opinion of history by revealing the fictional elements embedded in history. But it soon becomes evident that White's poetics of historiography essentially follows a path of thinking firmly established since the first Western poetics, that is, since Aristotle's *Poetics*. White's displacement and reclassification of the problematic of history entail a transferring to historiography of categories borrowed from the criticism of fiction. He dissolves the opposition between the real and the possible and between the episodic and the organic by giving history a plot that organizes events into a dynamic sequential narrative, with a beginning, a middle, and an end. Historical writing also embodies a vision of the history of humankind.

The principles of mimesis and plot play a central role in the work of another powerful contemporary thinker, Paul Ricoeur. Saint Augustine's teleological conception of time and Aristotle's notion of emplotment (*mythos*) are the major strands in his reflections on temporality, narrative, historiography, and fiction. The thesis of his three-volume study *Time and Narrative* is clear enough: "Time becomes human time to the extent that it is organized after the manner of a narrative; narrative, in turn, is meaningful to the extent that it portrays the features of temporal experience" (1: 3). It is through the configurational act of narrative that one achieves a temporal unity of the past, present, and future. In Ricoeur, emplotment is again given a quintessential importance in the organization of human experience in narrative. Emplotment is an act of "grasping together," a configurational arrangement. It "transforms the succession of events into one meaningful whole" and "imposes the 'sense of an ending' (to use the title of Frank Kermode's well-known book) on the indefinite succession of incidents" (1: 67). Ricoeur's thinking on narrative does not depart from Aristotle's mimetic theory of art but only reworks it into a broader three-level scheme. It is impossible to go into the complexities of his arguments here; suffice it to say that for him an individual or a collectivity aspires to the coherence of a story with a plot. Historical agents "prefigure" their lives as stories with plots; historians retrospectively "configure" these historical actions into sequences of events with a beginning, a middle, and an end; and finally readers mentally "refigure" lives, events, and actions and endow them with meaning. With Ricoeur's formulation of the problematic of history and fiction, the Western mimetic theory of narrative has come full circle in its emphasis on the unity of the text and the coherence of representation.

2

Rectifying the Terms, II

"NARRATIVE," "HISTORY," AND "FICTION" IN CHINA

People of varied kinds signify to each other, and the names
and substance of varied things entwine; the noble and humble
are indistinguishable, and sameness and difference are
undifferentiated. If this be the case, understanding the intention
of others will necessarily become a problem, and the disaster of
failing to pursue anything to the end will necessarily arise.
—"The Rectification of Names," *Hsün Tzu ku-i*, 618

M y purpose here is to trace the early definitions and uses and
subsequent metamorphoses of the approximate Chinese
counterparts to such terms as "narrative," "history," and "fiction."
In this chapter, I focus on the institutional, social, and ideological
considerations of the Chinese on these kinds of discourse. I will
argue that such concerns are primary and never secondary to epistemological or representational questions in the Confucian approach, and this is especially true in the early stages of Chinese
history.

In later chapters, I engage the question of interpretation and
representation in Chinese historiography in order to look at the
issue from a different direction. In the final chapter, I discuss the
aesthetic and representational dimensions of the theory and criticism of "fiction" or *hsiao-shuo* in the Sung, Ming, and Ch'ing. At
that point, the justification for fiction has gone beyond the early
moral, social, and institutional considerations. Fictionality is af-
firmed for representational, epistemological, and aesthetic reasons.
The treatment of fiction in late imperial China is perhaps parallel

to the theoretical justification of poetic writings since the rediscovery of Aristotle's *Poetics* during the Renaissance in the West. In this chapter, however, I limit myself to the terminological and "discursive" aspects of these questions.

The mechanisms for controlling the production and dissemination of discourses had unique characteristics in traditional China. First, discourses were regulated to produce maximum cohesion and centripetal effects in society. Such an orientation entailed the institutionalization of literature: types of discursive formations are made into official organs of the state—for example, the Yüeh-fu (Bureau of Music), Pai-kuan (Office of Fiction), and Shih-kuan (Office of History), which became an increasingly important and integral part of the imperial state apparatus after the T'ang.[1] Second, discourses were handled and streamlined in a more direct fashion by means of categorization in official bibliographies. Unity and homogeneity were imposed on heterogeneous and at times heterodoxical discursive formations by cataloguing, classifying, dislocating, excluding, marginalizing, and other procedures. The systems of categorization gave an order to existing literary discourses and directed expectations about future literary productions.

The first problem in the comparative study of Chinese narrative theory is the want of a generic term equivalent to the Western term *narrative*. To be sure, the idea of narrative or narration frequently appears in critical discussions. Terms such as *shu*, *hsü-shu*, and *hsü-shih* mean to narrate, tell, transmit. But "narrative" never served as a literary category in genre studies and bibliographies. For a term that embraces the entire range of narrative writings, the choice can only be *shih* (history). Given the absence of epic and the late appearance of drama in the Chinese literary system, history occupies a central place. As is shown in the ensuing analysis, the Chinese conception of history is comprehensive enough to include diverse types of such "historical" and quasi-historical writings as fiction.

History was a political institution in ancient China. The term *shih* originally meant the officer or office of history. The *Shuo-wen chieh-tzu*, an early dictionary, explains *shih* etymologically as the officer who impartially records events and holds documents in his hands (Tuan, 117–18). Early records such as the *Shu* (Book of documents), the *Tso chuan* (Tso commentary), and the *Chou-li* (Rituals of the Chou) mention various offices of history and titles of historians and briefly describe their duties.[2] The *Chou-li*, for example, lists several titles for historians at the Chou court: *ta-shih* (grand historian), *hsiao-shih* (junior historian), *nei-shih* (inner historian), *wai-shih* (outer historian), *yü-shih* (royal historian), and *nü-shih* (woman historian). The duties of these historians were to record events and speeches, preserve archives and documents, draft state papers and edicts, read and announce governmental decisions, attend religious ceremonies and state rituals, and oversee astronomical matters such as making calendars and observing and recording natural phenomena. The early Chinese *histor* was less a free inquirer of the past than a state agent. Later, the word *shih* acquired other meanings. At least by the time of Ssu-ma Ch'ien, *shih* had begun to signify the records of the historian or historical records, and not just the records kept by such official historians as the Grand Historian (*t'ai-shih ling*).[3] Gradually, *shih* also came to indicate a category of reality.

Written language, books, documents, and writing in general have always been associated with the power of the state and the administration of the government in China. The Office of History has been part of state bureaucracies from the earliest times. It was the foremost duty of the historian to record everything said and done by the sovereign, a duty that in later times became that of the keeper of the *ch'i-chü chu*, a diary of the activities of the emperor that was the primary source for the imperial annals in the official dynastic histories. Herein lay the social and moral function of the historian. The historian "punished" with his pen by impartially recording the wrongdoings of the emperor; he "praised" by celebrating the ruler's virtuous acts. The institution of history, as such, was said to provide the moral measure of the world. Through the mechanism of the "department" of history, the sovereign perpetuated his rule from above and his subjects voiced their remonstrances from below.

Generally speaking, the Chinese have entertained two distinct and yet related conceptions of "fiction" or *hsiao-shuo*. *Hsiao-shuo*— "small talk," "minor discourse"—has been regarded as either a minor philosophical discourse or a type of unofficial, inferior history. The first conception classifies fiction within the corpus of philosophical works, and the second makes it a species of the genus history. Be it philosophy or history, the Chinese have harbored an ambivalent attitude toward it. As usual in Confucian approaches to things, it is the social function that determines the acceptability of fiction in Chinese culture. Seen as a philosophical persuasion, fiction could be both a subversive and an instructive force. But since fictional discourse spreads heterodoxical principles and dissents from Confucian ideology, its dissemination in society must be controlled and regulated. Nevertheless, insofar as fictional discourse may supplement existing knowledge and provide new information for the governing of public affairs, it should not be rejected outright by the broad-minded Confucian gentleman. As a special type of history, fiction is something to be both guarded against and utilized appropriately. On the one hand, fiction is trivial, untrustworthy, and ignoble to the mind of the historian since it consists of gossip, popular opinion, unreliable sources, fabrications, and subject matter unsuitable to high historiography; on the other hand, fiction may be incorporated in official Chinese culture since the stories and satires of fiction may be read as an index of popular sentiment. It voices the will of the common people and thus performs the positive function of remonstrance.

The earliest extant appearance of the word *hsiao-shuo* can be found in the *Chuang Tzu*. "If you parade your little theories [*hsiao-shuo*] (to fish for renown), you will be far from the Great Understanding" (296, trans. modified). In the chapter "On the Rectification of Names" ("Cheng-ming") of the *Hsün Tzu*, one finds the expression *hsiao-chia chen-shuo* ("the strange discourse of the minor school") (Yang Liu-ch'iao, 637), which comes close to *hsiao-shuo* in meaning. In the contexts of these philosophical discussions, *hsiao-shuo* and *hsiao-chia chen-shuo* are contrasted to great understanding (*ta-ta*), the Tao (*tao*), and wisdom/knowledge (*chih*).

Hsiao-shuo is also associated with *hsiao-tao*, meaning "byway" or "minor art," a term that appears in the *Lun-yü* (Analects 19.4). Commentators have interpreted the term differently. Chu Hsi (1130–1200) took it to mean the arts of farmers, gardeners, physicians, and fortunetellers (Chu Hsi, 10.1b). Liu Pao-nan (1791–1855) interpreted it as *i-tuan* (heterodoxy) (Liu Pao-nan, 22.1b). It has also been taken to designate the doctrines of the minor philosophers of the Spring and Autumn and the Warring States periods (770–221 B.C.). Although commentators explain the term differently, *hsiao-tao* obviously carries a pejorative connotation and implies either a discourse that is petty, misleading, and inconsequential or an occupation that the gentleman disdains to pursue.

Confucianism, as in the theory of Hsün Tzu (fl. 298–238 B.C.), holds a "conventional" view of language as opposed to the mimetic view of language in Plato's *Cratylus*. In the chapter "On the Rectification of Names," *Hsün Tzu* states that names and words are invented and imposed on things by human beings. There is no inherent a priori correspondence between things and names. Language is a matter of human convention. Names, labels, and words are not representations of things, as was long held in the West. They are instituted by human beings and can be changed by them at any time.

There is nothing inherently appropriate about names. They are things agreed upon. Once the agreement is made and the habits are fixed, they are considered appropriate. If they deviate from the agreement, they are considered inappropriate. There is nothing inherently real about names. They are things agreed upon. Once the agreement is made and the habits are fixed, they are considered real. There is nothing inherently good about names. (Yang Liu-ch'iao, 624)

For Hsün Tzu, language does not necessarily derive from or represent reality; rather, it constitutes, regulates, and produces reality. Linguistic disorder is coextensive with disruptions in the social hierarchy and a direct cause of them. Confucians are particularly cautious of the danger of the production and circulation of false names, wrong ideas, and "fictions."

The low estimate of *hsiao-shuo* in Chinese culture in part results from the element of fabrication it putatively contains. Readers of Chinese literature are familiar with passages in the *Lun-yü* in which Confucius expressed his respect for facts, for verification, and for what happened actually rather than hypothetically. He pronounced himself reluctant to speak of the afterlife, spiritual entities, the strange, the supernatural, violence, and anomalies (7.21). Confucius proclaimed himself a transmitter of cultural and literary legacies rather than a creator (in the famous line *shu-erh pu-tso*; 7.1) *Hsiao-shuo* has been identified with unfounded fabrications, rumors, and gossip (*tao-t'ing t'u-shuo*). Fiction as such is deceitful and dangerous, for as the Master said, "The gossip-monger [*tao-t'ing erh t'u-shuo*] is the outcast of virtue" (17.14, 146).

It is important to note that *hsiao-shuo* is only an approximation to the Western "fiction," never an equivalent. Such ordinary dichotomous distinctions as history/fiction, fact/fabrication, literal truth / imaginative truth have quite different conceptual premises and carry different literary implications in the two cultures. The following remarks by Victor Mair help clarify some of the meanings embedded in the Chinese term *hsiao-shuo* and demarcate the differences between Chinese notions of *hsiao-shuo* and Western ideas of "fiction."

[The] Chinese term for "fiction" is *hsiao-shuo* (literally, "small talk" or "minor talk"). This immediately points to a fundamental contrast with the English word which is derived ultimately from the past participle of Latin *fingere* ("to form" or "to fashion," "to invent"). Where the Chinese term etymologically implies a kind of gossip or anecdote, the English word indicates something made up or created by an author or writer. "*Hsiao-shuo*" imports something, not of particularly great moment, that is presumed actually to have happened; "fiction" suggests something an author dreamed up in his mind. By calling his work "fiction," an author expressly disclaims that it directly reflects real events and people; when a literary piece is declared to be "*hsiao-shuo*," we are given to understand that it is gossip or report. For this reason, many recorders of *hsiao-shuo* are at great pains to tell us exactly from whom, when, where, and in what circumstances they heard their stories.[4]   (Mair, 21–22)

It is interesting to search for the cultural, political, and ideological presuppositions that underlie the different approaches to literary and historical discourse. In China and the West, the specific rules for the formation and regulation of discourse point to different directions in literary development. In the Chinese case, political as well as literary considerations of what constitutes official discourse and non-official discourse appear to determine the nature, status, and range of Chinese "fiction."

Pan Ku's (A.D. 32–92) treatment of the category of *hsiao-shuo* in the "I-wen chih" (Treatise on the arts and writing) in the *Han-shu* (History of the Former Han) is especially revealing of the Confucian approach to fiction. First, Pan listed *hsiao-shuo* writers in the "philosophers section" (*chu-tzu lüeh*) and placed them last among the ten "schools" (*chia*), which include Confucianism, Taoism, Mohism, Legalism, and yin-yang theory. In this scheme, *hsiao-shuo* becomes the same type of discourse as, say, Confucianism or Taoism. The classification of fiction under "philosophy" initiated by Pan Ku was maintained in all subsequent bibliographical sections in the dynastic histories. With the compilation of the *Sui-shu* (History of the Sui) in the seventh century in the T'ang dynasty, Chinese historians began to categorize all writings as belonging to one of four divisions. This system, devised by Hsün Hsü (d. A.D. 289), became standard in all ensuing Chinese dynastic histories, including the last one, the *Ch'ing-shih kao* (Draft history of the Ch'ing dynasty), written in the early twentieth century. In the tetrapartite division, *hsiao-shuo* is a subcategory in the "philosophy section" (*tzu-pu*). Fiction has been seen as a philosophical and sophistic persuasion that competes with and challenges the predominant discourse of the Confucian canons (*ching*).

The second significant fact in Pan Ku's discussion of *hsiao-shuo* is his tracing of the origin of the *hsiao-shuo* "school" to the ancient office of *pai-kuan*, a minor historian-official whose responsibility was to channel the gossip of the back alleys and streets to the court. The *fictor* is a low-level, minor *histor*. The humble status as well as the usefulness of *hsiao-shuo* as an institution is seen in the function that it performs in Confucian society. The double-edged nature of *hsiao-shuo* is well explained by the following ambivalent and condescending comments of Pan Ku:

> The *hsiao-shuo* writers succeeded those officers of the Chou dynasty whose task it was to collect the gossip of the streets. Confucius said: "Even byways [*hsiao-tao*] are worth exploring. But if we go too far we may be bogged down." Gentlemen do not undertake this themselves, but neither do they dismiss such talk altogether. They have the sayings of the common people collected and kept, as some of them may prove useful. This was at least the opinion of country rustics. (Pan Ku, 1745; trans. Lu Hsün, 3)

Hsiao-shuo is a discourse of limits. It constitutes the furthest point to which official discourse wishes to go, the point from which it must step back. The office of *hsiao-shuo* is a legitimate establishment if and only if it contributes to the rule of the sovereign by fulfilling the tasks of social reporting, "reportage," and admonition.[5] Although at the far end of the spectrum of historical discourse, *hsiao-shuo* borders on the trivial, spiteful, and worthless. Confucian gentlemen should never get entangled in fiction.

Further back in time, the *Tso chuan* records one of the earliest discussions of the function of "narrative" in an interesting dialogue between the master musician K'uang and the Marquis of Chin in the fourteenth year of the reign of Duke Hsiang of the state of Lu. In the text, K'uang defines and illuminates social relations, the proper places of sovereign and subjects, the function of art, and the uses of history and story.

Heaven, in giving birth to the people, appointed for them rulers to act as superintendents and pastors, so that they should not lose their proper nature. For the rulers there are assigned their assistants to act as tutors and guardians to them, so that they should not go beyond their proper limits. Therefore the son of Heaven has his dukes; princes of States have their high ministers; ministers have their collateral families; great officers have the members of the secondary branches of their families; inferior officers have their friends; and the common people, mechanics, merchants, police runners, shepherds, and grooms, all have their relatives and acquaintances to aid and assist them. These stimulate and honor those when they are good, and correct them when they are wrong. They rescue them in calamity, and try to put away their errors. From the king downwards, everyone has his father, elder brothers, sons and younger brothers, to amend and watch over his government. *The historiographers make their records; the blind make their poems; the musicians recite their satires and remonstrances; the great officers admonish and instruct, and the inferior officers report to these what they hear; the common people utter their complaints;* the merchants display their wares in the market place; the hundred artificers exhibit their skillful contrivances. Hence in the *Hsia-shu* it is said, "The herald with his wooden-tongued bell goes along the road, proclaiming, '*Ye officers, able to instruct, be prepared with your admonitions. Ye workmen engaged in mechanical affairs, remonstrate on the subject of your business.*' In the first month, at the beginning of spring, this was done." (Modified from Legge, 466–67; italics added)

All social institutions and human positions are defined relationally and functionally. The ruler stands to his people as "superintendent" and "pastor." The subject reciprocally renders service to the ruler in the role of "tutor" and "guardian." Among the subjects of the ruler are the poet, the musician, the historian, the reporter. Their common duty is to remonstrate, admonish, instruct, and correct. The phrase "inferior officers report what they hear" has been taken as an indication that *hsiao-shuo* derived from an ancient institution. The modern scholar Yü Chia-hsi has amply documented this view with passages from other early records (see Yü Chia-hsi, 265–79). The court official who gathered and reported stories of popular origin is a proto-*hsiao-shuo* writer. The contention that there were officials whose function was to collect and air the sentiments and opinions of the people for the ruler seems to confirm Pan Ku's theory of the genesis of *hsiao-shuo*. Whether there was a historical connection between the court reporter of the Chou dynasty and the *hsiao-shuo* writers of later times is an open question, one I will not address here. The significance of such a view for this study is that it reflects a Chinese way of conceptualizing fiction. For fiction to have a place in the order of things, it must be circumscribed sociologically, functionally, and institutionally. Its right to exist depends on the effect that it may have on the social hierarchy.

As noted above, the "Ching-chi chih" (Treatise on the Classics and documents) of the *Sui-shu*, which was compiled between 629 and 656, used a new bibliographical system that set the pattern for all later dynastic histories. Writings are grouped in four categories: *ching* (Classics, canonical writings), *shih* (histories), *tzu* (philosophical discourses), and *chi* (belles lettres, literary collections). The treatise follows the lead of Pan Ku in making *hsiao-shuo* a subcategory of *tzu-pu*. The comments on the *hsiao-shuo* entries, which I present in full below, consist largely of quotations from the *Tso chuan* and Pan Ku.

Hsiao-shuo were the talk of the streets. Thus the *Tso chuan* quotes chair-bearer's chants, and the *Shih* (Book of Poetry) praises the ruler who consulted rustics. In days of old when a sage was on the throne, the historians made their records; the blind made their poems; the musicians recited their satires and remonstrances; the great officers admonished and instructed, and inferior officers reported to these what they heard; the common people uttered their complaints. Clappers sounded in early spring as a search was made for folk songs, and officers on tours of inspection understood local customs from the popular songs; and if mistakes had been made, these were rectified. All the talk of the streets and highways was recorded. Officers at court took charge of local records and prohibitions, and the officers in charge of civil affairs reported local sayings and customs. Thus Confucius said: "Even byways are worth exploring. But if we go too far, we may be bogged down."   (trans. Lu Hsün, 4, modified)

These comments reflect the tradition of regarding the fiction writer as a minor officer of history invested with the functions of reporting, record-keeping, remonstrance, and rectification. The brief summary at the end of the *tzu-pu* repeats the old position in respect to the nature, uses, and abuses of the various schools and arts.

The *I ching* says, "There are different paths in the world, but they all lead to the same destination; there are hundreds of occupations, but they all are for the same end." Confucianism, Taoism, and *hsiao-shuo* were the teachings of the sages, with special emphases. The military arts and medicine were part of the politics of the sages, with different applications. For the ruling of the world, various offices were instituted. When chaos came in later times, the officers left their posts. Some of them attempted to gain favor from princes with their skills and persuasions. Each respected what he himself practiced and traveled on separate roads at the same time. However, if they are gathered with none omitted and are measured in accordance to the right way, they may also be the means of civilization and regulation. The *Han-shu* has the sections for philosophy, the military arts, mathematics, and crafts. Now they are combined and set forth, all in fourteen categories, being called the division of philosophy [*tzu-pu*].   (Wei et al., 1051)

Again there is a double perception of the nature of various forms of discourse. They could be a source of potential danger and subversion if not properly regulated. Their free circulation may result in social disorder and doctrinal dissension. But if they are domesticated and incorporated as part of the institutions of the empire, they may prove to be a civilizing and cohesive social force, as in the days when the sage-kings ruled China. In being disciplined as a loyal subject and in being institutionalized as an "official" of the ruler, the *hsiao-shuo* writer is transformed into an imperial agent serving the interests of the state.

The generic category closest to Western narrative in the Chinese tradition is obviously "history." Genre criticism and literary classification have been associated with the making of anthologies, the compiling of bibliographies, and the cataloging of books. Literary anthologies like the *Wen-hsüan* (The literary anthology) and works of literary criticism such as the *Wen-hsin tiao-lung* (The literary mind and the carving of dragons) do not provide the answer to the question of narrative since historical and fictional works receive only minimal treatment there. The *Wen-hsin tiao-lung*, for example, makes only one, passing reference to *hsiao-shuo*. Rather, it is the historians who occupy themselves with the varieties of "historical works" and historical materials. Extant and newly created historical records, political documents, popular stories, biographies, geographical works, anecdotes, miscellaneous notes, and dialogues are all subsumed under the rubric "historical writings." The Chinese historians take a decidedly historical attitude to all narrative materials. Their job is to define the nature of each group of "histories," delimit its range, and locate it in the proper class.

A significant development in Chinese fiction came during the Six Dynasties period (265–588) in the genesis of a corpus of writings labeled *chih-kuai* (records of anomalies). Broadly speaking, the *chih-kuai* are anecdotes about supernatural and mystical happenings or about southern barbarian mores and customs. The *Sou-shen chi* (Records of the supernatural), a *chih-kuai* anthology compiled by Kan Pao (fl. 317–22), head of the Office of History at the Eastern Chin court and compiler of the official dynastic history of the Chin, the *Chin chi* (Annals of Chin). In the preface to the *Sou-shen chi*, he declares that these stories of supernatural and extraordinary events are not inventions but rather historical records. These "records" should be subjected to the same kind of criticism as some early histories have been if any defects, discrepancies, and omissions are found in them. Such faults would arise because of defects in the collection and selection of historical materials, problems of verification, and the lack of direct access to past events. Thus, the same historian has written both an official history and an unofficial account of anomalies, and they exist side by side at the two extremes of the broad spectrum of historical works.

Kenneth J. DeWoskin has advanced several propositions about the Six Dynasties *chih-kuai* works:

1. The techniques by which these works were created seem in the main to be those of the historian, that is, the systematic collection and arrangement of material from a variety of sources. There are frequent appeals to sources and much specificity about time and place. This is not writer as *fictor*, a fact with ramifications for virtually all later Chinese narrative.

2. The affinity to history notwithstanding, the *chih-kuai* were recognized as something different by their authors and were set

aside in special works or in special sections of larger works. In a number of prefaces written to *chih-kuai*, the authors hint strongly that their materials may be faulty in a historical sense.

3. The Six Dynasties *chih-kuai* were "records" of supernatural events set forth in a plain, unencumbered narrative style.

4. The recording of anomalies had a legitimate precedent and a precise formal model in the dynastic history tradition. In earlier times, the historian and the astrologer were one, charged with the responsibility of observing ordinary and extraordinary phenomena in nature and interpreting them as they bore on the emperor's administration of government among men (DeWoskin in Plaks, *Chinese Narrative*, 39–40).

Evidently, the *chih-kuai* were evaluated not as imaginative works, with their own characteristics, but rather as defective history, unofficial history, supplemental history, and sources for history.

The T'ang historian Liu Chih-chi (661–721) made a systematic classification of the vast amount of miscellaneous narrative writing known to him. He devoted a special chapter of his theoretical work *Shih-t'ung* (Generalities on history), "Tsa-shu" (Miscellaneous narratives), to the amorphous body of quasi-historical writings outside the corpus of canonical and official histories. He wrestled with these semi-official and non-official histories and *hsiao-shuo* materials and arranged them into ten types: (1) "special records" (*p'ien-chi*), which are incomplete dynastic histories limited to the contemporary period rather than the whole of history; (2) "short notes" (*hsiao-lu*), a type of biographical sketch; (3) "lost records" (*i-shih*), which are either rediscovered ancient histories or later fictional works describing aspects of life excluded from official histories; (4) "trivial talks" (*so-yen*), works of fiction, dialogues, and collections of sayings and anecdotes, such as Liu I-ch'ing's (403–44) *Shih-shuo hsin-yü* (New stories of the world); (5) "prefectural histories" (*chün-shu*), biographies of eminent local individuals; (6) "family histories" (*chia-shih*), pedigrees, private biographies of family members; (7) "separate biographies" (*pieh-chuan*), biographies of eminent individuals such as virtuous women, filial children, pious ministers, and recluses; (8) "miscellaneous records" (*tsa-chi*), stories of strange, extraordinary, and supernatural events, which include the aforementioned *Sou-shen chi*; (9) "geographical books" (*ti-li shu*), which describe the social customs, scenery, and natural resources of local regions; and (10) "books of capitals and cities" (*tu-i po*), which describe the architecture, palaces, and designs of dynastic capitals. Some of these types of histories, for example, "family histories and pedigrees" and "geographical books," overlap with some of the eleven types of miscellaneous histories beyond "standard history" and "ancient history" in the history division of the "Ching-chi chih" of the *Sui-shu*. There are also works in Liu's list, such as the *Shih-shuo hsin-yü*, that are treated as *hsiao-shuo* and appear in the *tzu-pu* of the *Sui-shu*. Chinese historians and bibliographers have found the line of demarcation between history and *hsiao-shuo* difficult to establish in regard to certain problematic texts. Some works have been shuffled back and forth between the *tzu* (philosophy) division and the *shih* (history) division.

Liu Chih-chi speaks disparagingly of all ten types of miscellaneous histories. To his mind, the canonical histories and official histories (*cheng-shih*) such as *Tso chuan*, the *Shih-chi* (Records of the Grand Historian), and the *Han-shu* are the standard by which to measure all narrative works. In comparison to these timeless, monumental achievements, the heterogeneous, unorthodox histories are all defective and of dubious historical value. Liu finds many faults with them from a strictly historiographical point of view: fabrication and thus untruthfulness, bad taste, inelegant narrative style, portrayal of low subject matter, superstitiousness, immorality, expression of biases, exaggeration of facts, and lack of serious intent. In the chapter "Ts'ai-chuan" (On selection and composition), he says that "the writer detests the gossip and talk of the streets and alleys that deviate from truth and distort facts" (Liu Chih-chi, 150). These heterogeneous works are of uncertain worth as serious history and are unreliable as data for historical research.

Despite his mistrust of these miscellaneous narratives, Liu does not altogether deny their potential usefulness. After attacking these suspect forms of histories, he appeals for a degree of tolerance toward them. Speaking with the usual condescending tone of a superior and enlightened Confucian historian, Liu opines that these works may benefit scholars and historians by broadening their knowledge. But the historian must be cautious about what are often misleading historical materials and choose what is relevant and reliable for his purpose. The "Miscellaneous Narratives" chapter concludes with the following words:

But the sagacious king always consults the words of rustics, and the poet does not discard the humble styles. Thus, there are scholars who have a vast knowledge of ancient events and a great understanding of things of old. If one does not look into other records and search for different books but studies only the chapters and sentences of the Chou dynasty and Confucius and stubbornly sticks to the annals and biographies of Ssu-ma Ch'ien and Pan Ku, how could he accomplish anything? And Confucius did say that knowledge based on broad learning and the careful discrimination of what is good will succeed. If this is true, it does not matter whether the books are uncanonical and the words unorthodox. Broad learning results from choosing that which is good.   (Liu Chih-chi, 366–67)

Liu Chih-chi's understanding of "types of histories" is but another assertion of the ambivalent Chinese attitude toward the existence and proliferation of the unofficial discourse of Chinese fiction. He emphasizes both the exclusion of fiction from the realm of culture because of its perversity and the possibility of limited appropriation of fiction by official historical discourse.

The Ming scholar Hu Ying-lin (1551–1602) was one of the first to attempt a classification of *hsiao-shuo* genres. He listed six types of *hsiao-shuo*: (1) *chih-kuai* (records of anomalies), (2) *ch'uan-ch'i* (stories of the extraordinary), (3) *tsa-lu* (miscellaneous notes), (4) *ts'ung-t'an* (collected talk), (5) *pien-ting* (inquiries), and (6) *chen-kuei* (admonitions) (Hu, 374). He made no mention of vernacular fiction, which was flourishing at the time. We do not know his central criterion for classifying fiction. Helpful and heuristic as they are, the six genres of *hsiao-shuo* are by no means exhaustive and absolute categories. Hu himself pointed out the fluidity of *hsiao-shuo* genres and the difficulty of literary classification.

It is extremely easy for the two types *ts'ung-t'an* and *tsa-lu* to get conflated. They usually incorporate the other four kinds too. But in most cases the four kinds stand in their own right and do not contain these two types. As for *chih-kuai* and *ch'uan-ch'i*, it is very easy for them to intermingle. They may both be present in the same story or co-exist in a single event. I am only mentioning the obvious examples.

Hsiao-shuo belongs to the branch of philosophical writings. But in discoursing on principles and truth, some come close to the Classics and other resemble commentary. In recording and narrating events, some interpenetrate with historiography, and others resemble the record and the biography. Anecdotal poems by Meng Ch'i and the lyrics by Lu Huan are sampled in poetic criticism [*shih-hua*] and literary discussions and appended to the division of *belles lettres*. But an investigation of their style and format would show that they really belong to the branch of *hsiao-shuo*. As for the miscellaneous writings in the division of philosophy, they are much entangled with the *hsiao-shuo*. [Cheng Ch'iao, 1103–62, a Southern Sung historian] said that there were nine kinds of ancient and modern writings that could not be distinguished from each other, but he did not know that the easiest one to get mixed up was the *hsiao-shuo*. (374)

Hu attempts a categorization of works of *hsiao-shuo* even while he perceptively points to the futility of such an effort. *Hsiao-shuo* cannot easily be assigned to a proper place in the existing grid of discourses and writings. Although it has been placed in the division of philosophical writings by bibliographic custom, its presence is also felt in the Classics, the histories, and belles lettres. It is both inside and outside the tetrapartite scheme of classification. The subgenres of *hsiao-shuo* itself also interpenetrate and interchange. One would be hard-pressed to pinpoint where a subgenre begins and ends. It is no exaggeration to say that Chinese fiction is an antigenre and anti-discourse in that it breaks down the hierarchies of the literary canon; it has always been an unsettling force to the literary establishment.[6]

Not unexpectedly, Hu's attitude to *hsiao-shuo* is also ambivalent. *Hsiao-shuo* is something both useful and dangerous. One must distance oneself from it insofar as it distorts facts and propagates deceit and immorality. But at times *hsiao-shuo* is worthy of being a supplement to history and the Classics since it collects and records otherwise omitted stories and penetrates the depths of human affairs in its own way. The idea that *hsiao-shuo* is "supplemental history" (*pu-shih*) is a commonplace in Ming and Ch'ing literary criticism. As for the increasing popularity of fiction among all people, not only the populace but also the educated upper class, Hu Ying-lin has an interesting explanation:

As for the gentlemen of great taste, they know the absurdity [of the *hsiao-shuo*] in their heart, but rush to tell it with their mouth. In the daylight they repudiate its erroneousness, but in the dark they quote and use it. It is like licentious sound and beauty in women; people hate it but cannot stop loving it. The more the people love it, the more the people tell it. And the more the people tell it, the more the authors write it. Why should it be strange? (374)

Here, an analogy is made between *hsiao-shuo* on the one hand and sex and women on the other hand. Men's love and hatred for fiction are comparable to their love and hatred for sex and beauty in women. The comparison recalls a passage from the *Lun-yü*: "I [Confucius] have yet to meet the man who is as fond of virtue as he is of beauty in women" (9.18, 15.13). In Hu's moralistic view, the spread of fiction is perfectly natural: "Why should it be strange?" Yet something demands more explanation. If we pursue his logic further, the conclusion is that fiction is a supplement to history and the Classics in the same way sex with women is a supplement to the Confucian gentleman. Here, one is reminded of Derrida's critique of Rousseau's notion of "supplement."[7] For Rousseau, writing is a supplement to speech, education a supplement to nature, and masturbation a "dangerous supplement" to normal sexuality. The supplement is a superfluous accessory to the original. It is a defect, an unwanted addition to the presence and the fullness of the original being.

The prejudice against the supplement is, however, ultimately reversed, for "people hate it but cannot stop loving it." The very existence of the supplement requires a felt lack in that which is being supplemented. The "external supplements are called in to supplement precisely because there is always a lack in what is supplemented, an originary lack" (Culler, *On Deconstruction*, 103). Fiction can be compensatory, a supplement to historiography and the Classics, only because historiography and the Classics are already marked by the qualities attributed to fiction: absence, deficiency, inaccuracy. Indeed, "inessential" fiction is called upon to help because the official literary canon buttressed by Confucian ideology is far from self-sufficiency, plenitude, and completion. Fiction is not and cannot be a defective addition to the official order of discourses; rather, it reveals the defectiveness of that very order. Fiction exists as a troubling and subversive force in the literary and philosophical system and cannot be eliminated or even comfortably located in a proper place. It remained the fortune of Chinese fiction to grow and survive on the margins of acceptable discourse throughout history.[8]

3

Chinese Historical Interpretation in the Reading of Narrative

What is prized in historiography is meaning, what are
recorded are events, and what are employed are words.
—Chang Hsüeh-ch'eng, *Wen-shih t'ung-i*, 144

Could we ever narrativize without moralizing?
—Hayden White, *The Content of the Form*, 25

What I hope to accomplish in this chapter is to contribute to
the investigation of what might be called the Chinese "historical paradigm" in the reading of narrative. Narrative here includes writings we would classify as either historical or fictional. I
see two further polarities within the Chinese historical approach,
two sets of premises and expectations in regard to historical narrative and narrative in general. When they are played off against
each other, they are mutually contradictory and self-deconstruc-
tive. Each questions and undermines the consistency and validity
of the other. More often than not, however, these two strains interpenetrate and interlock in the thought and work of most traditional Chinese historians and critics. Only in a few cases, such as
in the reflections of Liu Chih-chi and Chang Hsüeh-ch'eng (1738–
1801), is there an acute awareness of the divergence of the two
polarities, and the consequences of each are pursued to their logical
conclusions.[1]

Within the Chinese historical paradigm for the reading of narrative, one may postulate two distinct and yet related approaches
to history: the "hermeneutic" approach and the "historiographical" approach. Both derive from the *Ch'un-ch'iu* (Spring and autumn annals), traditionally thought to be the work of Confucius.

The annals itself has the double status of being at once a Classic and a history. As one of the Six Classics, the annals falls in the domain of *ching-hsüeh*, the "study of the Classics." But as a historical text, it also belongs to the realm of *shih-hsüeh*, "historical studies." Whereas the hermeneutic approach grew out of exegesis of the Classics, the historiographical approach emerged from the discipline of history.

This divergence further harks back to a difference among the three earliest commentaries on the *Ch'un-ch'iu*, a difference between on the one hand the exegetical texts of the *Kung-yang chuan* (Kung-yang commentary) and the *Ku-liang chuan* (Ku-liang commentary) and on the other hand the narrative text of the *Tso chuan* (Tso commentary). The first two commentaries are oriented toward revealing the hidden dimensions of meaning beyond the literal level. Classical scholars assumed that the text of the annals followed the rule of "great principles hidden in tiny words" (*wei-yen ta-i*). The aim of interpretation is to penetrate the obscurities, euphemisms, and circumlocutions of this secretive historical record so as to discover the deeper layers of meaning put there by Confucius. The *Ch'un-ch'iu* is not to be read as a simple annals; the historical text is a pretext for personal expression and political intervention. This hermeneutic approach recognizes a discrepancy between word and meaning and permits "euphemisms" (*hui*) to express ethical and metaphysical truths. Events themselves can be represented in a number of ways, depending on the nature of the historian's moral and political message.

But although events can be represented from different perspectives and reality can be viewed from varying angles, fabrication is not permitted. Confucianism is opposed to invention, the making up of "empty words" (*k'ung-yen*); rather, it recommends the transmission of the cultural legacy and values concrete, substantive deeds (*shih-shih*). Events and characters cannot be invented in a historical text. The ultimate significance of the particular event resides in the timeless general principles it points to. Here historiography is subordinated to philosophy, ethics, and politics. The Ch'ing historian and philosopher Chang Hsüeh-ch'eng is to a large extent indebted to the hermeneutic, commentarial, exegetical approach to history. He is especially concerned with the interpenetration of historical discourse and other modes of discourse among the Six Classics.

In contrast, the focus of the "historiographical approach" is less on interpretation and more on the art of narration. The difference between the two approaches is that between a historical hermeneutics and a poetics of historical narrative. The beginning of the second tradition can be traced to the *Tso chuan*, and the most outspoken advocate of this approach is perhaps the T'ang historian Liu Chih-chi. Unlike the other two commentaries on the *Ch'un-ch'iu*, the *Tso chuan* is itself a historical work, the first Chinese chronicle (*pien-nien*). It consists of a series of self-contained short narrative pieces appended to entries in the annals that explain the individual entries in the Classic by fleshing out the stories behind them.[2] Professional historians have viewed the commentary as a model for their work, for it is at once an objective account of the past and a highly graphic, vivid narrative. Objectivity in recording, accuracy in details, and an aesthetics of realistic narration are the ideals of Chinese historiography. Historical objectivity demands a respect for facts and a suppression of personal, subjective feelings. Any deliberate misrepresentation of facts, of the kind found in the *Ch'un-ch'iu*, is to be avoided. Historiography is not the occasion for the expression of some truth other than that of the reality of the past in all its specificity. Truth in historiography is the truth about the past. The historians believe that once the past is rendered objectively, the patterns of good and evil and the laws of human relations will become self-evident. The meaning of history is not to be recovered through the tortuous procedures of interpretation; it emerges freely and naturally from a well-structured historical narrative. The "real" will manifest itself in historical texts.

The exegetical tradition assumes that meaning in narrative is not directly accessible but is to be recovered through a hermeneutic of the sign. The exegete goes through the interpretive procedures of contextualization and totalization in order to unveil the full sense of the text and the meaning of history. In contrast, the historiographical tradition repudiates the discrepancy between text and meaning. It attempts to ground the transparency of historical discourse in a poetics of realistic description and faithful recording. The ideal of historical discourse is an artful and yet truthful transcription of the real. Each orientation exposes the illusion and falsehood of the assumptions of the other. The divergence of methods and goals constitutes, as it were, the "aporia" of Chinese historical thought.[3]

In the remainder of this chapter, I discuss the hermeneutic tradition. In the next chapter, I present an analysis and a critique of the historiographical approach. Also, in the final part of the next chapter, I focus on these issues in the context of contemporary literary theory in order to reach some conclusions.

Origins of Historical Interpretation in Classical and Historical Studies

The "hermeneutic" mode of historical interpretation originated in Classical studies (*ching-hsüeh*), was widely used in historiography, and was then carried deep into the reading of other literary genres and forms of narrative, such as fiction. In such an interpretive pattern, the readers bring a set of general literary and cultural presuppositions and expectations as they confront the narrative text. They acknowledge first a gap and then a correspondence between the surface text and a hidden meaning, or between the seemingly impartial, objective record of personages and events and the latent "historical" paradigm behind it. The task of reading is to grasp the "meaning of history," to apprehend the deep moral, ideological, and political structure behind the historian's acts of recording and editing and beneath the symbols, signs, indexes, and configurations in the historical narrative. This properly Confucian hermeneutic began with the exegesis of the *Ch'un-ch'iu* and continued to the very end of pre-modern Chinese historical thought, figuring prominently in Chang Hsüeh-ch'eng's philosophy of history and his stress on the "meaning of history" for understanding the past. The resilience and pervasiveness of this line of interpretation became all the more evident when it was applied to the reading of a variety of popular literary genres beyond official historiography.[4]

Generally speaking, the Confucian hermeneutics I delineate was the officially valorized mode of interpreting narrative works, both historical and fictional. Nevertheless, there were periods in which this paradigm suffered erosion as well as periods in which it was consolidated. With the emergence of alternative modes of reading history and the challenge of Taoism and Buddhism, and with the flourishing of fictional narrative, Confucian hermeneutics, which was solidly grounded in Classical studies and official historiography, gradually lost its predominance. Although still the official discourse, it was in reality nothing more than one approach among many to narrative.

The *Ch'un-ch'iu* is the official annals of the ducal state of Lu during the Spring and Autumn era (770–476 B.C.) of the Eastern Chou dynasty (770–221 B.C.). Its entries cover a period of 242 years from the first year of Duke Yin (722 B.C.) to the fourteenth year of Duke Ai (481 B.C.). Confucius was believed responsible for the final version of the text. Closely associated with the text are the three oldest and canonical commentaries on the annals: the *Tso chuan*,[5] the *Kung-yang chuan*, and *Ku-liang chuan*. The *Ch'un-ch'iu* has been regarded as the fountainhead of Chinese historiography, and Confucius himself is said to have taken great pride in his redaction. It has served as a cultural myth cherished by all Confucians. According to the traditional account, amid the political turmoils and moral degeneration of his age, Confucius edited the annals of his native state of Lu; in it, he presented his vision of history and humanity and passed his judgment on political events. The goal of exegetes for two millennia has been to elucidate the textual structure of "great principles hidden in tiny words" in the annals in order to discover the hidden political criticism. The great historian Ssu-ma Ch'ien (ca. 190–145 B.C.) expressed a sentiment shared by generations of Chinese historians:

Above, it [the *Ch'un-ch'iu*] makes clear the way of the Three Kings, and below it discusses the regulation of human affairs. It distinguishes what is suspicious and doubtful, clarifies right and wrong, and settles points which are uncertain. It calls good good and bad bad, honors the worthy, and condemns the unworthy. It preserves states which are lost and restores the perishing family. It brings to light what was neglected and restores what was abandoned. In it are embodied the most important elements of the Kingly Way. (Watson, 51)

At first glance, the seemingly uninspired, matter-of-fact, and extremely terse entries in the annals may discourage anyone intent at looking for the goals, uses, and methods of Chinese historiography. The entries themselves are punctuated by days, months, seasons, and years, and record in very few words the notable events that happened in the state of Lu and in other states in the Chou kingdom. Without the explanations in the commentaries, one would have no clue as to the "Kingly Way" embodied in the text. The commentators have studied the entries, the lines, and the words with the utmost care in an attempt to discover the deep layers of meaning.

The commentary on the opening lines of the *Ch'un-ch'iu*, which deal with the first year in the reign of Duke Yin, will give some idea of the Confucian hermeneutic and its characteristics. The first entry of the annals reads:

> The first year, spring, the king's first month.
> *Yüan-nien, ch'un, wang cheng-yüeh.*

It is all too easy for the untrained eye to miss the "deep significance" of these six Chinese characters. Luckily the commentaries inform the reader of the context of the first entry. Many commentators have taken this brief entry as the *point de départ* for a discussion of the question of "legitimacy," a key concept in Chinese historiography. Behind this terse record lies a troubled history of succession to the dukedom of Lu. The *Kung-yang chuan* offers the following explanation of this passage:

> What is meant by [*yüan-nien*]? The first year of the ruler.
> What is meant by [*ch'un*] (spring)? The first season of the year.
> What is meant by [*wang*] (the king)? It means king [Wen].
> Why does the text first give "king," and then "first month"? [To show that] it was the king's first month.
> Why does it [so] mention the king's first month? To magnify the union of the kingdom [under the dynasty of Chou].
> Why is it not said that the duke came to the [vacant] seat? To give full expression to the duke's mind.
> In what way does it give full expression to the duke's mind? The duke intended to bring the State to order, and then restore it to [Huan].
> What is meant by restoring it to Huan? Huan was younger, but nobler [than the duke by birth]; Yin was grown up, but lower [than Huan by birth]. The difference between them in these respects, however, was small, and the people of the State did not know [their father's intention about the succession]. Yin being grown up and a man of worth, the great officers insisted on his being made the marquis. If he had refused to be made so, he did not know for certain that [Huan] would be raised to the dignity; and supposing that he were raised to it, he was afraid that the great officers might not give their assistance to so young a ruler. Therefore the whole

transaction of Yin's elevation was with a view [in his mind] to the elevation of [Huan].

But since Yin was grown up and a man of worth, why was it not proper that he should be made the marquis? Among the sons of the wife proper, the succession devolved on the eldest, and not the worthiest and ablest. Among a ruler's sons by other ladies of his harem, the succession devolved on the noblest, and not the eldest.

In what respect was [Huan] nobler [in rank] than Yin? His mother was of higher position [than Yin's mother]. Though the mother was nobler, why should the son be [also] nobler? A son was held to share in the nobility of his mother; and a mother shared in the [subsequent] nobility of her son.   (Legge, "Prolegomena," 55–56)

The commentary reflects on the significance of the individual words and their ordering, proceeds slowly and gradually from the effects to the causes, and supplies the missing links and the historical context for the entry, all toward a complete clarification of the record.[6] The *Kung-yang* notices an interruption, a silence in the entry. It does not record that the duke took the throne in the first month of the first year. Step by step the commentary reveals the story of a disputed succession. Huan, the intended successor, was too young to take the throne at the time of his father's death. His older brother Yin assumed the position of the duke temporarily, intending to step down when Huan grew up. This is the reason, according to the commentator, that Confucius did not record Yin's inauguration in the "first year" of his reign. The *Kung-yang* explains this extraordinary event by invoking the rules for a legitimate succession and consequently endorses the legitimacy of such a power transition.

Commentators have seized upon the importance of *cheng-yüeh* in the entry. *Cheng-yüeh*, "first" or "proper" month, is commonly contrasted to *jun-yüeh*, "intercalary" or "improper" month. The proper month is associated with legitimate, regular reigns—regna—and the improper month with illegitimate, irregular reigns—interregna. Through the adoption of new calendars and reign titles (*nien-hao*), kings and emperors in part grounded their legitimacy on the regularity of the cosmic movements. Illegitimate rulers are not appointed by the Heaven and are classed as irregularities in the natural order. Confucius reputedly began the annals with the phrase "the king's first month" in order to show respect for the proper rule and authority of the House of Chou over the ducal states.

An example from the *Tso chuan* will illustrate the differences and the relationship between the hermeneutic and the narrative approaches to history. The following entry, a line of six characters, occurs under the twenty-eighth year of Duke Hsi: "The king [by] Heaven's [grace] held a court of reception in Ho-yang" (Legge, 207). The line might be better rendered as "The heavenly king hunted in Ho-yang." (Some commentators read *shou* "to receive" [i.e., to receive guests in a formal reception] as *shou* "to hunt.") The line itself gives no clue to either the political background or the moral content of Confucius' remarks. The *Tso chuan* unfolds the story of the troublesome political situation underlying this record of an otherwise simple event.

As to the assembly here, the marquis of Tsin called the king to it, and then with all the princes had an interview with him, and made him hold a court of inspection. [Confucius] said, "For a subject to call his ruler to any place is a thing not to be set forth as an example." Therefore the text says,— "The king held a court reception at Ho-yang." (Legge, 212)

One can think of other ways to record this historical event. At the time, the Chou court had lost control of China, and various feudal states technically subordinate to the Chou were vying for power and hegemony. Perhaps a more faithful statement would have read "The marquis of Chin [Legge's Tsin] summoned the king to meet the princes in Ho-yang," or simply "The king was called to Ho-yang." But Confucius' decision to record the event in the way he did was a political one. Alleged instances of Confucius' deliberate "distortions" and "misrepresentations" are numerous and point to a Confucian conception of history. Historiography, like every other form of discourse, is a political practice, a concrete act of the "rectification of names" (*cheng-ming*). In Confucius' "sociolinguistics," things should correspond to their names, and human beings to their titles and ranks. For a subject to issue orders to a sovereign violates proper human relations. It is the conviction of the commentators that every paragraph, every line, every word, in this historical text is charged with deep meaning.

A basic premise of the *Ch'un-ch'iu* commentators is that a discrepancy between word and meaning, between the "letter" and the "spirit," exists in the text. The exemplarity of this unique historical work to a large extent lies in the fact that it is not a historical record in the ordinary sense. It has, for want of better terms, a "mythic," an "allegorical," dimension that must be revealed by exegesis. It was the common view that Confucius used these historical records as a vehicle to express his vision of human history and to pronounce his judgment on the world. Juan Chih-sheng, a modern scholar in the *Kung-yang* tradition, asserts that underlying the annals is the rhetorical figure of *k'uang* ("exempla"; Juan, 123–35). The Han Confucian scholar Tung Chung-shu (ca. 183–115 B.C.) was the first to use the word *k'uang* in the discussion of the text: "The language of the *Ch'un-ch'iu* uses many exempla [*k'uang*]. This is why its writing is brief but its rules are clear" (Lai, 1). In *k'uang*, one "illustrates principles by using events" (*chieh-shih ming-i*; Juan, 125). Since the times prevented Confucius from speaking openly, he conveyed his thoughts through the medium of historical writing. The interpreter must penetrate the euphemisms, evasions, innuendoes, insinuations, and circumlocutions replete in the text to reach the great principles of Confucius. By studying the textual patterns of the annals—the omissions, deletions, gaps, fragmentations, repetitions, and juxtapositions—the reader may gradually discover the hidden sense of the hermetic annals.

As some Classical scholars have indicated, one reads the *Ch'un-ch'iu* in a way similar to the way one reads the *I ching*. Just as one moves from signs toward meaning in the *I ching*, so one moves from events toward principles in the *Ch'un-ch'iu*. The *Ch'un-ch'iu* consists of exempla (*k'uang*) and the *I ching* of signs (*hsiang*), but the exempla and the signs are indexes to the latent principles and meanings in the respective texts. In the words of Chu Hsi, "The *I ching* and the *Ch'un-ch'iu* are the Tao of heaven and man. The *I ching* articulates the physical with the metaphysical, and the *Ch'un-ch'iu* articulates the metaphysical with the physical" (quoted in Juan, 206). Philosophy, politics, and history join hands in the meeting place of the hermeneutics of signs. The use of historical events in Chinese literary and historical interpretation to illustrate truth and principles does not, however, involve a denial of the historicity and reality of the events. The events belong to the general course of history. Just as the Tao and the signs are inseparable in the *I ching*, the events and the principles signified by them are also ontologically contiguous in the *Ch'un-ch'iu*. The principles of the world are embodied and observable in concrete historical events and situations. Grasping the "meaning of history" requires a contextualization of the events behind the entries.

Orthodox Confucian historical hermeneutics found expression primarily in the reading and theorizing of historical narratives, a process complete before the rise of vernacular Chinese fiction. Chinese historical interpretation has always presupposed a notion of legitimacy. Ideas of legitimate succession and legitimate rule have been read into historical works in order to make sense out of the processes of history.[7]

Ou-yang Hsiu (1007–72) of the Sung (960–1279) initiated a new round of debate over political legitimacy in Chinese history. He elaborated his view in several important treatises. "On the Origin of the Theory of Legitimacy" ("Yüan cheng-t'ung lun") introduces his moralistic concept of legitimacy:

The [*Kung-yang*] Commentary says: "The superior man augustly commands an upright position" [*ta chü-cheng*]. It also says: "The king majestically inaugurates a unification" [*ta i-t'ung*; Legge: "magnify the union of the kingdom" ("Prolegomena," 55)]. The upright [*cheng*] is the one that rectifies [*cheng*] the deviations in the world, and the unifier [*t'ung*] is the one that brings together the divisions in the world. The theory of legitimacy [*cheng-t'ung*] has been advanced because of the deviations and divisions.   (Chao, 78; my translation)

Ta chü-cheng comes from the entry for the twelfth month of the third year of Duke Yin in the *Kung-yang chuan*. Ou-yang Hsiu broke the word *cheng-t'ung* (legitimacy, legitimate succession) into its component characters and thus traced its origin to the commentary. The compound *cheng-t'ung* first appeared in Pan Ku's *Han-shu*. In early China "legitimacy" or "legitimate succession" implied more the correct blood filiation of the successor and was part of a cyclical, alternating conception of dynastic change found in the Five Processes (*wu-hsing*) theory. By the Northern Sung, "legitimacy," as exemplified by Ou-yang Hsiu's passage, had largely come to mean an upright, benevolent rule and the ability of the ruler to unify China.

Two other related terms for legitimacy achieved currency from the Sung on. *Chih-t'ung*, "political succession," confers legitimacy on those rulers who demonstrated benevolence and competence rather than a correct genealogy. *Tao-t'ung* roughly means the "legitimate transmission of the Tao." Although China had been at times subjugated to illegitimate, "irregular" rulers and barbarian invasions, history, according to this view, did not belong to them but to those Confucian scholars who preserved and transmitted Confucian learning and the Tao. Legitimacy became a political problem in the writing of official dynastic histories when the historians dealt with periods of disunion and foreign rule. They had to decide which ruling house was the legitimate one and whether the non-Chinese reigns deserved separate official histories. Complications encountered by the historian include the problems of periodization, of overlapping and simultaneous reigns among rival states, and of dynastic interruptions and resumptions.

Historical discourse is again a crucial political weapon. The historian may be a "conservative" in recognizing the legitimacy of a given reigning house or a "loyalist" in risky defiance of dominant foreign rule. The opposition between *cheng* (proper, legitimate) and *jun* (intercalary, illegitimate) has been a leading principle in historical interpretation since the Sung. One of the best-known instances is Chu Hsi's correction of Ssu-ma Kuang's (1019–86) *Tzu-chih t'ung-chien* (Comprehensive mirror for aid in government), a monumental general history of China from the beginning of the Warring States period (403 B.C.) to the end of the Five Dynasties (A.D. 959). In writing about the period of the Three Kingdoms (220–65), Ssu-ma Kuang chose to follow the events of the state of Wei rather than those of the rival states of Shu and Wu. Chu Hsi, in his abridged version of the *Comprehensive Mirror*, the *Tzu-chih t'ung-chien kang-mu*, emphatically maintained the distinction between legitimate and illegitimate rule, and made the Shu rather than the Wei the legitimate successor to the Han dynasty.

The apex of the historical approach or "historicism" can be found in the work of Chang Hsüeh-ch'eng. His synthetic and seminal work has been regarded as a summa of Chinese historical thought.[8] His times were the heyday of textual scholarship (*k'ao-cheng*) and the revival of Classical studies. He attempted in his theory of historiography to reunite the separate strains of historical and Classical studies. As a historiographer, he examined the Classics from a critical historical point of view; as a Classical scholar, he ultimately required history to illustrate metaphysical truths. An exploration of Chang's philosophy of history will serve to clarify the Confucian conception of meaning in historical discourse.

Chang's magnum opus, the *Wen-shih t'ung-i* (The general meaning of literature and history) begins with a startling leveling of genre distinctions among the Six Classics, the *I ching*, the *Shu*, the *Ch'un-ch'iu*, the *Shih*, the *Li* (Book of rites), and the *Yüeh* (Book of music). Chang denied the disciplinary separation between Classical and historical studies and re-established the ground of all discourses by uniting a theory of signs and a philosophy of history. He advanced two important theses: all the Six Classics are (1) history and (2) signs. Thus, *ching-hsüeh* (the study of the Classics), the highest form of learning in traditional China, becomes a historical discipline and a study of the phenomena of signs. Chang's historical approach to the Classics is clear from the opening sentences of his book: "The Six Classics are all histories. The ancients did not write books. The ancients did not speak of truths apart from events. The Six Classics are all the political documents of the early kings" (1).

Although Chang was not the first to express the view that the Classics can be read as history, his exposition has far broader implications. For him, the totality of the natural world and human activities constitutes the very matter of history. The Six Classics are the traces, signs, and documents of historical life and bygone political institutions and social customs. They are themselves not the Tao but the "vessels" that "carry" the Tao and thereby allow us to know the Tao. Here Chang invokes a distinction in Chinese philosophy between the "metaphysical" and "physical," or, to use the Chinese terms, between the Tao and the "vessel" (*ch'i*), between "that which is beyond form" (*hsing-erh shang*) and "that which is within form" (*hsing-erh hsia*). Books of poetry, politics, rites, music, astrology, and divination from the past are, more than anything else, historical signs. A study of these ancient texts may reveal the vestiges of the Tao, the principles held fast by the ancients, and the truths of the universe. It may be said that the Six Classics are the "indexes" of the past and the Tao.

Chang Hsüeh-ch'eng held that one can never have direct access to the ultimate principles and the Tao; access is possible only through an intermediate investigation of their gradual, successive unfolding in history, that is, through their manifestations in social institutions and human relations. Chang rarely defined the exact meaning of the Tao; rather, he only suggested it in various terms. In one of the best-known passages of the *Wen-shih t'ung-i*, he gave the following highly imaginative account of the genesis and condition of the Tao.

[The state] before heaven and earth I cannot come to know. Heaven and earth gave birth to men, and there the Tao came into being but without a form. When three people lived in a house, the Tao had a form, but it was still indistinct. There were fives and tens of people, and then hundreds and thousands. And when one house could not contain them and they were organized and assigned to different posts, the Tao became manifest! The distinctions of benevolence, righteousness, loyalty, and filial piety, and the institutions of jurisdiction, government, rites, and music, all afterward appeared ineluctably. (34)

Chang further explains the formation of the Tao in ostensibly social and historical terms. The life of three people living in a house serves as a miniature model of society. They need to open the door in the morning and shut it in the evening; to cook, someone has to cut wood and fetch water. From all this emerge order and the division of labor. When quarrels occur, they perforce select the eldest man to be the leader and the judge. Herewith begin social hierarchy and the concept of jurisdiction. In observing the movement from the dealings and interactions of three people to those of hundreds and thousands, and in examining the historical evolution of communities and their customs and institutions, the patterns of the Tao become perceptible and intelligible.

Chang's philosophy of history is further substantiated by an ingenious theory of signs or by what amounts to be a "historical semiotics."[9] The scope of historical studies is immensely widened by the inclusion of the study of signs. Not unexpectedly, Chang's reflections on signs issue from his study of the *I ching*. The idea of *hsiang*, which I translate "sign," is one of the guiding principles in that work, which has extensive discussions of the nature of signs, their interpretation, and their relation to the Tao.

Earlier, the philosopher Wang Fu-chih (1616–92) had extended the "semiotic" viewpoint of the *I ching* to the other Classics: "What fills the world is nothing but signs [*hsiang*]. The similes [*pi*] and the evocative imageries [*hsing*] of the *Shih*, the political affairs of the

Shu, the names and distinctions in the *Ch'un-ch'iu*, the proprieties of the *Li*, and the tunes of the *Yüeh* are nothing but signs. But the *I ching* grasps and contains their principles" (213).

Chang also worked toward a general theory of signs, but with greater consistency and clarity, by reinterpreting the other Classics in the light of the *I ching*. "What the signs cover is vast. They contain not only the *I ching*, but also the Six Arts [Classics]. [The signs] are the *imminent formation of the Tao as it has not manifested itself*" (*Wen-shih t'ung-i*, 5; my italics). Under this expanded notion of signs, all phenomenal manifestations, images, poetic figures, historical events, social institutions, however unrelated they may be, are without exception signs. The symbols in the *Shih*, the natural and social events recorded in the *Tso chuan*, and the dreams, omens, divinations, and political speeches in the *Shu* are special varieties of signs or what may be called instances of "semiosis."

Chang divides signs into two categories: natural signs and mental signs. "There are the natural signs of heaven and earth [*t'ien-ti tzu-jan chih hsiang*] and the signs of mental construction [*jen-hsin ying-kou chih hsiang*]" (5). Natural signs exhibit an iconic resemblance to what they signify or what they are signs of. Mental signs are products of free human invention. The *I ching* contains a great many natural signs of heaven, earth, and man; the *Shih* is filled with poetic figures (*pi* and *hsing*) and mental signs. Chang's twofold division of signs recalls an earlier distinction between "real signs" (*shih-hsiang*) and "imaginary signs" (*chia-hsiang*) made by K'ung Ying-ta (574–648) in his commentary to the *I ching*, the *Chou-i cheng-i*.[10] As Chang explains, however, these two types of signs are also interrelated:

The human being is stationed between heaven and earth and cannot but be affected by the ebb and flow of *yin* and *yang*. Mental constructions are wrought by changes in feeling. The changes in feeling are responses to the structure of the human world and the result of riding on the tides of *yin* and *yang*. Therefore, the signs of mental construction also originate from the natural signs of heaven and earth.   (*Wen-shih t'ung-i*, 5–6)

The two types of signs are connected through a chain of perceptual and psychological processes; "mental signs" ultimately derive from "natural signs." One cannot understand one sign system without understanding the other. The ability to read the signs and grasp their meanings in political and historical texts such as the *Shu* and the *Ch'un-ch'iu* requires a knowledge of the signs in the *Shih*. The profuse, varied signs of the Six Classics are mutually implicated and interpret each other through categories and correspondences. "The *I ching* measures human affairs with the Tao of heaven, and the *Ch'un-ch'iu* corresponds to the Tao of heaven with human affairs" (*Wen-shih t'ung-i*, 5). The goal of the historian is to comprehend the structure and functioning of the diverse, multifarious signs and locate them within a single, all-encompassing perspective.

The important questions are What exactly is a sign? What is the relationship between the sign and the Tao? The sign and the Tao seem to be the two sides of a same thing. Chang at times attempts a semiotic definition of the Tao.

The Tao is called the formation of signs.   (44)

As the myriad events and things just begin to change from tranquillity to movement, their forms and traces are still indistinct. But their signs are visible. Thus, the Tao cannot be seen. What people think they hazily see as they seek the Tao are all signs of it.   (5)

The Tao, in the singular or plural, is inscrutable. It underlies the cosmos, all natural existence, and the human world, but it remains hidden and unknowable. The Tao is accessible to us only through its external manifestations, its "configurations" in the natural and cultural realms, its "textualization." One cannot see the Tao itself, only the signs of it. The joining of the theory of signs and the philosophy of history renders inevitable the conclusion that history consists of signs and signs are fundamentally historical. Human beings cannot infer the Tao other than by reading the intermediary links (historical signs) and through the interpretive efforts of totalization. Historical signs embrace both cosmic and cultural manifestations: natural occurrences, astronomical records, the movements of heavenly bodies, historical monuments, ancient texts, social institutions, political affairs, human relations, and so on. By way of an investigation of historical signs, historiography preserves the past, anticipates the future, and understands changes; in brief, it unifies time.

Chang was not, however, satisfied with a simple description of the state of signs. Faithful to the role of the historian, he was concerned foremost with the uses and the meaning of history. The task of historical interpretation is still to move from an initial semiotic description of the object of study toward a definitive hermeneutic of the meaning of history. Like his predecessors, he believed that the study of the signs of the past should be oriented toward the apprehension of the meaning of history and the mutual illumination of past, present, and future. For him, historiography is, in the final analysis, in the service of metaphysical truths. He confessed that his vocation was to illustrate the "tao" of the Neo-Confucian philosophers Chu Hsi and the Ch'eng brothers with the art of the great historians Ssu-ma Ch'ien and Pan Ku.

Chang repeatedly emphasized the centrality of meaning in the writing and reading of historiography. He distinguished among "meaning" (*i*) or "principle" (*i*), "events" (*shih*), and "words" (*wen*). "What is prized in historiography is meaning, what are recorded are events, and what are employed are words" (*Wen-shih t'ung-i*, 144). The mere recording of events with words is not enough; rather, the historiographer must search for the meaning that can be drawn from the events. The words signify "external" historical events. But beyond both the signifiers and signifieds is the "significance" of the recorded events, which is a matter of the subjective judgment on the part of the historian or interpreter.[11] Chang explained the relationship among meaning, events, and words as follows:

Confucius wrote the *Ch'un-ch'iu*. It is said that the events deal with [Duke] Huan of Ch'i and [Duke] Wen of Chin, its writing is historical, but its meaning is underscored by Confucius as he himself says. The events are what are respected by the philologists of later ages; the words are what are noted by the essayists of later ages; but what is underscored by Confucius does not reside here but elsewhere. Thus, is it possible that the way of historical writing does not aim at significance and meaning?   (134–35)

Here Chang falls squarely within the tradition of Chinese historical thinking shaped by the early commentaries on the *Ch'un-ch'iu* and continuously confirmed by later historians. The historians in this tradition hold that historical research is in the final analysis guided by a moral, political, "ahistorical" standard. The supreme craft of the historian lies in art of "editing" (*pi-hsiao*), which was first masterfully demonstrated by Confucius' recension of the *Ch'un-ch'iu* in the sixth century B.C. The task of all subsequent historians is to imitate this primal historico-political act of editing and interpretation.

Historical Interpretation in *Hsiao-shuo* Criticism

The historical paradigm is pervasive in the interpretation of literary works, especially narrative works. Ideas and expectations about historiographical writings soon lent themselves to the reading of historical romances. A conspicuous case of the use of the theory of legitimacy in fiction criticism is Mao Tsung-kang's (fl. 1670) "Tu *San-kuo chih* fa" (On the methods of reading the *Romance of the Three Kingdoms*). Mao maintains that this popular novel was written in emulation of Confucius' *Ch'un-ch'iu*. The purpose is to praise the pious and the worthy and condemn the impious and the wicked. At the beginning of his study, he reminds the readers of the difference between "legitimate rule" (*cheng-t'ung*) and "interregnum" (*jun-yun*) and "usurped rule" (*chien-kuo*) in the historical romance (Chu and Liu, *San-kuo yen-i*, 293). In this regard, he recommends that readers follow Chu Hsi rather than Ssu-ma Kuang. The Shu was the legitimate state, the Wu and the Wei were the usurpers, and the Chin (265–419) was the interregnum. Although the Wei occupied the central plains and the Shu was squeezed to the southwestern corner of China, the Shu was the legitimate successor to the Han dynasty in principle.

In Chinese vernacular fiction, events seemingly become meaningful if and only if they are related to a historical or, perhaps more appropriately, an ahistorical context. This or that particular episode makes sense insofar as it can be situated in some grand scheme of history. Thus, the Mao Tsung-kang version of *The Romance of Three Kingdoms* begins by invoking a timeless lesson. The narrator proclaims that "the general tendency of a world is that a long division will inevitably end in union, and a long union will inevitably end in division." Then he cites examples from China's past to illustrate this idea.

Moreover, beneath the vicissitudes of the past lies a deep moral logic. The Wan-li (1573–1620) edition of the *Chin P'ing Mei*, the *Chin P'ing Mei tz'u-hua*, begins by alluding to early historical examples. The narrator brings up the story of the Han founder Liu Pang and his arch-rival Hsiang Yü and cautions the reader against the attractions of feminine beauty. The dangers are amply illustrated in the novel as Hsi-men Ch'ing's sexual indulgence leads to his self-destruction. By telling the story in such a fashion, the narrator alerts the reader to a great, transhistorical moral paradigm. This is also true of Chang Chu-p'o's (1670–98) commentary to the *Chin P'ing Mei*, which directs the reader's attention to the importance of the underlying structural recurrence of filial piety and brotherly love. The first chapter begins with the idea of brotherly love (*t'i*). While Hsi-men Ch'ing and his friends swear "brotherhood," Wu Sung meets his elder brother Wu Ta and his sister-in-law Pan Chin-lien. The beginning as well as the bulk of the novel offers an upside-down picture of true brotherhood. But in the final chapter, the son of Hsi-meng Ch'ing, the "filial brother" (Hsiao-ko), becomes a monk, thus redeeming his father from sin. It seems that a moral-historical paradigm lies beneath the countless episodes of the novel.

Chin Sheng-t'an (1608–61) constantly drew on the terminology and methods of historical interpretation in his criticism of the *Shui-hu chuan*. As a self-proclaimed "editor," Chin placed himself within the tradition of Confucius and Ssu-ma Ch'ien. His recension of the novel is to play a role similar to that played by the *Ch'un-ch'iu* and the *Shih-chi*. It is true that in the *tu-fa* (method of reading) essay and the preface forged by him but attributed to Shih Nai-an, he suggests that the author might not have had the deep-seated resentment (*fen*) other readers such as Li Chih (1527–1602) thought. Shih wrote the novel as a pastime and a literary game. But throughout the entire commentary, Chin gives us multiple hints as to the grand import of the book.

Chin begins his commentary on the Prologue (*Hsieh-tzu*) of the 70-chapter version of the novel by reflecting on the unusual title of the novel. The name of the novel must be clarified, "rectified," at the outset. The title "Water Margin" (*Shui-hu*) seems to have a deep meaning. The purpose of the Prologue (which incidentally was written by Chin) is after all to lead up to and bring forth some great moment. What is involved here is an issue of positionality. "Water margin" indicates a remote location away from the center. The story narrates actions occurring far away from the rule of law, civility, society, and the Confucian ideal of benign government: "In the entire realm, all people are the subjects of the king; under the heaven, all land is the king's." But the novel tells about 108 rebels who reside on the margin of the empire. The characters should have been protected by the benign rule of the Sung empire and been able to live peacefully. But they were forced to shun society and civilization. It is precisely at this juncture of marginality and centrality that Chin thinks the deep meaning of the novel, and by extension the meaning of fictional discourse in general, may be sought after. "If the [108] people did not really exist, I do not know how much injustice and suffering that the author of the book has to bear. He had to invent 108 people with words and locate them on the water margin" (*Shui-hu chuan*, 38). The author must have had a great purpose in writing a grand book of 70 chapters about 108 heroes.

In his commentary on the first chapter of his version of the story (the second chapter in the 100-chapter and the 120-chapter editions), Chin notes that the novel does not begin with any of the 108 Liang-shan heroes, although they are supposed to be the subject of the novel. Nor does Sung Chiang, the head of Liang-shan bandits, appear until much later in the work. Instead, the story begins with Kao Ch'iu, a corrupt and powerful minister in the court, and Wang Chin, a martial arts tutor in the imperial army. This becomes another opportunity for Chin to trace the deep significance of the novel. For Chin, beginning with a high minister like Kao Ch'iu indicates that the disorder in the empire originates from "above." It is governmental malfeasance that causes the uprising. A law-abiding, filial person, Wang Chin was persecuted by his superior Kao Ch'iu and forced to flee the capital city. This sorry state of affairs seems to be the origin of the uprising of the 108 heroes.

At this juncture, Chin reflects upon the nature of fiction (*hsiao-shuo*). The *Shui-hu chuan* belongs to the category of "unofficial history" (*pai-kuan*). "Allegories" (*yü-yen*) and "unofficial histories" are also "histories" (*shih*). The fiction writer is also a historian of a sort, though not officially appointed. Unlike official histories, unofficial histories are written by commoners (*shu-jen*). Under normal circumstances, commoners would not dare write histories or discuss state affairs. They do so because of the disappearance of the kingly way. Fiction, a marginal discourse, takes the place of official historical discourse because of a lack, an absence in the center. As an unofficial history, the *Shui-hu chuan* "records" the deeds of the 108 heroes.

In his commentary on Chapter 2, Chin takes another step closer to the origins and causes of the rebellion in the empire. He marvels at the talent and ability of the rebels. "Their talents are fit for the court, and their strength is fit for the battlefield. But they all entered the marshes against their will. Whose fault is it?" (81) Examining the novel chapter by chapter, Chin inquires into the layers of meaning beyond the surface level. Close reading becomes a process of retrieving hidden significance.

Chin draws parallels between canonical texts such as the *Ch'un-ch'iu*, the *Shih*, the *Tso chuan*, Ch'ü Yüan's *Li sao*, and Ssu-ma Ch'ien's *Shih-chi* on the one hand and great fictional texts such as the *Shui-hu chuan* on the other.[12] He discovers the methods of the *Ch'un-ch'iu* and the "historian's pen" (*shih-pi*) at work in the many instances of euphemisms and hidden expressions in the novel. He even attempts at times to explicate sections of the novel in the fashion of the *Kung-yang chuan*, *Ku-liang chuan*, and the *Li-chi*.[13] In the depiction of the characters, Chin Sheng-t'an finds the use of both the "straightforward style" (*chih-pi*) and the "circuitous style" (*ch'ü-pi*). Except for Sung Chiang, all the other 108 heroes are described in a straightforward fashion. Their good or bad qualities can easily be seen. But Sung Chiang is the character most difficult to understand. Although there is not a single word, sentence, section, and chapter in the entire novel that attributes negative qualities to him, Sung appears to Chin Sheng-t'an not as being a filial and trustworthy man but as the most hypocritical of all characters. This is due to the fact that the novelist used the indirect approach. "Praise and blame are necessarily lodged beyond words. *Hsiao-shuo* and standard history employ the same methods."[14]

In another place, Chin finds that, contrary to usual practice, the death of Luan T'ing-yü, the martial arts master, at the hands of the heroes of Liang-shan is not directly described and the hero who killed him is not named. This is because, according to Chin, the novelist adopted here the principle of the *Ch'un-ch'iu* of using evasive and euphemistic phrases in recording the deeds of the "honorable" (*tsun-che*), the "closely related" (*ch'in-che*), and the "worthy" (*hsien-che*). Out of respect for the dead, the story of the final combat is not told directly; in order to cover up the "crime" of the worthy hero, his identity is withheld.[15]

In his truncated 70-chapter version of the *Shui-hu chuan*, Chin points to the novel's underlying pattern of movement. As a result of his own editing, "the great book begins with peace in the empire and ends with peace in the empire." After many years of violence and disorder, harmony is re-established in the end. Chin subscribes to the Confucian moral-political vision of history, which is a cyclical process alternating peace and disorder.

A final example of this kind of reading procedure may be seen in Ch'i Liao-sheng's (ca. 1732–92) "Preface to the *Hung-lou Meng*," the first-known preface to the novel. The running theme of the Preface is the idea that double meaning is present throughout the work. The sense of a segment of the story never exhausts itself but develops into another sense, which is often the opposite of the first sense. In a description of prosperity, one already sees the impending decline; in the grace and beauty of the inner chambers of the women, one perceives voluptuousness and unseemliness; in the portrayal of Chia Pao-yü's licentiousness and silliness, one discovers his noble sentiment and intellectual awakening. The countless instances of double meaning in the novel are seen as analogous to the "hidden diction of the *Ch'un-ch'iu* and the circuitous style of the historian. . . . I say that the author has a twofold intention and the reader should have a single [perceiving] mind" (I Su, 27–28).

In all the examples of reading narratives, fictional or historical, discussed above, interpretation implies a surface-depth textual structure. The heterogeneous elements and various components of the narrative text are given a conceptual unity and structural closure. The exegetes and commentators, in an attempt to mediate and bridge the ambiguities, discrepancies, inconsistencies, and gaps inherent in a narrative, relate all details to an all-encompassing, totalizing paradigm. The ultimate ground of intelligibility for such a moral-historical hermeneutics remains a notion of history. For Confucian readers such as Chin Sheng-t'an, Mao Tsung-kang, and Chang Chu-p'o, the challenge of reading the Chinese novel lies in penetrating the surface level of the text to discover a hidden ideological, moral, historical, or, better still, an "ahistorical" and "metahistorical" dimension of meaning.

The Poetics of Historiography

Liu [Chih-chi] speaks of the methods of historiography, but I
speak of the meaning of history; Liu discusses the redactions and
compilations by offices and bureaus, but I discuss the writings of
one school. These are totally different paths that do not intersect.
—Chang Hsüeh-ch'eng, Wen-shih t'ung-i, 333

When Liu Chih-chi stated that the function of historiography
was to eulogize the upright and castigate the wicked, he was
merely expressing a commonplace of Chinese historical criticism,
a position that by his time had been upheld for about a thousand
years. Like all Chinese historians, he believed that the role of the
historian is to judge the past. But what distinguishes Liu is his
critical approach to historiography, which he expounded in the
Shih-t'ung, a work whose scope and insight went unmatched until
Chang Hsüeh-ch'eng's *Wen-shih t'ung-i*. Later critics have given
his work mixed notices. While condemning him for being unorthodox, disrespectful, and iconoclastic, they have revered him for his
extraordinary historical talents and pungent analysis of specific
historical issues.[1]

As I stated earlier, Liu formulated and represented an extreme
approach to history, a "historiographical" approach. One may speak
of a critical hermeneutics, a "hermeneutics of suspicion," in his
case. To be sure, he believed in the authority of Confucius and
respected the status of the Six Classics. But where he differs from
others is his insistence on separating rather than conflating the
study of history and the study of Classics. In historical research, he
held that the *Shu* and the *Ch'un-ch'iu*, whatever their status as
sacred classics, must be examined and questioned from a strictly
historiographical point of view. "Unhistorical" elements, distor-

tions of facts, and demerits of any sort in previous histories, including Confucius' *Ch'un-ch'iu*, should be exposed and criticized.

The central principle of Liu's historiography is the direct recording of events as they really are (*shih-lu*). The historian should forgo euphemism, indirection, and misrepresentation. History is the simple, plain, and unadorned recording of facts, of things that actually happened. In writing history, one should give preference to "straightforward writing" (*chih-pi*) over "circuitous writing" (*ch'ü-pi*). The reader of histories must exercise independent judgment, an inquiring spirit, and some skepticism toward the past and the Classics. One should "question the old" (*i-ku*) and "puzzle over the Classics" (*huo-ching*). The *Tso chuan*, a text he loved and memorized as a boy, becomes the model for historical writing. He criticizes the other two commentaries on the *Ch'un-ch'iu* for redundancy, farfetched interpretation, and "non-narrativity." The *Ch'un-ch'iu* entries are made explicit and tangible by the *Tso chuan*'s narratives. The transparency and luminosity of the historical characters and events are rendered in a laconic and yet effective narrative style. One learns more about the natural connections between events, and about their causes, motives, development, and results by reading the stories in the *Tso chuan* than by following the speculative, hairsplitting exegeses of the *Kung-yang chuan* and *Ku-liang chuan*.

Liu thinks that in a well-written historical narrative, such as the *Tso chuan*, the meaning of the recorded events is self-evident and interpretation is superfluous. The historian does not need to comment on events and point out what is right and what wrong. A faithful, objective recounting of the past will enable the reader to see the moral inherent in the events. A perfect historical narrative obviates the need for interpretation. Good historical writing is characterized by a lucid, succinct style in which a few words evoke a plethora of meanings. In a chapter entitled "Narration" ("Hsü-shih"), Liu explained the desired style:

There are the manifest and the hidden in the language of writings. The manifest [*hsien*] is that which employs luxuriant words and elaborate statements and therein exhausts its principles. The hidden [*hui*] is that which saves words and makes short its composition, and its events thus spread outside the borders of the sentences. . . .

[In all these expressions,] the words are near, but the imports are far-reaching, the language is shallow but the principle is profound. Although the statements have already ended, the latent meaning is not exhausted. In making the reader know the kernel by looking at the surface and discern the bone by touching the hair, and in allowing him to perceive the event in the sentences and understand the three sides beyond the words, isn't the urgent significance of hidden [*hui*] expressions great indeed?   (Liu Chih-chi, 223, 225)[2]

Liu's view of the structure of language and meaning in historical narrative is completely different from the hermeneutic tenet of "great principles hidden in tiny words." With him, there is no discrepancy between language and meaning. He opts for a narrative language with the virtues of directness, plainness, transparency, laconism, and parsimony. Meaning and principles arise naturally, unobtrusively, and "effortlessly" from such a language; there is no need to resort to laborious interpretation. "Hiddenness" in language here means brief and clear narration in the style of the *Tso chuan*, not distorted recording as in the *Ch'un-ch'iu* or contorted interpretation as in the exegetical tradition.

Liu is critical of Confucius and the *Kung-yang chuan* and *Ku-liang chuan* for errors of fact and for farfetched interpretations of historical events. For instance, in the winter of the twentieth year of Duke Hsi, what really happened was, according to the *Tso chuan*, that the Duke of Chin summoned the Chou king to a meeting. Confucius' entry, "The King held a court of reception at Ho-yang," violates the rule of historical objectivity and is therefore bad historiography. Liu thinks that Confucius committed another mistake in an entry for the second year of Duke Min.[3] Confucius wrote: "The twelfth month, the Ti barbarians entered Wei" (*Ti ju Wei*). The *Tso chuan* reveals that the barbarians attacked and conquered the small Chinese state of Wei. In employing an euphemism—the barbarians "entered" Wei—Confucius showed respect to Duke Huan of Ch'i, the hegemon of the Chinese states at the time. Since Huan was considered a worthy ruler, Confucius did not blame him for his failure to protect a Chinese state from a barbarian conquest. For Liu, the moral lessons from the two incidents would have been all the more obvious had Confucius recorded them in straightforward manner.

The curious point in Liu's historiography is his belief in a natural, inevitable link between language and meaning, and between signifier and signified. His fundamental assumption is that human relations are grounded in the nature of things and events. Once the stories of the past are narrated "objectively," the reader can draw moral lessons from what he reads. Interpretation becomes superfluous once objective historical discourse locates everything within a transparent, natural perspective. At this point, his initial "negative hermeneutics of suspicion" apparently transforms into a positive poetics of *vraisemblance*. In the end objective narration and realistic description support the existing conventions of representing history. The writing of history does not constitute the "real" but creates, in Barthes's words, a "reality effect" (Barthes, "Historical Discourse," 154).

Chinese historians have long been conscious of the question of verisimilitude in historical discourse. Liu distinguished two types of narratives in the section entitled "Imitation" ("Mo-ni"). Some narratives resemble the depicted objects in appearance but are remote from them in essence (*mao-t'ung erh hsin-i*). Others may appear different from the represented objects in form but capture their essence (*mao-i erh hsin-t'ung*). He considers the second type superior for its capacity to represent reality more truthfully. Chang Hsüeh-ch'eng made a similar point in discussing fabrication in historical discourse.[4] In the recording of events, addition and creation are forbidden. However, in the presentation of the speeches of historical characters, there is allowance for inventiveness. The following, often-quoted passage explains Chang's views:

In regard to the method of recording speeches, there is no invariable rule for addition and reduction. It all depends on what the author wants. But the [author] must infer what was in the speaker's mind on that day. In that case, the addition of a thousand words is not too many. But when [the author] comes up with what was not in the speaker's mind on that day, the addition of one word is fabrication as well, even if the words make up a good composition. (Chang Hsüeh-ch'eng, *I-shu*, 14: 126)

As Chang admitted, fiction is not entirely absent in history.[5] The historian may invent, fabricate, and fictionalize within certain limits so long as his presentation produces a "reality effect," an atmosphere of verisimilitude. The historical representation of reality mixes both the real and the probable. Despite Liu's insistence on the centrality of *shih* (the real, the factual, the actual) in the writing of history, elements of the *hsü* (the imaginary, the empty, the invented) are indispensable. Historical events become intelligible only in historical discourse. History "means both the *historiam rerum gestarum* and the *res gestas* themselves, both the events and the narration of the events. (It means both *Geschehen* and *Geschichte*)" (Hegel, 75).

Generations of readers have acclaimed Ssu-ma Ch'ien as a historical genius. Although faulted for a love of the exotic and the strange, a fondness for describing unconventional characters, and an unorthodox outlook, he has been hailed for his faithful, straightforward recording of historical events [*shih-lu*]. Pan Ku left the following assessment of Ssu-ma Ch'ien:

Since Liu Hsiang and Yang Hsiung, who had erudite knowledge of books, all have acclaimed Ssu-ma Ch'ien as having the talent of a good historian. They admire his expertise in relating the principles of events, his being argumentative but not superficial, unadorned but not vulgar. The writing is direct, and the events are verifiable. He did not indulge in empty praise, nor did he conceal evils. This is why it [the *Shih-chi*] has been called truthful recording (*shih-lu*).[6]

Ssu-ma Ch'ien himself disclaimed any creation or authorship on his part; he understood his work as a record of the past. "I call it the narration of past affairs and the sorting out of what has been passed down over generations, not what is called creation" (Takigawa, 10: 5207). Yet, the historian's matter-of-fact recording of past events does not explain the tremendous aesthetic appeal of the *Shih-chi*. The *Shih-chi* has been admired for its vivid descriptions of historical conflicts and canny psychological insights into individual characters. Readers have been enthralled by the lifelike, verisimilar depictions of remote historical events. In his letter "Discussing Writing with Governor Ts'ai Pai-shih," the Ming critic Mao K'un (1512–1601) documents his contemporaries' responses to the *Shih-chi*:

When people today read the biography of the knights-errant, they care less about their own life; when they read the [joint] biography of Ch'ü Yüan and Chia I, they want to weep; when they read the biography of Chuang Chou and Lu Chung-lien, they want to leave the world; when they read the biography of Li Kuang, they want to fight with strength;

when they read the biography of Shih Chien, they want to be humble; when they read the biographies of Han Hsin and the Lord of P'ing-yüan, they want to befriend gentlemen. How does this happen? It is because [Ssu-ma Ch'ien] has captured the nature of the objects and the heart of the characters.   (Huang Tsung-hsi, 1552)

The literary affects and emotional appeals of Ssu-ma Ch'ien's prose have elicited empathy and identification from countless readers. In the process of reading, the reader is engrossed by the ethics and heroism of the historical world; he or she begins to identify with the model characters. Historical recording, literary effect, and socio-pragmatic function conjoin in the *Shih-chi*.

It is difficult to pinpoint the surreptitious transition from faithful recording to an aesthetic of verisimilitude in historical discourse. For historians, the vantage point is invariably the degree of fidelity to the past in a historical "record." It is, rather, the *hsiao-shuo* commentators who shed light on the poetics of historiography by proceeding from the nature of fictional discourse. The inspired commentaries of Chin Sheng-t'an and Chang Chu-p'o frequently erase the distinction between historical and fictional narrative. The *Shih-chi* and the *Shui-hu chuan* and *Chin P'ing Mei* are said to share many techniques of composition. Chin's "Tu ti-wu ts'ai-tzu shu fa" (How to read the fifth book of genius) and Chang's "*Chin P'ing Mei* tu-fa" (On the method of reading the *Chin P'ing Mei*) alert the reader to common methods of reading history and fiction. An understanding of the methods of the novels may enhance appreciation of the mechanisms of the *Shih-chi*, and a familiarity with the structural principles of the historical work may be in turn beneficial for the reading of fictional works.[7]

Readers of Chinese histories are impressed by the intricate, systematic organization of materials. The standard dynastic history does not revolve around a central theme but systematizes and categorizes primary sources and historical materials. The materials seem at times to be unprocessed, "unworked up," and of a highly authentic, objective nature. In comparison to Chinese histories, Greek histories look much more literary and fictive. In a seminal essay, Jaroslav Průšek compared Chinese and Western historiography. Greek histories, such as those of Herodotus and Thucydides, follow the epic model and unfold along a central narrative line.

Historical narrative is a powerful flow, "*eine Art fliessender Hand-lung*" (a flowing storyline), "*ununterbrochener Fluss*" (unbroken flow). Primary historical materials are "deformed" and subordinated to a continuous narrative stream, a unifying theme, a subject, or a main conflict, for example, the Peloponnesian War. In contrast to the Western fictional handling of history, Průšek finds that "the Chinese historian does not work up his historical sources, he does not combine the facts he has found in successive chains, *he does not fictionalize* them, but arranges them into certain categories. He does not strive at creating some sort of artistic picture of the past, but in presenting the material that has been preserved in the most accessible form to the reader" (Průšek, "History and Epics," 24; italics added).

Chinese historians have adopted one of two forms: the "chronicle" (*pien-nien*) and the composite "annals-biography" (*chi-chuan*). The latter, first established by Ssu-ma Ch'ien, has been used more frequently and became the standard for dynastic histories in later times. A dynastic history usually includes (1) annals of the imperial house (*pen-chi* or *ti-chi*); (2) treatises (*shu* or *chih*) on such matters as astronomy, geography, ritual and rites, music, literature and arts, and the economy; (3) biographies (*lieh-chuan*) of prominent individuals such as empresses, ministers, officials, generals, writers, and scholars, and descriptions of foreign states that had contact with or were known to the dynasty; and (4) chronological tables (*nien-piao*). Unilinear chronology is broken down into "segmented steps" (*Treppenabsatz*) and stratified multi-temporal sequences.

The intricate interweaving of annals and biographies gives a multiple perspective on historical events and personages from shifting angles. A set of annals or a biography incorporates original materials of all sorts—imperial edicts, necrologies, official papers, quotations. The effect is to evoke an aura of realism and authenticity. Dynastic histories set out to conjure up a vivid picture of all aspects of life under a dynasty and to some extent they succeed. The reader is overwhelmed by the vast amount of historical data and by the deceptively impartial, omniscient narration of past events and personages. When the voice of the historian-narrator finally intrudes upon the scene in brief summary remarks at the end of the annals and each biography, the moral and conclusions seem reasonable, natural, and inevitable. A hierarchical organization of materials in conformity to specific social and political standards is made to appear natural, unconventional, and unproblematic by a realistic poetics of historiography. As Andrew Plaks has pointed out, "the sense of an essentially *impersonal*, unmediated, setting forth of the facts as they actually happened is an aesthetic illusion that remains a constant model for other narrative genres further along the spectrum towards the fiction pole" (*Chinese Narrative*, 326).

Therefore, it seems incorrect to say that the Chinese historian does not fictionalize. The reality presented in a historical work is an artifact, reflecting a specific conception of the "real." As Průšek noted in his analysis of Chinese biography, the biographer

usually gathers a few anecdotes from the life of the given person, often of very problematic historical value, and on the whole without an attempt at chronological order. He selects, however, the kind of stories that are in accordance with the general image and stylization the given person has created by tradition. It is not a description of a concrete life, be it real or created out of fantasy, but the creation of a certain impression, the placing of this person in a specific pattern of thought and emotion. ("History and Epics," 29)

The historian cannot render the past as it is, but offers at best a perspective on or an impression of the past. Chinese historical discourse appears to be another arbitrary convention of representation, despite its claim to truth, fact, and objectivity. The realistic poetics of historiography creates an aesthetic illusion: an optical "middle distance" that "neither brings us too close to the object nor lifts us too far above it but views it in precisely the way that we ordinarily do in the daily business of living" (Culler, *Structuralist Poetics*, 143). What is perpetuated is no less than an ideology: a system of representations, images, myths, and ideas.[8] The Chinese historical convention ultimately naturalizes and legitimates the prevalent ideology and existing social order.

It has been pointed out that the modern Western historical discipline has been from the beginning in the service of the political interests of the bourgeois nation-state (White, *Content of the Form*, 58–82). The existence of historical discourse presupposes such notions as the legal subject, the agent, the state, the law, and moral consciousness. The "philosophy of history" and the "philosophy of right" are closely related. Hayden White asks, "Has any historical narrative ever been written that was not informed not only by moral awareness but specifically by the moral authority of the narrator?" (*Content of the Form*, 21) White's rhetorical question may be answered in the positive when we turn our eyes to the Chinese tradition. Historical discourse has always been a highly politicized activity in China: it has had to be at once objective and normative. The ideal of historical objectivity, the pragmatic concerns and didactic purposes of the historian, and the desired ameliorative social effects of the historical work are mixed into one single process. History may be called the grand metanarrative of legitimation and self-legitimation. Its authority is warranted by its self-defined function of truth telling. The legitimacy of official historical discourse in Chinese culture is secured in the transparency of such seemingly tautological statements as "Let the ruler be a ruler, the subject a subject," and "Call good good and bad bad." It legitimizes the "legitimate" rulers and subjects, sanctions the genealogical succession of reigns, and opposes the transgression of established social positions.

Hok-lam Chan postulates five levels in the legitimation process: procedural, coercive, semantic, scholastic, and popular. He argues that the semantic and scholastic have been the most conspicuous forms of legitimation in China and are richly documented in historical records. Semantic legitimation is the "articulation of extraordinary signs of a predominantly symbolic character indicative of the command of legitimate authority. These include ritual enactments, portentous events, concrete objects, or formulae of language that are derived from the religious, intellectual, and political traditions embraced by the elite groups, if not also by the general populace." Scholastic legitimation involves "the articulation and manipulation by the ruler or his agents of the concepts from the predominant religious, intellectual, and political traditions to confirm his claim to the mandate" (Chan, 17). Theories and ideas of legitimacy have evolved largely in the body of historical writings in China. Debates on questions of legitimacy have dealt with specific historical events and dynastic reigns. Apparently, historiography itself is the very matter and process of semantic and scholastic legitimation or, in other words, "semiotic" and "ideological" legitimation.

In China official history (*cheng-shih*) in its grand style constitutes and perpetuates the ideologies of legitimacy by drawing upon various sign systems and by borrowing concepts from all branches of existing knowledge. It includes special treatises on the calendar, astronomy, geography, the economy, the legal system, government offices, music, and rites, as well as charts of dynastic successions, catalogues of all existing books, the annals of the emperors, the categorization of the biographies according to status and vocation, and so forth. The official dynastic histories purport to represent the entirety of each dynasty in all dimensions: intellectual, political, ideological, economic, literary, and military. When read as a great composite narrative discourse, a historical work tells stories of legitimacy and illegitimacy through a series of narrative units, "semes," "narremes," and "ideologemes."

It is time to examine Chinese historical interpretation and the "poetics of historiography" more closely in the light of literary theory in order to reach some provisional conclusions. At the center of the present investigation is the question of interpretation or the relation between text and meaning. The Chinese and Western traditions are equally concerned with the unseen and deeper dimensions of meaning beyond the surface configurations of the text. There are, however, important and subtle divergencies as well as obvious convergencies in the interpretive procedures adopted by the respective traditions. These similarities and differences in textual interpretation are intimately tied to more basic epistemological and ontological assumptions. I begin by discussing the issue of multi-layered meaning in the context of allegory, allegoresis, or "allegories of reading," a mode of composition and interpretation that fell into disrepute with Romanticism but has regained an honorable place in recent literary criticism. In the comparative study of Chinese literature, one encounters both the temptation to apply the Western concept of allegory to the analysis of Chinese works and resistance to its use.

The titles of several of Plaks's studies, such as *Archetype and Allegory in the "Dream of the Red Chamber"* and the chapter "Allegory in *Hsi-yu Chi* and *Hung-lou Meng*" in *Chinese Narrative* seem to endorse an allegorical approach to Chinese narrative. In his research on Ming and Ch'ing vernacular fiction, Plaks noticed a preoccupation with "hidden meaning" (*yü-i*) or "deep significance" (*shen-i*) among the traditional commentators. According to these commentators, the authors had lodged specific meanings in their compositions. The reader's task is to be attentive to the areas of indirection and suggestion so as to catch the hidden meaning. The modern Chinese translation of "allegory" is *yü-yen*, a term whose locus classicus is the *Chuang Tzu*. *Yü-yen* are parables or *exempla* told by philosophers for didactic purposes. What Plaks has in mind as allegory are sustained narrative works invested with hidden meanings by the authors. Allegory is "a mode of composition in which extended structural patterns of a narrative text are intended to refer, in their overall configurations, to correspondingly complex patterns of intelligibility on some level not directly presented" (*Chinese Narrative*, 165).

Plaks also sets forth significant contrasts in epistemological and ontological assumptions between the Western conception of allegory and Chinese views of interpretation. A fundamental ontological dualism underlies Western allegory. The West posits a separation of two orders of existence, a distinction between a material, visible world and a spiritual, invisible world. "The function of allegory, in this system, then, is to define the multiple links, or correspondences, by means of which events and relations within one plane are made intelligible on the basis of analogous relations known to hold in the second" (*Archetype*, 87–88). This two-level cosmology is absent in the Chinese tradition. The Chinese do not subscribe to a view of an existential disjunction of two realms; rather, they understand the world as a continuous and contiguous whole. They are more baffled by the sheer vastness of space, the great expanse of the totality of existence facing the short span of human life. They strive to transcend the mortal's finite mind and move toward a "total vision" of the universe. The Chinese style of interpretation is therefore characterized not by a temporal projection and progression from one level to a higher level but by an increase in the breadth of vision.

In *The Reading of Imagery in the Chinese Poetic Tradition*, Pauline Yu also highlights the basic Western assumption of a disjunction between the visible and invisible, the contingent and the real, and text and sense in literary interpretation. "Western allegory creates a hierarchical literary universe of two levels, each of which maintains its own coherence, but only one of which has ultimate primacy" (21). Again, the root of the matter harks back to the Western conception of art. Art is poeisis, mimesis, fiction, creation, fabrication. The poem or the literary artifact is made in relation to a reality that is more substantial and yet ontologically distinct from it. The work is separated both from the level of concrete reality and from the realm of immutable Ideas. The structure of allegory partakes of the same relation generally assumed between the poem and the reality signified by it and lying beyond it. "Saying one thing and meaning another," allegory cannot be taken at face value as a literal record of actual events. "It is a system of signs whose very meaning consists in asserting their fictiveness and their function as signifiers for something beyond the text" (20– 21). The concrete, the literal, the historical, and the contingent are subordinated to a level of meaning and existence that is abstract, eternal, timeless, and divine.

Yu also mentions another medieval interpretive tradition—figural or typological interpretation. In this type of interpretation, as elucidated by Erich Auerbach, both the sign and what it signifies are taken as real, concrete historical events.

> Figural interpretation establishes a connection between two events or persons, the first of which signifies not only itself but also the second, while the second encompasses or fulfills the first. The two poles of the figure are separate in time, but both, being real events or figures, are within time, within the stream of historical life. Only the understanding of the two persons and events is a spiritual act, but this spiritual act deals with concrete events whether past, present, or future, and not with concepts or abstractions; these are quite secondary, since promise and fulfillment are real historical events, which have either happened in the incarnation of the Word, or will happen in the second coming. (Auerbach, *Scenes from the Drama*, 53)

Figural interpretation does not deny the historicity of the two sets of events. The earlier events and persons are not considered contingent vehicles for the expression of higher truths but are themselves significant stages in real, historical, and divine processes. The historical aspect of figural interpretation is no less important than the allegorical, dualistic presupposition between what is said and what is meant.

Yu also outlines some unique features of the Chinese "historical" mode of literary interpretation. The Confucian process of reading poetry is one of *contextualization*, in which the preferred mode is to read a poet's works as literal records of actual experience from which a biography can be constructed. The moral lesson "arises from a specific context, and for a specific historical reason" (Yu, 76). Traditional Chinese readers of poetry attempt to determine and illumine the original contexts of the poems, the biographical and social occasions behind them, contemporary conditions, and the possible lessons to be drawn. Chinese exegetes of poetry are interested in learning about concrete, historical experiences of this world. As we will see, these findings also bear upon aspects of Chinese historical interpretation of narrative.

To be sure, the Western teleological or eschatological conception of history is largely absent in Chinese historical thought. Western historical interpretation, stemming from Judaeo-Christian thinking, in the sundry forms of allegorical exegesis, figural interpretation, the dialectic of the Spirit, and "neo-Marxian hermeneutic," presupposes successive stages of history and describes history as a temporal progression from a beginning to a final destiny. It posits a corresponding hierarchization of interpretive horizons and fixes textual meaning within some ultimate level of intelligibility. Hence, the Western critic speaks of history as a relation of "promise and fulfillment," "fall and redemption," and thinks of the text in terms of "prefigurations," "traces," or "anticipations" of moments of history, such as the Final Judgment, the Second Coming, or the succession of Modes of Production.

Western historical consciousness is predetermined by visions of history and is necessarily cast in metahistorical terms. Disparate past events can be located within the process of "history" only through particular conceptions of the nature and destiny of humanity. Thus, Hayden White tells of "modes of emplotment" or styles of writing in nineteenth-century Western historiography in his book *Metahistory*. History may be variously emplotted as romance, comedy, tragedy, and satire, depending upon the vantage point of the historian. In later work, White reflects on the possibility of a "sublime" Western notion of history, "an apperception of history's meaninglessness" (*Content of the Form*, 72), in which one cannot weave the spectacle of human events and terrors into a coherent, meaningful whole. But in general, Western historians and philosophers of history have created "myths" of history that exhibit clear patterns of progression or regression. History can be and has been read along various master plots, such as comedy, romance, human emancipation, progress, fall and redemption, or the eventual resolution of conflicts.

The contemporary Western "historical" or "hermeneutic" approach to the study of narrative is unable to fall back securely upon an epistemology of representation, say, in the manner of Georg Lukács or Erich Auerbach. Nor is it able to retain wholesale the premises and assumptions of the old historicist notion of understanding, for example, that of Hegel or Dilthey.[9] But it still retains some of the historical and mimetic intentions and goals of literary and historical studies. Critics holding this position would not dissolve the text into a limitless playground of the weaving and unweaving of meaning without any extra-textual references. They look for traces of historical processes, potential meanings and lessons, and above all vestiges of "History" through the mechanisms, arduous and even imperfect, of textual mediation and totalization.

A good instance of the historical approach in contemporary literary criticism is Fredric Jameson's new "Marxian hermeneutic." At the opening of *The Political Unconscious*, Jameson states that the one absolute and even "transhistorical" imperative of all dialectical thought is to "always historicize." The reader comes to know, however, that now "History" is an "absent cause," no longer directly accessible, and stands to a large extent as a "narrative category" (102). Analogous to Chang Hsüeh-ch'eng's Tao, Jameson's history is not representable; even so, human beings must keep alive the necessity of representing it somehow. History is, according to Jameson, "fundamentally non-narrative and non-representational; what can be added, however, is the proviso that history is inaccessible to us except in textual form, or in other words, that it can be approached only by way of prior (re)textualization" (82). The conceptual difficulty is that on the one hand history as a real and objective social process, like Lacan's "Real," "resists symbolization absolutely"; on the other hand, it is apprehensible only through narrativization and textualization.

In an operation reminiscent of Western "teleological" thinking, and in an explicit evocation of the medieval fourfold allegorical scheme of exegesis, Jameson establishes a hierarchy of interpretive levels, or what he calls the three "distinct semantic horizons." The first horizon of the object of interpretation or the "text" is the *symbolic act*, which is the level of political history or the sequence of political events. The second horizon is the *ideologeme*, the level of the antagonistic collective discourses of social classes. The third and final horizon is the *ideology of form*, the level of the "symbolic messages transmitted to us by the coexistence of various sign systems which are themselves traces or anticipations of modes of production" (*Political Unconsciousness*, 75–76). What is to be noted here is a more general structure of interpretive procedures, not the specific Marxist shading in Jameson's hermeneutic. Jameson presupposes first a gap and then a correlation between the literary text and a much broader and substantial historical referent. Narratives are treated as symbols, indexes, prefigurations, "traces," and "anticipations" of real socio-historical processes even though they are not direct representations or "pictures" of the latter. The text always says something other than its literal truth. It is given a historical content, interpreted with a master code, and endowed with an overarching meaning.

The ambitions as well as the difficulties of historical hermeneutics can also be seen in Paul Ricoeur's recent multivolume study *Time and Narrative*. In attempting a "hermeneutics of historical consciousness," Ricoeur considers the ways in which a "poetics of narrative" may conjoin and respond to the "aporetics of temporality." At the conclusion of *Time and Narrative*, he proposes three aporias of temporality that narrative ultimately confronts and attempts to resolve. The first, "narrative identity," appears to result from a gap between phenomenological time and cosmological time, or between the private time of the soul and the public time of the world. Narrative activity creates a narrated "third time" that mediates and bridges the two initially separate times. This "third time" in a narrative work, as a result of the interweaving of the respective referential intentions of history and fiction, gives narrative identity, be it a character, an individual, or a historical community, a self-constancy, a cohesion, that partially overcomes the original temporal rift.

Ricoeur's second aporia of temporality, "totality and totalization," results from a tension between time as a collective singular and a dissociation in the three ecstasies of time—the future, the past, and the present. In order to achieve a oneness of time amid multiplicity, a "discordant concordance," Ricoeur dismisses the possibility of returning to a Hegelian notion of the *totality* of history. Instead, he suggests the necessity of *totalization*, "an imperfect mediation between a horizon of expectation, the retrieval of past heritages, and the occurrence of the untimely present" (3: 250). In other words, the new historical hermeneutics is "an open-ended, incomplete, imperfect mediation, namely, the network of interweaving perspectives of the expectation of the future, the reception of the past, and the experience of the present, with no *Aufhebung* into a totality where reason in history and its reality would coincide" (3: 207).

With the third and last aporia of temporality, Ricoeur reflects upon the "inscrutability of time and the limits of narrative." The question at stake is the very *unrepresentability* of time in narrative. Narrative seems to engage us in an impossible task. It attempts not only to represent something that remains unknown and impossible to represent, but also to refigure something that exceeds the ability of narrative as a genre or a mode of discourse to capture. Despite the limits of narrative, however, Ricoeur is far from willing to give up on it in the search for the unity and meaning of history. Compelled by an ethical and political imperative, he holds that "the reaffirmation of the historical consciousness within the limits of its validity requires in turn the search, by individuals and by communities to which they belong, for their respective narrative identity" (3: 274). The poetics of narrative is called upon by the politics of interpretation to offer possible solutions to the aporetics of time.

This "historical" approach to narrative is not only taken by many critics in relation to "literary" works but also underlines the very writing and reading of properly "historical" or historiographical works. Insofar as history is not satisfied with being a record of events but aspires to be a narrative, to give an explanation of things, to render meaning and coherence to the past, it is "a product of *allegoresis*." Historical narrative "figurates the body of events that serve as its primary referent and transforms these events into intimations of patterns of meaning that any literal representation of them as facts could never produce" (White, *Content of the Form*, 45). By an act of the will—an imposition of meaning through an interpretive scheme—historiography is always already figuratively allegorical in offering us a "truth" about the past arising above the surface literal level.

This short digression into the Western tradition may provide a backdrop against which to understand some important aspects of Chinese historical interpretation. Undoubtedly, my inquiry has benefited from the insights of earlier studies such as those of Plaks and Yu. Since I am, however, more inclined toward discovering patterns of the "politics of interpretation" in the Chinese critical tradition, my pursuit proceeds in another direction. Several characteristics of a mode of interpretation associated with the Confucian historiographical tradition, which is, after all, the valorized, official discourse in pre-modern China, emerge from my study. First, Chinese "historical" interpretation is concerned with the socio-historical contexts of the text. It attempts to disclose the background and origins of specific human actions in history and the reasons behind them. It is oriented toward the concrete, the particular, and the real in the past. Although the events and characters in a historical narrative are sometimes read as "allegories" or pretexts for the expression of some higher truths, they are the records of real, authentic, and historical occurrences and agents. Nevertheless, none of this implies that the historical disposition of the Chinese critical tradition is free from metaphysical and metahistorical presuppositions.

The attention and value given to the discovery of the contexts and details of concrete social and historical events is only half of Chinese historical interpretation. This preoccupation with the historically "real" is first animated by and then directed toward an "ahistorical" paradigm of interpretation.[10] From the viewpoint of the traditional exegete, this interpretive paradigm is perfectly natural, realistic, and inevitable. From the perspective of an outsider, however, the imposition of this scheme of interpretation upon narratives is by no means any less accidental or arbitrary than the imposition of Western allegoresis. The historical-minded Confucian readers are also equipped with a vision of history. The "is" and the "ought" are intertwined and become inseparable in historical interpretation. Behind all intentions of objectivity and empiricism in Chinese historical inquiry exists a deep-seated "political unconscious." A moral, ideological, and political measure underlies all search for the actual and real in history. For instance, one fundamental assumption of Chinese readers and writers of history is the central notion of "legitimacy": the legitimacy of social positions and the legitimacy of the succession of royal houses and dynasties. Indeed, Chinese historiography is an extension of Confucius' dictum "Let the sovereign be a sovereign, the subject a subject, the father a father, the son a son." It may be said that Chinese historical interpretation largely remains a hermeneutic of the story of legitimacy.

Not unlike Western allegoresis, Chinese historical exegesis imposes upon narrative an arbitrary "other meaning" beyond the surface events and personages. Here, I would like to highlight the post-structuralist sense of allegory. First, allegory is opposed to "symbol" and "imagery" in its resolute renunciation of any nostalgia and desire for an organic unity between text and meaning and between the object and the subject. Second, allegory is seen as a general feature of literature in its recognition of the distance and difference between sign and meaning. In allegory and all figural language, "the relationship between sign and meaning is discontinuous, involving an extraneous principle that determines the point and the manner at and in which the relationship is articulated. . . . The sign points to something that differs from its literal meaning and has for its function the thematization of the difference" (de Man, "Rhetoric of Temporality," 192).[11] The arbitrary link and non-coincidence between the signifier and the signified and between the referent and meaning reminds the reader of the internal difference within each and every narrative, be it historical or fictional. There always exists an inevitable difference between "events" and "principles" in Chinese narrative, a fact duly noticed by the exegetes.

Despite this acknowledgment of the non-identity of text and meaning, it is also part of the Chinese historiographical enterprise to create a semblance of the immanence of meaning in the text. The exegetes attempt to mediate the incongruent segments of the text, bridge the unavoidable distance between the signifier and the signified, and relate all details to a totalizing moral paradigm. All this is intended to narrate a credible story of the "rectification of names," of the establishment of lawful identities, and of the positioning of subjects in relation to a social hierarchy. Chinese historiography, as a grand metanarrative of legitimation, aims at rendering human social institutions such as the Patriarch, the Emperor, the Father, the State, and the Law into natural, transparent, and universal relations.

Reading T'ang Fiction as
History, Allegory, and Fantasy

But I cannot forget that, at other times, I have been deceived in
sleep by . . . illusions; and, attentively considering those cases, I
perceive so clearly that there exist no certain marks by which the
state of waking can ever be distinguished from sleep, that I feel
greatly astonished; and in amazement I almost persuade myself
that I am now dreaming.
—René Descartes, *Meditations on the First Philosophy*, 114

The T'ang period is one of the high points in the history of
Chinese narrative. New narrative genres emerged and flourished, and historians and literary critics developed an awareness of
the multiplicity of narrative forms. As mentioned early, Liu Chih-
chi wrote a chapter entitled "Miscellaneous Narratives" ("Tsa-
shu") in his *Shih-t'ung* to deal with what he considered ten types
of narrative materials outside the standard histories. The "Ching-
chi chih" of the *Sui-shu* lists 217 titles in the category "miscellaneous biographies" (*tsa-chuan*) and treats them as one of thirteen
types of "historical writings." In both instances, the historian-bibliographers adopted a historical approach toward various narrative materials and basically regarded them as marginal forms of
history.

In this chapter I analyze T'ang modes of reading fiction in an
attempt to reconstruct them. I ask how potentially subversive fictional texts were naturalized, appropriated, and accepted by the
literati and what were the modes of reading that allowed fictional
writings to be positively interpreted and used by the official culture.

Every reader of a narrative brings to the reading a particular conception of truth and reality. He or she will decide whether a given narrative is plausible, true, or approximately true (verisimilar, *vraisemblable*) in accordance with a set of assumptions and expectations about the nature of language and literature. The question of plausibility in narrative is not to be understood as a correspondence between language and some extra-linguistic reality. Rather, it has to do with a communication network between the sender/writer and receiver/reader. The "real" is not that which corresponds to "reality" but that which appears to be real in the eye of the reader. What confronts narrative theory is the issue of, not truth per se, but truth-saying, appearing-to-be-true, causing-to-appear-to-be-true. A. J. Greimas, in his discussion of semiotic theory, created the concept of "veridiction," or the veracity of narrative discourse. "By shifting our apprehension of the realm of the 'true' from a locus of referentiality external to language and into the context of the utterance itself, we become involved with a highly specialized discursive construct, whose primary function is being recognizable as being the constitution of a *meaning effect of truth*" (Maddox, 662). A narrative appears to be real and true precisely because it is able to create an effect of truth and gain the trust of its audience. In a roughly homogeneous culture, there exists "a more or less stable equilibrium arising from an implicit agreement between [the sender and receiver,] these two actants of the communication schema" (Greimas, 653). Greimas calls this tacit agreement the "veridiction contract."

As I suggest in Chapters 3 and 4, Chinese historical discourse had to meet two major criteria to appear plausible to the reader: a poetics of narrative that was realistic, naturalistic, and verisimilar, and a hermeneutic that established a meaningful pattern for the course of human history. Historical writings that met these two conditions were taken as credible discourse about the real by the general reading public. Official history was the norm against which the truthfulness of other, minor types of narrative was measured. Its view of things conformed to "common sense" and public opinion. Such "public opinion" is what constitutes discursive *vraisemblance* for Genette: "Such 'opinion,' real or supposed, is precisely what is today called ideology, that is to say, a corpus of maxims and prejudices that constitutes at the same time a vision of the world and a system of values" ("Vraisemblance et motivation," 6).

Any narrative that violates such a "vision" and "system of values" is regarded as non-historical or anti-historical and as belonging to the categories of the strange, the supernatural, the fantastic, and the exotic.

By the T'ang, biographical writings existed in great numbers. Despite their diversity, and at the risk of conceptual and classificatory confusion, all were placed under the same generic heading of *chuan* (biography). Bibliographers subdivided the category into *lieh-chuan* (historical biography), *pieh-chuan* (separate biography), *tsa-chuan* (miscellaneous biography), and so forth. The assumption was that the separate and miscellaneous biographies were not as plausible and real stories of people as the official historical biographies were. "Biographies" of demons, animals, inanimate objects, and supernatural beings were considered even further removed from the realm of truth. There seems to have been a wide spectrum of "biographical" writings, ranging from the credible to the less credible, the incredible, and the very incredible.

It remains an important task to examine the degrees of "credibility" and the kinds of "meaning-effect" in these stories. Should, for example, the reader interpret Han Yü's (768–824) "Mao Ying chuan" (Biography of the fur point) in the same way as, say, Liu Tsung-yüan's (773–819) "Ho-chien chuan" (Biography of Ho-chien)? Is Li Kung-tso's (fl. 810) "Nan-k'o t'ai-shou chuan" (Biography of the governor of South Branch) as historically true as his "Hsieh Hsiao-o chuan" (Biography of Hsieh Hsiao-o)? Does the representation of a virtuous fox-woman in Shen Chi-chi's (ca. 741–ca. 805) "Jen Shih chuan" (Biography of Miss Jen) have the same kind of claim to truth as the historical discourse of *lieh-nü chuan* (biographies of virtuous women) has? In what way does fiction reaffirm the ordinary "horizon of expectations"? Or how might it restructure and question the prevalent ideas of the true and the *vraisemblable*? The answers to questions like these speak directly to the issue of the possible relation between the literary text and the original conditions of its reception and lead to an analysis of the mechanism of the "veridiction contract." All the T'ang figures mentioned and examined in the following are contemporaries or near-contemporaries. A study of the contrasts and similarities apparent in an intertextual comparison should make clear the nature of the various kinds of narrative discourse.

A perplexing problem in the reconstruction of historical conditions of reception is the question of whether there existed one "horizon of expectations" or several. As critics have pointed out, a model for a historically oriented reception study, such as Hans Robert Jauss's, may be one-sided and misleading in positing a single, homogeneous horizon of expectations at the expense of other literary and cultural currents. For the purposes of this discussion, however, it suffices to think of a normative, widespread, and officially valorized conception of narrative discourse that directs the production, circulation, and reception of writings. A text becomes subversive when it collides with that official notion of truth and provokes a controversy in literary circles. An initially controversial and defamiliarizing text may ultimately be received, after years or centuries of "naturalization," interpretation, and reinterpretation, as a standard and familiar text. The anti-canonical can become canonical as a result of internal structural adjustments within the hierarchy of writings.

Since the *Shih-chi*, the historical biography (*lieh-chuan*) has been a major constituent of the "annals-biography" form of dynastic histories. The historical biographies followed a predictable formal pattern. They relate the life stories of illustrious personages such as empresses, imperial concubines, members of the nobility, court officials, high-ranking ministers, generals, and famous scholars. In toto the biographies render a broad panoramic view of the dynasty by recording the life of individuals from a wide spectrum of society. It is also clear that the biographies are intended to be not only representational of the real life of individuals but also illustrative of general patterns in human history. They furnish models, exemplars, exempla, and ideal types. "The biography would serve either as a model to be emulated, suggesting to posterity courses of action likely to lead to success and approbation, or less commonly as a minatory example illustrating errors to be avoided" (Wright and Twitchett, 29). Many biographies are categorized into biographies of special types of people, for instance, "good officials," "harsh officials," "filial ministers," "trustworthy friends," "virtuous women," "Confucian scholars," "members of the literary garden," and "recluses." The biographer groups and schematizes historical figures in terms of their social status, profession, or moral standards.

The principles of the historical biography are perhaps best defined in several succinct statements by Liu Chih-chi. Liu muses on the connotations of the Chinese character *chuan* and explores its meaning for the biography. In "Six Schools" ("Liu-chia"), the first chapter of the *Shih-t'ung*, Liu writes: "The biography [*chuan*] is to transfer [*chuan*], to transfer the ideas of the Classics one has received to posterity. Some say that the biography [*chuan*] is to perpetuate [*ch'uan*], that which is to be perpetuated and made known to future generations" (Liu Chih-chi, 14). The conflation of the two meanings of the *chuan* as "commentary" to the Classics and as "biography" is not unique to Liu Chih-chi. In fact, *chuan* may mean both things in the *Tso chuan*, the origin of the term. In the *Wen-hsin tiao-lung*, Liu Hsieh (ca. 465–ca. 522) discussed the creation of the *chuan* form in the *Tso chuan*. In Chapter 6, "Historical Writings" ("Shih-chuan"), he states, "By *chuan*, or to comment, is meant to *chuan*, or to transfer the ideas of the Classics one receives to those who come after one" (Liu Hsieh, 169). This point is further elaborated in Chapter 6, "Lieh-chuan" (Historical biography) of the *Shih-t'ung*.

The annals-biography form begins with the *Shih-chi* and the *Han-shu*. The annals make a chronicle of the years. The biography [*chuan*] records events. The chronicle lists the years and months of the emperors, as, for example, the entries of the *Ch'un-ch'iu* do. The record of events registers the conduct and behavior of the subjects [*jen-ch'en*], as in the commentaries on the *Ch'un-ch'iu*. In the *Ch'un-ch'iu*, the commentaries elucidate the entries. In the *Shih-chi* and the *Han-shu*, the biographies [*chuan*] explain the annals. (49)

Another passage reveals Liu's conception of characters suitable to be entered into a historical record. Chapter 30, "Characters" ("Jen-wu"), opens with the following words:

As for the life of men, there are the worthy and unworthy. If one's wickedness is enough to be a warning to the world, or if one's goodness is enough to provide a paragon for posterity, and if his name is not heard on the day of his death, whose fault is it? It is the responsibility of the historian. (315)

Several notable features of the historical biography emerge from the preceding discussion. The biographer tends to give a "formulaic" treatment to historical figures. Individuals are cast into prearranged patterns of life and categories of people, such as "recluse," "Confucian scholar," "good official," "bad official," "empress," "imperial concubine," "virtuous woman," and so forth. The biographies are essentially portraits of social positions rather than of individual beings. The task of the biography is, as Liu Chih-chi states, to relate the "conduct and behavior of subjects." The reader is brought to the realization that characters in a dynastic history function as the subjects of the emperors performing specific social roles. The effect of reading history is, in the end, a problem of identification, namely, the reader's identification of himself as a subject. Again, Liu's wordplay on biography as perpetuation and transference is highly suggestive of the ideological function of historiography. Historical biography sets out to transmit identities to posterity and to produce and reproduce social positions and lawful subjects for the state. Historical events and characters provide examples, models, values, roles, and ideals for present and future generations.

The idea that the biographies serve to explain the annals of the emperors in a dynastic history just as commentaries explain the Classics is also revealing of a historical hermeneutic. The reader must correlate the stories of individual historical subjects meaningfully to the whole history of a given dynasty. Historical sequence consists in dynastic cycles and the alternation of imperial reigns, and historical time is punctuated by the days, months, and years of the reign of the emperor. The deeds and conduct of individuals happen in the historical-imperial time of the reigning emperor and revolve around the world-historical actions and events of the imperial court. The subjects of the biographies are defined in relation to and therefore subjugated to the sovereigns of the imperial annals in historical interpretation.[1]

It might be said that in the dynastic history, the ideological function of the annals is the legitimation and perpetuation of the imperial rule, and that of the biographies is the formation of subjects. The subjects are represented as unified, rational, and self-conscious characters in full mastery of themselves.[2] In this respect, the Chinese biography resembles Plutarchian biography in the West, which is "almost the perfect complement of realistic fiction.[3] Its subject is real, a 'historical' personage, but its substance is highly fictionalized in the interest of emotion and moral instruction" (Scholes and Kellogg, 66). The biography is oriented toward an organizing idea, a specific "character" or personality. The biographer illustrates the character of the historical figure through his deeds and statements. And for this purpose, one or two exemplary episodes from the life of a given personality suffice. Historical figures are not presented in their contradictoriness at crucial moments of history. Biographical time merely serves as a means to disclose character in deeds and words. The biography is a portrait of a well-rounded, stable, and unified subject with great moral strength.

At its first appearance, Han Yü's "Mao Ying chuan" was seen as a new, unfamiliar kind of writing. There was no predictable pattern of response for readers to follow. "Mao Ying," a writing brush, was personified as a servant of the First Emperor, Ch'in-shih Huang-ti (259–210 B.C.). Some readers found this personification, historicization, and possibly allegorization of a trivial inanimate object unsettling and scandalous. Chang Chi (ca. 765–ca. 830) criticized Han Yü, his revered master in the archaic-style (*ku-wen*) prose movement, for writing this "biography." For Chang, to indulge oneself by writing something like the "Mao Ying chuan" was inappropriate and unserious, a departure from the Way of the sages. The defenders of the piece also invoked the authority of the Classics and Confucius. They contended that even the sages themselves had had time for relaxation, amusement, and jokes. In letters by Han Yü defending himself against Chang Chi's charges of impropriety, and in Liu Tsung-yüan's remarks on his impressions of the "Mao Ying chuan" ("Postface After Reading the 'Biography of Fur Point' by Han Yü"), Han and Liu justified the writing of unofficial biographies as a literary game, a play on words, and a humorous amusement for themselves and friends (Ma T'ung-po, 76–79; Liu Tsung-yüan, 366–67). Liu Tsung-yüan's reading of Han Yü's story was less allegorical and moralistic. He viewed the story primarily as a play on the subject of writing itself and as an expression of a vivid imagination. There was much pleasure to be derived from such literary activity. It took a contemporary to enjoy the "inside joke" and "laughter" within these writings (Nienhauser, "Allegorical Reading," 172).[4]

Li Chao (fl. 818) in the *T'ang kuo-shih pu* (Supplementary history of the T'ang) praised Han Yü for displaying the talents of a good historian in "Mao Ying chuan": "Shen Chi-chi wrote the 'Chen-chung chi' (The world inside a pillow), which was in the vein of an allegory [*yü-yen*] by Chuang Tzu. Han Yü wrote the 'Mao Ying chuan.' Its writing was exceptional, not below that of the historian Ssu-ma Ch'ien. The two pieces were by people with a real talent for history" (Li Chao, *chüan* 3, 8).

Li Chao approached the two fictional works within the generic expectations of historical and allegorical works. For him, the literary standard for fiction writers was historical discourse. He praised these two writers because they showed a talent for writing history. Shen Chi-chi was a court historian, and his "Chen-chung chi" was included as an "allegory" (*yü-yen*), a subcategory of *chi* (record), in the great Sung literary anthology, the *Wen-yüan ying-hua* (Fine flowers of the literary garden). Han Yü's "Mao Ying chuan" was included in the biography section (*chuan*) of the same anthology.

There seem to be two major modes of reading and appropriating fictional works in the T'ang: the historical and the allegorical (in the sense of *yü-yen*). I discuss the historical mode of reading in Chapter 3. The necessary condition for the historical mode is that the events and characters described in the unofficial "fictional" biographies must appear sufficiently real so that they can be accepted as real by readers. Most so-called *ch'uan-ch'i* tales do not meet this condition and thus have been read as stories of the supernatural, the strange, and the inexplicable.

When the historical mode of reading is no longer suitable, the reader passes to the "allegorical" mode in order to make sense of the text. "Allegory" here is understood in the narrow sense of Chinese *yü-yen*, which has been both a genre of writing and a kind of reading since Chuang Tzu's *yü-yen*. In Chapter 4, I touch on the notion of allegory in the context of post-structuralist criticism and take it to describe a general feature of literature and language. Allegory reveals the arbitrary, conventional relation between signifier and signified, between words and meaning. This certainly holds true for Chinese *yü-yen* as well. But in the present discussion, I limit myself to allegory as a literati strategy for reading literary texts.

In China allegory is deemed a weaker and lower kind of writing than history because of its association with the anecdotes and fables of pre-Ch'in philosophers. Its origin is non-Confucian, Taoist, "heterodoxical." Allegorical reading was, however, a common mode of reading among the Confucian literati. In such a mode, the reader recognizes the fictionality of the stories and thus does not take them as historically true. The stories become meaningful at the didactic and philosophical level. They may teach a moral lesson. Stories about weird dreams, ants, foxes, and dragons were not believed to be literally true despite the simulated historical rhetoric of the narrator. Once these stories are not taken to be historically real, they may be read allegorically. For instance, the "Nan-k'o t'ai-shou chuan" and the "Chen-chung chi" may be read as Taoist allegories that reveal the meaninglessness of the busy career of a Confucian civil servant and point to the true Way. By the same token, the "Mao Ying chuan" may be read as a "Confucian" allegory about the relationship between the minister and the sovereign. It criticizes the sovereign's lack of virtue in forsaking an aged loyal minister. For a militant Confucian, however, Taoist and Buddhist allegories were still unacceptable. The term *yü-yen* did not find "wide acceptance in the lexicon of the traditional Chinese critic" (Hartman, 25).

A story that cannot be reasonably construed either historically or allegorically is meaningless, frivolous, exotic, devious, subversive. This was the fate of numerous fictional narratives that could not be understood within the official cultural code. Here we arrive at the "fantastic," a label that characterizes an uncertain attitude in both the text and the reading process.

The Historical Mode of Reading

The "Hsieh Hsiao-o chuan" by Li Kung-tso, author of the "Nan-k'o t'ai-shou chuan," was one of the few unofficial fictional biographies read in the historical mode and appropriated as history. Li Kung-tso relates the life of an extraordinary woman and his personal involvement in the story. Hsieh Hsiao-o is born into a rich merchant family and marries Tuan Chü-chen, a gallant knight-errant. On a business trip, her father and husband are robbed and killed by bandits. In a dream, Hsiao-o is visited by her dead father and husband, who present her with two word puzzles in twelve Chinese characters that are clues to the identity of their murderers. She vows to avenge the murders. For many years, she asks various people for help in solving the puzzles, but nobody can decipher them. Li Kung-tso happens to visit the area and meets Hsiao-o. He solves the puzzles for her and reveals the identity of the murderers, the brothers Shen Lan and Shen Ch'un.

Hsiao-o disguises herself as a man and manages to find work as a servant in the house of Shen Lan. Her diligence wins the trust of the brothers, who never suspect that she is a woman. She notices that half the treasures in their house formerly belonged to her family. One night when the brothers are drunk, she kills them and brings about the capture of the entire bandit gang. The city magistrate is so moved by Hsiao-o's noble deeds that he pardons her for the killing. She declines many proposals of marriage from the rich and famous and becomes a nun. Many years pass before she and Li Kung-tso meet again. She then relates to Li what has happened to her since their first meeting.

At the conclusion of the "Biography of Hsieh Hsiao-o," Li Kung-tso made the following comment, imitating the voice of the historian in the *Tso chuan*:

The gentleman [*chün-tzu*] says: to swear an oath without betraying it, and to avenge father and husband, this is integrity; to be a servant in the midst of others without revealing her female identity, this is chastity. The career of a woman can begin, end, and complete itself in nothing but integrity and chastity. [A woman like] Hsiao-o is enough of a warning to those intent on rebelling against principles and violating human relationships, and enough of an exemplum of the integrity of chaste husbands and filial wives. I related past events in detail, elucidated the hidden words, correlated them with the secrets of the supernatural, and complied with the principles of human affairs. Knowing virtuous acts without recording them is against the principles of the *Ch'un-ch'iu*. Thus I wrote this biography in order to praise her. (Wang Pi-chiang, 95)

The frame of the narrative, especially the concluding section, closely resembles that of a historical biography. The narrator's comment draws a moral from the events and sets up the protagonist as a paragon of virtue. The seriousness of intent and the factuality of the story, underscored by the authority of the voice of a dutiful historian at the end, seem to indicate that what has been told is history rather than fiction.

The story appears to have been widely known and believed to be true. Li Fu-yen (fl. 830–40) retold the events, citing Li Kung-tso, in the tale "Ni Miao-chi" (Sister Miao-chi) in his collection of stories *Hsü Hsüan-kuai lu* (Records of the mysterious and strange, continued). Later adaptations of the story are not hard to find. In the Ming, Ling Meng-chu (1580–1644) wrote a vernacular version of the story, which appeared as the nineteenth piece in the *P'ai-an ching-ch'i* (Slapping the table in amazement). Wang Fu-chih's *Lung-chou hui tsa-chü* (The meeting of dragon boats) is an early Ch'ing dramatic adaptation of the story. However, conclusive evidence of the belief in the historical authenticity is its incorporation into the "Lieh-nü chuan" (Biographies of virtuous women) chapter of the *Hsin T'ang-shu* (New T'ang history) compiled in the Northern Sung dynasty. The *lieh-nü chuan* genre was inaugurated by Liu Hsiang, a scholar of the first century B.C. It was part of the body of Confucian pedagogy, prepared by a scholar to inculcate the proper values in women. The *Hsin T'ang-shu* devotes a short section to the "wife of Tuan Chü-chen." The historical narrative is much shorter and much less dramatic compared to the original story. Whereas Li's account is first-person, "autodiegetic" (narrator as a principal character), and full of emotion and sentimental comment, the historical narrative is an impersonal, insipid, and plain record devoid of dialogue and dramatic scenes of action. Parts of the biography by Li Kung-tso—coincidences in the plot line, the decipherment of a dream—read like a fictitious story. The author of the section on Hsieh Hsiao-o in the collective biography of women has expurgated and downplayed the fictional elements and appears to tell the story of a real historical figure and something that really happened in the past.

The historicity of the story of Hsieh Hsiao-o need not concern us here. Whether Li Kung-tso made it up or recorded an actual event is irrelevant. The point is that the story *appeared* more or less real and true to some of his contemporaries or near-contemporaries and to future historians. The storyteller was able to marshal compelling evidence to support his story. The text itself gives many "veridiction marks": specific dates for events, real places and settings, details on the parentage and family background of the protagonist, and the storyteller as participant and eyewitness in the developments of the events. Another factor working for its acceptance as history must have been the edifying message that emerged naturally from the logic of the narrative. The concluding remarks reinforced and conformed to contemporary maxims concerning women and virtue. The particular story refers to a general moral, and the general moral in turn explains the particular story. The lesson at the end of the story is a natural continuation of the preceding account. The significance of the story seamlessly merges with the signification of the story. Thus the story is both historically credible and morally edifying. The historical mode of reading works perfectly well in this case.

By being incorporated into official history, the fictional work fulfilled the highest role it could aim at. After a process of selection and editing, fiction was elevated from the humble position of *hsiao-shuo*, unofficial history, supplemental history, and historical source to the status of history itself. The "Biography of Hsieh Hsiao-o" portrays the life of a woman who comes close to the image of a filial and virtuous female established by society. This fictional text is therefore not excluded from official discourse and assigned to oblivion; it is assimilated by history and transmitted to future generations. Hsieh Hsiao-o joins the company of a group of exemplary virtuous ladies in the *Hsin T'ang-shu*. As represented by historical discourse, she becomes a paragon of virtue and courage to be commemorated and emulated by posterity.

The Allegorical Mode of Reading

Liu Tsung-yüan, the famed master of the archaic-style prose movement, was a contemporary of Li Kung-tso and Shen Chi-chi and an occasional writer of unofficial and fictional biographies. One of the least remarked pieces in his oeuvre is "Ho-chien chuan," a story of a "lustful woman." In the story, Ho-chien is in the beginning a virtuous woman. Once married, she is a dutiful and respectful wife. She refrains from gossip, rarely appears in public, and does not step outside the house. However, her modesty and demeanor rouse the jealousy of her evil-minded in-laws and relatives, and they intrigue against her. They invite her out several times, to no avail. A year later, they finally succeed in persuading her to visit a remote Buddhist monastery. In the inner chambers of the monastery, there are food and entertainment. A handsome young man with a large penis waits on her and later attempts to ravish her. At first she cries and resists, but finally she gives in. She begins to like him and will not leave him. She departs only after repeated urgings by her people. After the episode, Ho-chien changes completely. She dislikes her husband and successfully plots his death. Her sexual appetite becomes insatiable.

Behind closed doors, she cavorted with licentious men, all naked, and indulged in lewdness. A year later, these men were exhausted. She became sick of them and drove them away. She attracted loose men from Ch'ang-an and had intercourse with them morning and night behind doors, still not tired. She also built a bar in the southwest. She herself lived on the upper floor. The door was left open so that she could secretly look down. A maidservant was used as a lure. Among those who came to drink, the big-nosed, the young and strong, the handsome, and those good at playing drinking games all came upstairs and copulated with her. She looked around even as she was copulating, afraid of losing a man. Moaning and dreamy all day long, she was still not satisfied. More than ten years later, she died of exhaustion of the bone marrow.   (Liu Tsung-yüan, 796)

Appended to the end of the biography is "Mr. Liu's comment." The moral lesson to be drawn from the story is the difficulty of preserving virtue and maintaining friendship. It is easy for people to change heart when circumstances prove coercive or profitable. Such is the case between husband and wife and "between friends; it is especially something to be feared in the relationship between sovereign and subject. Thus I wrote this on my own" (797). The story of the change from exemplary virtuous woman to monstrous sex maniac becomes an allegory of human relationships in a patriarchal society.

The lack in the "Ho-chien chuan" of the veridiction details that mark the "Hsieh Hsiao-o chuan" leaves the reader uncertain about the historicity of the story. The woman's name is not given. She is called Ho-chien because she is from the township of that name. Nothing is said about her background or her family. Temporal and spatial settings are not specified. The names of the other characters are unknown. The story hence reads more like a timeless allegory rather than a historical record. Yet the allegory is a forced and cumbersome one. Although the concluding statements are clichés and homilies, the unabashed description of female sexuality was offensive to the taste and the standard of decorum among the literati. Admittedly, the idea of a destructive and sexually obsessed female was as familiar as its opposite—woman as the epitome of virtue and self-constraint. Nevertheless, to overwhelm the reader with graphic descriptions of a sexually unsatiated woman in order to illustrate the plight of human relationships was considered excessive and unnatural. The biography deviated from the standard expectations of readers. Evidently, it has been an embarrassment to the commentators and editors of Liu's works. In his collected works, it is not listed in the section of biographical writings but is appended to the last section as one of a number of additional writings. The *Wen-yüan ying-hua* includes five of Liu's biographies but omits "Ho-chien chuan." In his monumental fourteen-volume study, *Liu-wen chih-yao* (A guide to the writings of Liu Tsung-yüan), the modern scholar Chang Shih-chao discussed all the biographies except this one. "Ho-chien chuan" has been a marginalized text because it violates the conventions of reading.

The Entwinement of the Historical and Allegorical Modes

The two images of the feminine—the epitome of chastity and the symbol of lust—are familiar to and commonly accepted by Chinese readers. The female character oscillates between the height of virtue as in the "Biography of Hsieh Hsiao-o" and the baseness of animal sexuality as in the "Biography of Ho-chien." The former story has been regarded as more credible and more real than the latter one only because it more closely approximates the historical convention of representation. Its veridictory utterances evoke an aura of historical authenticity more successfully.

Shen Chi-chi's "Jen Shih chuan" describes trafficking between the supernatural and human beings. The many T'ang tales of the supernatural can partly be understood within the generic conventions of the *chih-kuai*, a distinct tradition of fiction that began in the Six Dynasties period. From the historian's point of view, however, tales of the supernatural are untrustworthy and deceitful. A lucid statement of the criteria separating true narrative from false narrative can be found in the preface to Li Chao's *T'ang kuo-shih pu*. At the beginning of this work, which has been regarded as falling halfway between history and *pi-chi* (notebook) fiction, Li Chao explained his principles for selecting materials:

I completely exclude those that speak of retribution, relate ghosts and spirits, prove dreams and divinations, and describe matters concerning women; I include, however, those that record events and facts, investigate the principles of things, discriminate the dubious and the unclear, give admonitions and cautions, collect customs and folklore, and furnish material for discussion and entertainment. (Li Chao, *chüan* 1, 1)

Li Chao here reaffirms a conception of narrative that is only too Confucian and historiographical, a conception described in detail in previous chapters.[5] In this perspective, Shen Chi-chi's "Jen Shih chuan," along with many other tales of the supernatural and the fantastic, would be dismissed as frivolous and devious and excluded from the realm of serious narrative.

Shen Chi-chi's story might have appeared even more uncommon, unnatural, unreasonable, and incomprehensible because its relation of the story of a virtuous female fox-fairy was unprecedented. Contrary to the usual belief, Shen's female fox in human guise does not harm human beings but surpasses them in loyalty and chastity. The story raises certain difficulties of interpretation within the ordinary horizon of literary and cultural expectations.

Feminine sexuality, which is at once so incomprehensible, so attractive, and so dangerous to men, has been represented not only as the other of the male order but also as the supernatural, the other of the human order. The female has been portrayed as a fox-fairy, an evil temptress, in the vast number of stories on this species of demon in the Chinese literary tradition. The *T'ai-p'ing kuang-chi* (Comprehensive records compiled in the T'ai-p'ing reign period) contains nine *chüan* (chapters) of fox stories that existed at the time of its compilation. The fox demon is feared as a most dangerous species because of "his double capacity of originator of disease and of impostor under human guise" (de Groot, 596). Men especially need to guard against the female fox demon and its excessive sexual desire. Only by constantly drawing the *yang* from men by having intercourse with them can these seducers of unwary men sustain their own life. The traffic between the fox-fairies and human beings can be fatal at times. For instance, an entry in the *Hsüan-chung chi*, a collection of exotica from the Six Dynasties, unmistakably identifies the supernatural fox with certain qualities attributed to woman (*Hsüan-chung chi*, 227). The fox is beautiful, deceitful, and licentious, as is a woman presumably. The analogy is also true the other way: a woman is a foxy, bewitching, and dangerous creature.

Hence, it is a perfectly appropriate gesture for Pai Chü-i (772–846), a near-contemporary of Shen Chi-chi, in writing a "satiric admonitory poem" (*feng-yü shih*) to use the fox as a "natural" symbol of deception to caution the world. In "The Fox of the Ancient Grave" ("Ku-chung hu"), he warns that the false appearance of a female fox or a foxy woman should be as alarming as it is beautiful (Pai Chü-i, 87–88).

In the *T'ai-p'ing kuang-chi*, Shen Chi-chi's story is entitled "Jen Shih" ("Miss Jen") and is listed in the section of stories on "foxes" (*hu*) (Li Fang et al., 3692–97). The original title might have been that given in the *I-wen chi*, "Jen Shih chuan" or "Biography of Miss Jen" (Wang Meng-ou, 186–92). The title and the format of this "biography" are reminiscent of those in a standard *lieh-nü chuan* in a history. The immediate irony is that the object described in this elevated literary genre is the life of a non-human being. A biography of a fox-fairy is a contradiction in terms. An uncertainty in generic expectations is created at the start and remains unresolved throughout the reading process. One asks: Should the story be read as a "biography of virtuous women" or a parody of that very form?

The basic irony of the story is introduced in the very name of the character and in the first sentence—a simple declarative statement: "Jen, a female fairy." Her surname *Jen* is written with the "human" (*jen*) radical and is a homophone of both "human" and "virtue" (*jen*). Yet, Miss Jen is immediately qualified as non-human, a fox-fairy. Three orders of reality exist in the story: the supernatural world of fox-fairies, the ordinary world of human beings in the recent past, and the immediate world of political events at the very moment of the storytelling. Should one read the "Jen Shih chuan" as a fabulous story about a supernatural fox, or a record of some human beings, or a criticism of certain recent political events? Is the story to be read in the historical or the allegorical mode? Read in the first mode, the events in the story are to be taken as historically real and literally true; in the second, the events and characters are to be seen as fictitious but the story itself as meaningful in moral, philosophical, and psychological terms.

The story observes the structural pattern of a biography in a historical work. The main characters and their personal qualities are briefly introduced at the beginning. The large middle section consists of several major anecdotes. At the end the narrator identifies the source of his material and presents an appraisal of the recounted events, all in the fashion of a historian.

Like the narrator in Li Kung-tso's story, the storyteller gives many indications and veridiction marks of the historicity and factuality of the events. For example, specific times are attached to the events of the story: "in the middle of summer of the ninth year of the T'ien-pao reign period [750]," "during the Ta-li reign period [766–79]," and "during the second year of the Chien-chung reign period [781]."[6] The locales of the fictional events are well-known and historically verifiable places in Ch'ang-an, the T'ang capital, such as "Pleasure Gardens" (*Le-yu yüan*) and "New Prosperity Quarter" (*Hsin-ch'ang li*). Fictional characters and events imperceptibly entwine with real settings.

Toward the end of the story, the narrator, who merges with Shen Chi-chi, the historical author, reassures the reader that he learned about Miss Jen directly from his friend Wei Yin, who is portrayed as a real person in the story. Here the writer adopts a procedure of discursive manipulation rather common in T'ang *ch'uan-ch'i* tales. To use the vocabulary of Greimasian semiotics, the alternation of "subjectivizing camouflage" and "objectivizing camouflage" makes the narrative appear to be real. Subjectivizing camouflage bears the marks of enunciation and appears as discourse by a subject. The autobiographical "I" is the primary indicator of such discourse. Sentences start with "I say," "I saw," "I know," and so on. The "I" or the subject of enunciation passes itself off as the guarantor of truth. Objectivizing camouflage erases the subject of enunciation through impersonal utterances that seem to express the pure relation of things. The combination of these two discursive manipulations or, in the terms of narratology, the mixture of "heterodiegetic" narration (narrator absent from the narrative), "autodiegetic" narration (narrator as principal character), and "homodiegetic" narration (narrator inside the narrative, as in first-person stories) is designed to produce veridiction, a veracious discourse of things. Li Kung-tso used the same narrative procedure to great effect in the "Hsieh Hsiao-o chuan" and the "Nan-k'o t'ai-shou chuan." The impression left on the reader is that the storyteller did not invent anything but simply wrote up a true "record" of actual events.

In all these ways, the storyteller has set up his story so that it can be read in the historical mode. The story is, however, as much about the supernatural as it is about the human. There is no ambiguity as to the nature of Miss Jen. The declarative first sentence of the story makes her supernatural status emphatically clear. The fact that she does not belong to the human world is also implied through "free indirect discourse" and various "points of view." Their first night of lovemaking leaves the human hero of the story, Cheng, feeling that "her lovely appearance and beautiful body, each song or smile, her manners and movements, all were captivating, almost otherworldly!" The boy sent by Wei Yin reports that her beauty is beyond human parallel: "Uncanny! Like nothing in the world you've ever seen!" In the eyes of the store clerk Chang the Eldest, "she must be a fairy or someone from the royal house. . . . She can't belong to this mundane world!" All this seems to undermine historical rationality and encourage an allegorical reading. The narrator teaches an important moral lesson by telling the story of a supernatural being.

Miss Jen is the object of men's desire. Besides the appeal of her extraordinary beauty, her womanly virtues are of a kind rare in the human world. Her resourcefulness, foresight, personal integrity, and faithfulness to her lover are the exemplary qualities characteristic of the women of the *lieh-nü chuan*. The narrative devotes little space to Miss Jen's supernatural attributes and magical qualities. She is described more as an ideal type of human being. Cheng and Wei, two human beings who love Miss Jen, seem inferior to her—although they lead or will lead a successful official career. Whereas Miss Jen is described as possessing foresight, uncommon intelligence, and loyalty to a single lover, the two men are of mediocre intelligence, wanting in fidelity, shortsighted, and blind to her true nature. Their belated knowledge of Miss Jen's condition finally causes her tragic death. Miss Jen tells Cheng and Wei that it would be inauspicious, as the shamaness predicted, for her to accompany Cheng to his new post. Their response to her is a moment of supreme irony, "How can someone be as intelligent as you [Jen] are and yet be [deceived by a supernatural being]?" As Jen's death proves, men, not supernatural beings, are the ones who are blind to the nature of things. The contrast between the men and Jen amounts to a reversal of roles: a being from the supernatural order has assumed Confucian virtues lacking in the human world.

Toward the end of the story, the narrator imitates the voice of the historian and comments on the turns of events:

Ah, the principles of man can be found in the emotions of supernatural beings! To be accosted and not lose one's purity, to follow one man until death—even among the women of today there are those who could not measure up to this. Unfortunately, Cheng was not a very sensitive man. He only enjoyed Jen's beauty, and never fathomed her character. Had he been a man of truly deep understanding, he might have twisted the strands of fate, investigated the limits between spirits and humans, and written it up all beautifully to transmit his more abstruse feelings, rather than just surfeiting himself with her manners and appearance. What a pity!

The story may not be plausible to historically minded readers. But on the allegorical level, it can be meaningfully construed as a fable of *human* relationships. The narrator's concluding remarks make the story, which otherwise may appear frivolous and absurd, profoundly relevant to the predicament of human beings. The exhortation of men and women to conventional virtue and good character at this point provides a clue to the sense of what has been narrated so far. The story is intelligible at the allegorical level even if incredible at the historical level.

The story continues after those comments. The narrator–character–historical individual, Shen Chi-chi, is among a group of banished officials, ministers, and "subjects" of the emperor in the last section of the story. In the historical context, Shen and his friends are exiled for being associates of the once-powerful chancellor Yang Yen, who has lost favor at court. All the companions mentioned by the narrator—General P'ei Chi, Deputy Mayor Sun Ch'eng, Secretary Ts'ui Hsü, Censor Lu Ch'un, and former censor Chu Fang—are historical figures and associates of Yang Yen. Their lives are recorded in the *Chiu T'ang-shu* and/or *Hsin T'ang-shu*. A little earlier in the story, allusion is made to a momentous political event in the recent past. The site of Miss Jen's death is Ma-wei Slope, the same place Yang Kuei-fei, the consort of Emperor Hsüan-tsung, was killed twenty-five years before Shen Chi-chi wrote the story. The life of Yang Kuei-fei and the time of the story of Miss Jen are both set in the T'ien-pao reign period. And in both cases, beauty is made a scapegoat for the misconduct of men (Dudbridge, 61–80).

In the story itself, the fate of this group of banished Confucian officials is altogether different from that of Cheng, whose household prospers and who lives to the age of sixty-five, or from that of Wei Yin, who rises to high positions and dies "in office." The exiles show more sympathy to Miss Jen. "When the group had heard the events surrounding Jen, they were all dismayed. They asked me to write them up as a record of the unusual." They recognize themselves in the other, in a supernatural being outside the human order.

With the conjoining of the contemporary political situation and supernatural events, the story develops another dimension of meaning. The moralizing comments of the narrator seem to refer to specific historical events. In their own opinion, the members of the Yang Yen faction had been punished for their loyalty and dealt with harshly by their political enemies and the emperor. Just as Miss Jen was devoured by a pack of hounds due to the oversight of Cheng and Wei, the political careers of Yang and his associates were doomed because of the emperor's failure to discern true faith. As is quite common in Chinese literature, the love relationship between the sexes here becomes an allegory of the relationship between the sovereign and the minister. Moreover, a general allegory of human relationships turns into a specific allegory of real, historical events. Like the modern scholars Wang Meng-ou and Pien Hsiao-hsüan, one can pursue correspondences between the fictive characters in the biography and real figures in T'ang history. In such a reading, Miss Jen is an allusion to Yang Yen and his associates.

The allegory in the story becomes an allegory of contemporary political history. At the end, the story itself is true both as allegory and as history. The two are combined along the metaphorical as well as the metonymical axes of narrative. Metaphorically and paradigmatically, the story of the supernatural is an allegory of specific human events. Metonymically and syntagmatically, the allegorical part of the story about Miss Jen is continuous with the historical part of the story about the exiles. Allegory and history operate in the fictional text—for once—at the same moment.

The success of the historico-allegorical reading of "Jen Shih chuan" depends on a fundamental absence and lack. The projection of an ideal female rare in both beauty and morality onto the supernatural is a male wish-fulfillment and indicates a primary, originary absence, an absence that could be fatal to men and the social structure. Whereas "Hsieh Hsiao-o chuan" narrates the presence of virtue in this world, "Jen Shih chuan" displaces that presence to an ontologically different realm. What had previously been represented as a beguiling and harmful demon is now transformed into a trustworthy and beneficial being. The supernatural female fox becomes a mirror that provides a specular image of man. That image embodies the Confucian virtues prescribed by society and yet perpetually eludes the order of men. The biography of the fox-fairy is thus predicated upon a lack in the human world. "Nan-k'o t'ai-shou chuan" relates the alienation of the subject from the Confucian order, but "Jen Shih chuan" describes the alienation of the Confucian subject from a world in which Confucian ideals are absent. In the supernatural being Miss Jen, one sees a vision of something irretrievably missing and profoundly missed. And yet the otherness of the missing/missed object signals an *aphanisis*, the fading of the subject, the alienation of the human being from society. In the final analysis, the story articulates what is unconscious in official historical discourse, namely, the complete disappearance of the Confucian subject from the world.

The Impossibility of Interpretation: T'ang Tales of the Fantastic

If some contemporary readers, however few, could not understand a T'ang "fictional biography" meaningfully as either history or allegory, the story would pose an interpretive problem. It would create a hesitation, an uncertainty in the process of interpretation. In modern fiction criticism, the "fantastic" is characterized by such an ambivalent attitude of reading. Interestingly enough, a significant corpus of T'ang writings has been labeled by a similar name, *ch'uan-ch'i* (record of the strange, the extraordinary, the fantastic). A story that could not be fully comprehended with the familiar "horizon of expectations" would surely have ideological, social, and literary ramifications. Such fiction might enlarge the extent of signification in the existing literary system and subvert official ideology even as it ostensibly reinforces that ideology. In the following, I pursue the implications and consequences of the appearance of such works in the T'ang, especially dream stories.

From Chuang Tzu's butterfly dream to Ts'ao Hsüeh-ch'in's (ca. 1715–ca. 1763) *Dream of the Red Chamber*, there exists a distinct tradition of dream stories in Chinese fiction. The *T'ai-p'ing kuang-chi* contains seven *chüan* of stories under the heading "dreams." Such stories are further subdivided into "dreams of felicitous manifestations" (*meng-hsiu cheng*), "dreams of calamitous manifestations" (*meng-chiu cheng*), "dream adventures" (*meng-yu*), and "dreams of ghosts and spirits" (*kuei-shen*). Other sections of the anthology have many more stories involving dreams.

T'ang literati fiction has commonly been classed under the generic designation *ch'uan-ch'i*.[7] *Ch'uan-ch'i* may be taken as a specific case of *chuan* since most of the stories observe the structural pattern of the biography and a large number of them are labeled "biographies." A standard tale consists of a tripartite structure modeled on the *lieh-chuan* of historiography:

(1) an *introduction* which identifies the main character (or characters) by a somewhat formulaic enumeration of temporal and spatial settings, the main character's occupation and personal qualities (the last two items are not obligatory); (2) the *main body* of the narrative with one or more event sequences (the story itself); and (3) an *epilogue* which contains a meta-textual appraisal of the story recounted, an explanation of the source of the story, and, sometimes, a brief mentioning of the descendants of the main character, in the fashion of a historical biography.   (Kao, *Classical Chinese Tales*, 39–40)[8]

Yet within the structural confines of historical discourse, the writer of *ch'uan-ch'i* sets out to explore and articulate realities that the official historian is neither willing nor able to represent. Basic to the T'ang tale is the problematic of "fact and fantasy" that remains the fascination of the fiction writer.[9] Here my study follows several previous ones in examining *ch'uan-ch'i* as tales of fantasy and of the fantastic. Fictional discourse is the result of the interweaving of two worlds: a world consisting of ordinary facts governed by the logic of human rationality and made familiar by historical discourse on the one hand, and a world that transgresses the logical coherence of the first world and traverses the supernatural, extraordinary, and imaginary on the other hand. The complexity of the T'ang tale hinges on the creation of a third narrative world that mediates the contradictoriness of these two orders of reality within the restrictions of an essentially historiographical form. The underlying problem of this new kind of writing lies in the attempt to represent, using the rhetoric of the official historian, a world that is fundamentally non-historical, irrational, and supernatural. The tension within a tale builds upon the juxtaposition of a strictly historical, verisimilar, and matter-of-fact manner of representation with a represented non-historical, otherworldly reality. As a result, fictional discourse in the T'ang period stretches the boundaries of narrative and enlarges the limits of the signifiable. The writer endeavors to articulate an unutterable experience and represent the unrepresentable through the medium of fictional narrative.

One feature of T'ang tales of the fantastic is the epistemological uncertainty and the hesitation of the human subject to assume a social position. Exploration of this feature will allow us to analyze the precariousness of the subject or "character" in the fictional biography. Todorov's seminal definition of the fantastic still remains a heuristic guide: "The fantastic implies, then, not only the existence of an uncanny event, which provokes a hesitation in the reader and the hero; but also a kind of reading, which we may for the moment define negatively: it must be neither 'poetic' nor 'allegorical'." One does not take the story of the fantastic as a fable or allegory by reading it in another sense, nor does one take it as literally true in the fashion of reading figurative expressions of poetry. "The text must oblige the reader to consider the world of the characters as a world of living persons and to hesitate between a natural and supernatural explanation of the events described" (Todorov, *The Fantastic*, 32–33). The heart of the fantastic involves a sustained perceptual ambiguity. Reality or dream? Truth or illusion? "The fantastic opens on to a region which has no name and no rational explanation for its existence. It suggests events beyond interpretation" (Jackson, 25).

In the case of the Chinese fictional text, the events are beyond the interpretation of historical hermeneutics. There is also a semantic indeterminacy, a textual ambiguity that resists "naturalization" and interpretive appropriation. The classic Chinese example of the pure fantastic is Chuang Tzu's butterfly dream.[10] "Suddenly he woke up and there he was, solid and unmistakable Chuang Chou. But he didn't know if he was Chuang Chou who had dreamt he was a butterfly, or a butterfly dreaming he was Chuang Chou" (Chuang Tzu, 49). The uncertainty between being a human and being a butterfly is sustained throughout and remains beyond causal explanation or Confucian interpretation. There is a silence, a moment of non-signification, and a dissociation of the signifier and the signified as the result of a referential ambiguity.

Stories of dream adventures and transformation are common in T'ang tales. The problems of perception and of the interplay of dream and reality remain at the forefront of many well-known stories, such as Pai Hsing-chien's (776–826) "San-meng chi" (Record of three dreams), Shen Chi-chi's "Chen chung chi," Li Kung-tso's "Nan-k'o t'ai-shou chuan," Li Mei's (fl. 835) "Chang sheng" (Scholar Chang), Shen Ya-chih's (ca. 781–ca. 832) "I-meng lu" (Record of a strange dream) and "Ch'in-meng lu" (Record of a dream in the Ch'in), and Wang Tu's (fl. 614?) "Ku-ching chi" (Record of an ancient mirror) . In the "San-meng chi," Pai Hsing-chien wrote about three types of dreams. At the conclusion of the story, the narrator finds it impossible to explain dreams.

> In the *Ch'un-ch'iu* and books of philosophy and history many dreams have been mentioned, but they have yet to record these three types of dreams. The dreams that people in the world dream indeed must be innumerable, but they have yet to list these three kinds of dreams. Are they just coincidental, or are they caused by some law of predestination? That is something I cannot answer. I have written these down in detail so as to keep them as a record.   (quoted in Kao, *Classical Chinese Tales*, 196)

The discourse of the fantastic is, in the words of Irène Bessière, "la poétique de l'incertain" (the poetics of uncertainty). The borderline between reality and dream is no longer well defined as in historical discourse, and many tales assume the task of probing the limits of human experience and interrogating the conception of reality endorsed by the convention of historical narrative. They are inhabited by both the real and the unreal, the familiar natural world and the unseen supernatural world. One witnesses the multiple division of the self, the transformation of space and time, the collapse of the limit between matter and mind, the transgression of the boundary between nature and culture, and of relations between human beings and supernatural beings. Fiction scrutinizes the historically "real," questions the validity of social positions, discovers the edges of the culture, and pushes commonly accepted epistemological and ontological assumptions to their limits. The fantastic opens up new horizons of existence and creates visions of possible worlds beyond the conventionally known. All this contributes to a perceptual and conceptual disorientation and ultimately to the decentering of the homogeneous, autonomous Confucian subject.

The discourse of the fantastic, with its ideological disorientation and its fragmentation of the subject, presupposes for its purpose a specific formal structure, a language, an "aesthetic of presentation." "There was a change in literary awareness, in the attitude toward the processing of the represented reality" (Kao, *Classical Chinese Tales*, 4). The biographies are characterized by an intense literary self-consciousness, an awareness of the problematic nature of literary presentation itself. The adoption of the form of the standard historical biography for the telling of supernatural and fantastic happenings amounts to a critique and suspension of the reality unfolded in historical discourse. The modality of the storyteller's language and the principle of causal explanation are none other than the subjunctive. The subjectivity of the protagonist/subject resides in the *subjunctivity* of the narrated reality. At the level of language, the linguistic markers of "as if" (*jo, fang-fu*) are frequent. Unlike the declaratives of historical discourse affirming the factuality of past events, the subjunctives of the tales tell of what might and could have happened. Going even further than subjunctivity, one may also say that the fantastic is predicated upon a "negative subjunctivity." "Fantasy is fantasy because it contravenes the real and violates it. The actual world is constantly present in fantasy, by negation. . . . [Fantasy] is what *could not have happened*; i.e. what *cannot* happen, what *cannot* exist" (Russ, 52).

The discourse of the fantastic questions and negates the world that is taken as real in historical discourse. The storyteller describes possible worlds and impossible worlds and then cancels and denies their validity. He wavers between apologetic self-justifications and qualifications about the truthfulness of his story. Statements such as the following are characteristic at the beginnings or at ends of stories:

Knowing virtuous acts without recording them is against the principles of the *Ch'un-ch'iu*. (Li Kung-tso, "Hsieh Hsiao-o chuan")

The event traverses the strange and wondrous.   (Shen Ya-chih, "Hsiang-chung yüan-tz'u" [Lament from the Hsiang River])

The story speaks about spirits and the strange, and the events are unrelated to the way of the Classics.   (Li Kung-tso, "Nan-k'o t'ai-shou chuan")

Although it talks about prodigies, it is really based on fact.   (Huang-fu Mei [fl. 873], "Wang Chih-ku")

These narrators are attempting to justify the validity of fiction to an audience whose literary taste and expectations were conditioned by the Confucian classics and the tradition of historiography. In comparison to the Six Dynasties *chih-kuai*, which purport to record supernatural events and which have complete conviction in the recorded external events, the T'ang tales are concerned not only with representing extra-textual reality but also with activating intertextual relationships. The tale is distinguished by moments of self-reflexivity and allusions to prior narrative traditions and literary texts.[11] The fictional (inter)text enters a network of other literary texts and engages the entire linguistic, cultural, and philosophical matrix. Above all, it engages, invokes, and debates with the authority of Classics and the principles of historical narrative.

Stylistically, many biographies are a mixture of different genres and alternate poetry and prose. Chao Yen-wei (fl. 1190–1206) observed that a T'ang tale "contains many literary forms wherein one can see historical talents, poetic gifts, and discussions and arguments" (Chao Yen-wei, 111).[12] As in later vernacular narratives, the poetry sometimes expounds conventional wisdom and offers stylized images of human behavior counter to the thrust of the prose narrative, or sometimes represents pathos that deviates from the morality of the concluding comments. The storytelling frame (the narrator's moralizing comments in imitation of the historian's comments at the end of a historical biography) may be at odds with the story itself. The reporting speech of the storyteller may also conflict with the reported speech of the characters.

For example, Ch'en Hung's (fl. 829) "Ch'ang-hen ko chuan" (Biography of [Commentary on] the "Song of Everlasting Sorrow") is divided into halves. The first half is a prose biography of the imperial consort Yang Yü-huan written by Ch'en Hung, and the second is the famous narrative poem "Ch'ang-hen ko" by Pai Chü-i. The prose biography is said to be a "commentary" (*chuan*) on the poem. The great formal and ideological disparity between the parts of the story is obvious. Another case is Yüan Chen's famous story "Ying-ying chuan," which incorporates poems that recount the happenings of the story within the frame of the prose narrative. The prose frame and the lyric recounting of the story, the shifting stance of the narrator, and the divergent speeches of the characters constitute a unique story that has been found rather unedifying and confusing in moral principles. The juxtaposition of varied modes of presentation and the subtle differences in the tone of the narrator create a sedimentation of multiple layers of meaning and a complex textual pattern of intelligibility. This mixture of genres contributes to a heterogeneous textuality and a complex, sometimes contradictory attitude toward life in these fictional biographies.

In the following, I reread a *ch'uan-ch'i* story often cited as exemplary of the T'ang fictional biography and read as a study of the dilemmas and difficulties of the insertion of the subject into a world of pre-established Confucian values. The "Nan-k'o t'ai-shou chuan" by Li Kung-tso is a story of what Todorov calls "themes of the self," a story that deals with the relation between man and the world. At stake in themes of the self are issues of consciousness, perception, and the interplay of dream and reality. The reading is oriented not toward the recovery of unity and coherence but toward the discovery of the contradictions and inconsistencies inherent in the story.[13] The text is regarded as an instance of the intertextual, dialogic co-presence of various ideologemes that are indexes of different ideologies, worldviews, and philosophies. It offers an opportunity to trace the trajectory of the subject's ordeals and failures in identifying itself in relation to a world of conflicting values.

Of the many T'ang stories of dreams and dream adventures, Shen Chi-chi's "Chen-chung chi" and Li Kung-tso's "Nan-k'o t'ai-shou chuan" are among the best known. Both have been retold many times. Among the most famous adaptations are the Yüan play *Huang-liang meng* (A dream of yellow millet) by Ma Chih-yüan (ca. 1250–1323) and others; two Ming plays, *Han-tan chi* (A record of Han-tan) and *Nan-k'o meng chi* (A dream of South Branch), both by T'ang Hsien-tsu (1550–1616); and the short story

"Hsü Huang-liang" (Yellow Millet, continued) in P'u Sung-ling's (1640–1715) *Liao-chai chih-i.*

Scholars have found that these two stories and another T'ang dream story, "Ying-t'ao ch'ing-i" (The cherry maid in blue clothes), attributed to Jen Fan (fl. 840) and collected in the "Dream Adventures" ("Meng-yu") section of *T'ai-p'ing kuang-chi* (*chüan* 283), are similar in plot and theme. Some scholars have held that all three derive from the story of Yang Lin in the collection *Yu-ming lu* (Record of the dark and the dead) by Liu I-ch'ing (403–44) of the Liu Sung dynasty (420–79). The "Ching-chi chih" of the *Sui-shu* classifies the *Yu-ming lu* in the category "Miscellaneous Biographies" in the history section. In the *T'ai-p'ing kuang-chi*, the story of Yang Lin is classified as a *wu* (shaman) story; the "Ying-t'ao ch'ing-i" as a dream story; the "Nan-k'o t'ai-shou chuan" as an insect story; and the "Chen-chung chi," re-entitled "Lü weng" (Old man Lü), as a story of an *i-jen* (extraordinary person). The "Chen-chung chi" can also be found in the *Wen-yüan ying-hua*, but under the category *chi* (record), subcategory *yü-yen* (allegory).[14]

My reading focuses on the issue of character in the story. The question of the "character" or "protagonist" becomes a matter of the ideological determination of the "subject." I examine the subject as it is constituted or fractured by the fictional discourse of the fantastic. In terms of the methodology of reading, "the speaking person in the [story] is always, to one degree or another, an *ideologue*, and his words are always *ideologemes*," and the character himself is situated in a "heteroglossia," a "dialogized representation of an ideologically freighted discourse" (Bakhtin, *Dialogic Imagination*, 333). The character in a T'ang story is beset by "ideologemes" of different kinds: Confucian classics, Buddhist and Taoist scriptures, formulas of the dominant historical discourse, and echoes of earlier writings. Linguistic and literary expression becomes a semantic field for ideological conflict in and through the subject represented in the story. In brief, such an analysis is oriented toward the tracing of the signs of a decentered, fragmentary, and "atomized subjectivity" in the literary text (Coward and Ellis, 146).

In this study of dream stories and the fantastic in the T'ang, I pay special attention, first of all, to what narratologists call the "order" or time-order of narrative. This term refers to the discordances between different temporal structures. A dream story such as the "Nan-k'o t'ai-shou chuan" contains a profusion of divergent time schemes of unequal duration. The simplest level is that of "anachrony," or the difference between storytelling time and story time. The storyteller, such as Li Kung-tso, often pretends to tell a story that occurred in history by assuming the posture of a historian writing a record. This "historical storytelling time" collides with the story time in a struggle by each to frame the other. Within the story time itself, the clock time of the ordinary world is counterposed to the subjective time of the dream world. In other words, the central difference is between "cosmological time" and "phenomenological time," between the "time of the world" and "time of the soul," or more simply, between "waking time" and "dreaming time." The phenomenon implied by the second term of each of these pairs is much less prominent in historical narration. Each of these two temporal orders competes to assert its own validity. The character or the subject, such as Ch'un-yü Fen, is caught in the conflicting claims of these discordant times. A salient feature of the dream stories is the use of a "time-measuring device" to indicate the duration of time and to create the "illusion of time." As David Knechtges observes, "The story uses a material object to measure the amount of time that actually passes in the dream. For example, the dream may take the space of time it requires to cook a meal, saddle a horse, or wash one's hands" (Knechtges, 101).

A second major aspect of the tale to be studied is what is sometimes called "mood" or the modality of narrative discourse. Whereas the declarative dominates historical narration, the declarative, the interrogative, and the subjunctive are all present in the dream story. In imitation of the historical biography, the storytelling frame proceeds in the declarative. Yet within the frame, the story is replete with interrogatives and subjunctives. "Where am I?" "Where was I?" "What just happened?" These are the questions the character usually asks on waking from a dream. The subjunctive is perhaps the defining characteristic of stories of dreams and the fantastic. As noted earlier, it is marked by "as if" (*jo, fang-fu*). It plays with belief and disbelief, evokes wonder, introduces both the possible and the impossible, and invites uncertainty. "Could all this be a dream?" "Was the dream world more substantial than the 'real' world?" These are some of the questions posed or implied by the protagonist, the narrator, and possibly the reader. Once again, the protagonist, the narrator, and the reader are uncertain of the ontological status of the world(s) described in the story because of the mixture of these three modalities.

A third important area to be noted in T'ang tales is what narratologists have variously called "point of view," "narrative perspective," "focalization," and "voice." Events in the story are seen and told through different perception centers: the narrator, the protagonist, and other characters. The reader needs to judge the degree of truthfulness in each of the different descriptions of the dream world. The narrator himself could be as objective and detached as a heterodiegetic narrator or as entangled and involved as a homodiegetic narrator. The reader must ask whose account is more trustworthy. Can one believe the story and the moralizing of the narrator? Who is telling the truth? Are the perceptions of the characters any less truthful than the report of the narrator?

The fourth and last important area I consider is the language of a given story. The literati short story uses a homogeneous classical language. It is far more difficult to reduce the classical tale to its elements than, say, the vernacular story of the Ming and the Ch'ing. The vernacular story is a mixture of classical and vernacular language and a combination of various genres. The heteroglossia of different social positions, popular sentiment, and ideological contention is easily perceptible in the juxtaposition of and transition between languages, styles, and genres. The disparity between the moralizing and cautionary words of the storytelling frame and the story itself, between the narrator's reporting speech and the reported speech of the characters, is particularly notable. Nonetheless, internal differences in tone and connotation, though subtle, are not altogether absent in the T'ang tale. It requires an enormous effort to pick out the intertextual allusions. For instance, Glen Dudbridge and William H. Nienhauser, Jr., have shown the extent to which Pai Hsing-chien's "Li Wa chuan" ("Tale of Li Wa") and Li Kung-tso's "Nan-k'o t'ai-shou chuan" allude to the Confucian classics (*Ch'un-ch'iu*, *Li-chi*, etc.) and standard histories (*Shih-chi*, *Han-shu*, *Hou-Han-shu*). The rhetoric of the narrator is embedded in a network of textual relations. Historical discourse, Buddhist and Taoist discourse, and the discourse of the Classics are co-present in the story to various degrees. Analysis of the language and ideologemes will allow us to undo the seeming naturalness and homogeneity of the story and point to its ideological contradictions.

The title of Li Kung-tso's story as it appears in Ch'en Han's *I-wen chi*, a T'ang anthology of some forty-one *hsiao-shuo* titles, is "Nan-k'o t'ai-shou chuan" (Wang Meng-ou, 4).[15] In the great Sung anthology, the *T'ai-p'ing kuang-chi*, the story is entitled "Ch'un-yü Fen," the name of the protagonist, and is listed with insect (*k'un-ch'ung*) stories (Li Fang et al., 3910–15). The contradiction in title and subgeneric classification poses an uncertainty that permeates the entire process of reading. One asks: What is the nature of the being described? Is it human, animal, or supernatural? Is the story about a human being or an insect? Should the story be read as a literal "record" of a real figure or as an allegory (*yü-yen*), an insect story with a broader human significance?

The story closely observes the structure of a standard historical biography. It begins by briefly introducing the main character, his nativity, and his personal qualities. Ch'un-yü Fen is described as indifferent to the career of an official and social convention. The middle portion of the story consists of a series of episodes in the dream reality of the Acacia Kingdom. The format of the conclusion—with its authorial comments—is that of official history. Throughout the story, the narrator in the voice of a historian stresses the historicity and factuality of the story and attempts to leave no trace of invention and fictionality. As in a historical record, events are dated specifically: "one day in the ninth month of the seventh year of the Chen-yüan period" (A.D. 791), and "in the autumn of the eighteenth year of the Chen-yüan period (802)." At the end, the narrator merges with the real historical person "Kung-tso" and makes it known that the recorded events are true because they were told by the protagonist himself. The storyteller plays the role of a historian (*histor*), a researcher, a reporter, and even an eyewitness rather than that of an inventor of fiction. He emphasizes that the story is a real, historical event that happened within time and in this world.

Yet within the frame of a credible, historical record is another level of existence opposed to historical rationality. A new world is disclosed in the experience of a dream outside the ordinary state of mind. At first glance, the dream world of the Acacia Kingdom differs from the ordinary, familiar world of human beings. Significantly, the sense of otherness is seldom stated in direct discourse but more often described in "free indirect discourse" and through the perception and the limited point of view of the protagonist Ch'un-yü Fen. At the entrance into the Acacia Kingdom, "suddenly he saw mountains and streams, wind and clouds, grass and trees, and streets and roads, which were very different from the things in the human world." In the wedding ceremony, Ch'un-yü listens to the music played by the fairylike maidens and notes that "the soft tones and clear sound, and the melodies of melancholy and sadness, were not like those heard in the human world." There are indications in the text that what he has seen is indeed a different supernatural world.

There exists a plurality of temporal orders in the story. First, there is the time of storytelling. The narrator is an anonymous voice until the conclusion, where he identifies himself as "Kung-tso," thus foregrounding the temporality of the narration. Second, there is the time of the narrated story. The time of the story is further divided into "historical time" and "dream time." The historical time is basically the life span of Ch'un-yü Fen, from his existence as an idler at the beginning, through his dream, his awakening, and his interview with Li Kung-tso many years after the dream experience, till his death at the age of "forty-seven." The dream is only a short moment in the life of the protagonist. The short duration in historical time of his prolonged sojourn in the dream world is specifically indicated by a time-measuring device. When he woke up, "his servant was still sweeping the yard, while the two guests were sitting on a couch washing their feet. The slanting sun had not set in the west. In the cup standing beside the east window, the wine was still [warm enough to be] fragrant."

In historical rationality, the time of the dream is but a fleeting moment in one's life that lasts as long as one is asleep. It is over as soon as one wakes. This supposedly brief moment, however, occupies the bulk of the story. The dream takes up the major portion of storytelling time. In comparison, historical time is far shorter and much less meaningful for the protagonist's experience than the time of the dream. The discordance between historical time and dream time inverts ordinary experience. Dream lasts longer than history.

What makes the story even more complex as well as more interesting is that the dream time unfolds according to the logic of historical time. Everything that happens in the dream world follows the ordinary historical sequence. History in the dream world parallels history in the human world. The story renders an intricate pattern of both the antinomy and the interpenetration of historical time and dream time.

When Ch'un-yü Fen wakes up and returns to normal historical time in the human world, historical time in the dream world comes to a standstill. The logic of history resumes in one world even as it stops in another. This asymmetry between dream time and historical time and the split within historical time itself destroy the wholeness of temporal experience. In official historical discourse, time, that is, history, is continuous and homogeneous in the human and cosmological order, serving as the foundation and the chief source of experience and knowledge. But in the fictional dream world of this story, the reversal, distortion, and fragmentation of temporal orders abolish the unity and security normally expected in historical discourse.

In the storytelling frame, more precisely at the end of the story, the narrator attempts to mediate the discordances between the different time schemes by integrating the narrated events meaningfully into the historical moment of his own storytelling. He subsumes the dream time and the bygone historical time within the immediacy of his storytelling time. Story time and storytelling time can never coincide in a story, however, and their difference can never be erased by any effort on the part of the storyteller. The attempt to create a concordance out of discordances has limited success.

Although the storyteller writes within the general structural restrictions of the historical biographical form, his story does not reproduce a preconceived image of man but emphasizes the experience of knowing, the process of perception, and the different states of consciousness.[16] Although the historian often succeeds in emotionally swaying the reader with dramatic descriptions of schematized pathos and great set speeches of high morality, the fictional biographer devotes more attention to sensory experience and psychology. The following passages from the story are examples of descriptions of sensory and perceptual processes.

1. A drowsiness suddenly overcame his *senses*, and his *mind drifted as if* he were in a dream.
2. *Suddenly* he *saw* mountains and streams, wind and clouds, grass and trees, and streets and roads, which were very *different from the things in the human world.*
3. The soft tones and clear sound, and the melodies of melancholy and sadness, were not like those *heard* in the human world.
4. She was about fourteen or fifteen years old, *as* elegant and dignified *as* a goddess.
5. The mountains, hills, streams, meadows, and villages *looked* the same.

Words of perception and feeling appear in the story with great frequency. The character *yu* (there are/were) is also constantly used as the first word in sentences describing scenes and events that appeal to Ch'un-yü's senses. (For instance, "There were [*yu*] scores of supernatural maidens, playing varied and strange music. The soft tones and clear sound, and the melodies of melancholy and sadness, were not like those heard in the human world.") It is not clear whether the sentences beginning with *yu* are factual statements directly from the narrator or descriptions of events occurring in the subjective eye of the character. Objectivity is entangled in the vision of the protagonist, existence (*yu*) is enmeshed in perception, and ontology is qualified by epistemology.

The threshold between reality and dream and between the real and the unreal is not distinctly drawn. The transitions between the ordinary, familiar world of human beings and the supernatural, dream world of the Acacia Kingdom are marked by moments of epistemological and ontological uncertainty, by a blurring in perception. "A drowsiness suddenly overcame his senses, and his mind drifted *as if he were in a dream.*" "Ch'un-yü was much confused *as if he were in a deep sleep.*" "*It were as if one has just lived one's entire life in what happened so quickly in a dream.*" The many "as ifs" (*jo*) in the story suspend the certainty of the protagonist and the reader as to the ontological status of the worlds at stake.

As the story unfolds, Ch'un-yü Fen gradually comes to a new understanding of the utopia of the Great Acacia Kingdom of Peace. The happy story of his wish fulfillment in being chosen as the royal son-in-law ends in his return to the human world. As early as in the wedding ceremony, the height of his happiness, Ch'un-yü began to see that the supernatural order was governed in the same way as the human world. "The wedding ceremony that now followed, with its ritual greetings, its standing up and bowing, was in every way similar to that customary among human beings." The world of the Acacia Kingdom becomes less otherworldly and begins to resemble a miniature replica of the Chinese empire. To the reader of Chinese history, Ch'un-yü Fen's adventure in the dream world is told in much the same fashion as the career of a Chinese official is told in a historical biography. The sequence of events in the Acacia Kingdom—the rise from humble position to prominence, marriage with a princess, the trust and appreciation of the king, appointment as a provincial governor, the military campaign, the jealousy of other officials, the king's suspicion, and the predictable final fall—traces the standard "phenomenology" of the public career of a Confucian scholar. The otherworldly dream land is no different from the reality of the human world.

After Ch'un-yü's "awakening," he and his friends make another discovery about the subhuman world of ants. There is an exact correspondence between the "social" structure of the ants in the hollows of the big acacia tree outside his house and the sequence of events in the Acacia Kingdom. The prophecies in the dream are verified by happenings in the world of the ants. The layers of meaning and levels of existence—the human world, the supernatural world, and the subhuman world—are correlated and converge at the end. Ch'un-yü's initial state of "alienation" from Confucian officialdom and his imaginary transcendence of the human world through his entrance into the Acacia Kingdom seem to be no less degrading and "dehumanizing" than the existence of insects. The final resolution of the contradictions takes place through, interestingly enough, another retreat from the human world in a flight to Taoism. "Ch'un-yü felt the vanity and emptiness of South Branch and was awakened by the transience of human life. Thus he devoted his thoughts to Taoism and abandoned wine and women."

Yet the subject's "identification" with Taoism is not the final word it might seem but merely another contingent moment that dissolves in the network of intertextual relations.[17] Following a tradition of historical discourse established with the *Tso chuan* and the *Shih-chi*, the biography concludes with metatextual comments by the author. The storyteller resorts to the rhetoric of the official historian and draws lessons from what has been narrated. It is precisely at the juncture of the reassertion of Confucian values that there appears an incoherence, a slip of the tongue, a departure from the norm of historical discourse. "Even though the story speaks about spirits and the strange, and the events are unrelated to the way of the Classics, it may give a warning to those who covet high positions." The reference here is to the well-known statement in the *Lun-yü* that Confucius did not speak about prodigies, violence, disorder, and spirits. The fictional biography has spoken on a forbidden matter, has signified the unsignifiable, and thus deviates from the way of the Classics and historiography.

In the very reinstatement of Confucian morals (as opposed to those of Taoism), there is an authorial disavowal, a self-referential correction, a dismissal of the truthfulness of the story. The reader now wavers between two possible modes of interpretation. On the one hand, the storyteller has everywhere indicated the historicity of the narrated events and has therefore conditioned the reader to take them literally, in the same way as one reads a historical biography. On the other hand, the way is now open for an "allegorical" reading in which the reader does not accept the spirits and supernatural occurrences at face value but considers them as signifying some truth beyond the literality of the story. The simultaneous affirmation and denial of the factuality of the story produces an aporia of reading that makes interpretation an impossible task: one cannot integrate the multilayered discourse of the story into a definitive single horizon of meaning. But one result is clear: the heavy-handed reinforcement of Confucian morality at the conclusion of the story serves only to undermine the integrity of Confucian ideology.

6

From Historicity to Verisimilitude

THE EMERGENCE OF A
POETICS OF FICTION IN CHINA

Truth becomes fiction when the fiction's real;
Real becomes not-real when the unreal's real.
—Ts'ao Hsüeh-ch'in, *Story of the Stone*, Chap. 1, 55

Chinese attitudes toward *hsiao-shuo* or "fiction" began to change in late imperial China. Most significantly, the emergence of the long vernacular novel and the attendant commentarial and critical tradition changed Chinese notions of narrative. This new "poetics of fiction" developed out of the characteristics and standards of fictional narratives rather than those of historical narratives. This development ended fiction's dependence on the norms and aesthetics of traditional historiography. The flourishing of vernacular fiction in late imperial China constitutes another step in the "dehistoricization" of the Chinese narrative tradition.[1] In this chapter, I outline and assess the contribution of Chinese fiction to the development of the poetics of Chinese narrative, paying special attention to views of *hsiao-shuo* commentators on the nature of Chinese fictional narrative.

As we have seen, the privileged and dominant genre of narrative in traditional China was historical writing. Fictional narrative, or what is called *hsiao-shuo* in Chinese terminology, was a marginal, denigrated genre. The poetics or aesthetics of narrative was in reality a theory of historiography. Before the flourishing of fictional criticism in late imperial China, Chinese theories of narrative were centered largely on the model of historiography.

For Chinese historians, history writing was intended to be an accurate transcription of events. Ultimately, history was a mirror of human affairs; it offered patterns of success and failure and subsequently served a didactic function. The historian should aim at a faithful, straightforward recording of events and individuals. This quality of "faithful recording of events" (*shih-lu*) was often thought to be a distinguishing trait of good historians. The T'ang historian Liu Chih-chi, for example, praised Ssu-ma Ch'ien for this very quality. The value of historical writings lies in their accurate, faithful rendering of past events. Such a theory leaves little room for fabrication and invention.

The art of narration, or *hsü-shih* (narration of events), fascinated Chinese historiographers. One chapter in Liu Chih-chi's *Shih-t'ung* is even entitled "Hsü-shih." Liu states that "among the excellent histories of states, it is their narration of events which makes them well-formed, and skill in the narration of events lies chiefly in succinctness" (Sargent, 30–31). The narration of events, or the manner of composing narrative, changed significantly with the appearance of long, vernacular novels in the Ming and Ch'ing. My intent in the following is to pursue the question of how far the Chinese theory of fiction has traveled from earlier theories of narrative based on the model of historical writings.[2]

Beginnings of the Poetics of Fiction in the Sung

As we have seen, fictional biography flourished in the T'ang period. The stories are apparently not based on historical events, yet their authors attempted to deny the fictionality of their stories and insist on their historicity and factuality. Typically the narrator invites the reader to read the story as credible history. At this stage, there is little self-conscious differentiation between history and fiction. For historians such as Liu Chih-chi, fiction is simply an unofficial and unreliable form of history.

Even before the flourishing of *hsiao-shuo* criticism in the Ming and the Ch'ing, a new perception of fictional narrative is noticeable in the Sung period. During the early years of the Northern Sung dynasty at the orders of Emperor T'ai-tsung (r. 976–97), several major collections were compiled. The products of years of labor on the part of scholars and officials, these books testify to the attempt of a newly risen dynasty to systematize all current knowledge and regulate the varieties of discourse. The methods and ideas informing these projects embody the worldview and ideology of the dominant social class toward the organization of knowledge and discourse. The compilation of the *T'ai-p'ing yü-lan*, a *lei-shu* or encyclopedia, spanned some seven years, ending in 984 with a work of 1,000 *chüan*. The mammoth literary anthology *Wen-yüan ying-hua* was completed a few years later. It was modeled on the influential *Wen-hsüan* and included selections of literary works from all major genres, mostly from the T'ang period.

It was also during the T'ai-p'ing hsing-kuo reign period (976–83) that the *hsiao-shuo* anthology *T'ai-p'ing kuang-chi* was finished. This monumental collection contains fictional works of the Han to the T'ang dynasties. It comprises 500 *chüan* and is divided into 92 subgenres according to subject matter.[3]

A notable difference between the *Wen-hsüan* and the *Wen-yüan ying-hua* is the emergence of the *hsiao-shuo* genre of "biography," or *chuan*. To be sure, the *Wen-hsüan* contains such narrative and quasi-biographical genres as the "stone inscription" (*pei*), the "commemorative record" (*mu-chih*), and the "account of a career" (*hsing-chuang*).[4] But the *chuan* is excluded from the anthology for being a historical genre rather than a literary one. Chapter 12 of Liu Hsieh's theoretical treatise, the *Wen-hsin tiao-lung*, is devoted to the semi-biographical genres of "elegy" (*lei*) and "stone inscription" (*pei*).[5] Chapter 6, which deals with historical writings, briefly mentions the topic of the *chuan*. But neither the *Wen-hsüan* nor the *Wen-hsin tiao-lung* discusses the "biography" (*chuan*) in its diverse forms. It was, rather, the historians and bibliographers who were interested in defining and classifying the varieties of biographical writings. The "Ching-chi chih" of the *Sui-shu* lists 217 titles of "miscellaneous biography" (*tsa-chuan*) in the "History Section" and treats them as one of the thirteen types of historical writings.[6] The "Bibliographic Treatise" of the *Chiu T'ang-shu* basically follows the practice of the *Sui-shu* on this matter.[7] In the *Shih-t'ung*, Liu Chih-chi devoted a chapter, "Miscellaneous Narratives" ("Tsa-shu"), to the quasi-historical writings that cannot be included in the corpus of canonical and official histories. He considers "separate biography" (*pieh-chuan*) one of the ten types of non-official histories.[8]

In the *Wen-yüan ying-hua*, there is no lack of such old biographical and semi-biographical genres as *hsing-chuang*, *chih* (record), *pei*, and *ming* (commemorative record). A major change from previous anthologies is the incorporation of more than thirty fictional "biographies" by T'ang writers.[9] Fictional biography is now listed alongside the elevated official literary genres. This recognition of a humble fictional genre and its investiture by the official literary canon are not insignificant for the study of Chinese fiction. Before the Sung, biography and *hsiao-shuo* had been classified as forms of historical and quasi-historical writings and discussed from the point of view of historiography. The T'ang historian-bibliographers still followed the traditional view and regarded fictionalized narrative materials, works of *hsiao-shuo*, and fictional biographies as faulty and deficient genres of historical writings or as sources for history.[10] Beginning in the Sung, attitudes toward the nature of fictional biography and *hsiao-shuo* in general began to change, partly because of the vast output of fictional writings produced in the T'ang dynasty. This is indicated by several facts: first, the treatment of *fictional* biographies as a *literary* genre alongside other literary genres in the *Wen-yüan ying-hua*; second, the compilation of the special *hsiao-shuo* anthology, the *T'ai-p'ing kuang-chi*; and third, the nature of the titles listed in the *hsiao-shuo* section of the *Hsin Tang-shu*, which come close to the modern conception of fiction.[11]

The increased appreciation of *hsiao-shuo* in the Sung may be also seen in several brief and fragmentary discussions. Sung figures as diverse and different as Chao Ling-chih (1081–1134), Tseng Tsao (fl. 1136), Hung Mai (1123–1203), Chao Yen-wei (fl. 1190–1206), and Ch'en Chen-sun (fl. 1234) justified the importance of *hsiao-shuo* from one position or another (Huang Lin and Han T'ung-wen, 57–68). One of the most important developments in *hsiao-shuo* criticism in the late Sung, a development with important repercussions for later periods, is Liu Ch'en-weng's (1231–94) commentary on the *Shih-shuo hsin-yü*. For the first time, *hsiao-shuo* is worthy of a commentary, hitherto reserved for canonical texts such as the Classics and standard histories.

A crucial change visible in Liu's commentary is an awareness of the poetics of *hsiao-shuo*. Liu was one of the first not to defend *hsiao-shuo* on purely social and moral grounds. Rather, he sees a truthfulness, a verisimilitude, emerging from the aesthetics of the fictional text. His terminology features words such as *chen* (truthful, real, realistic), *wai-mao* (outer appearance), *shen-ch'ing* (facial expression), *shen-ch'i* (vivid manner), *feng-chih* (bearing), *ch'ang-ch'ing* (common way of things), *shih-ch'ing* (the way of the world), *hui* (paint), and *ch'i-shih* (extraordinary thing). Liu also compares the narrative art of the *Shih-shuo hsin-yü* and the craft of the historian and acclaims the *hsiao-shuo* text superior to the "historian's pen" (*shih-pi*). Liu's commentary pays close attention to the language of the text, the description of characters, problems of "representation," and the truthfulness of the narrated events. As Huang Lin and Han T'ung-wen point out (69–79), Liu's discussions mark the beginning of the poetics of Chinese fiction.

The widespread popularity of storytelling in the Sung was another important factor in the new turn in Chinese fiction criticism. The *pien-wen* texts discovered at Tun-huang in the early twentieth century show that popular narrative flourished in the T'ang. However, there is little critical material on how T'ang people thought about these popular narrative texts. We are more fortunate in regard to popular narrative from the Sung period. Certain passages from Nai Te-weng's (fl. 1235) *Tu-ch'eng chi-sheng* (A record of the prosperous capital), Wu Tzu-mu's (fl. 1274) *Meng-liang lu* (A record of the dream of millet), Lo Yeh's (no dates known) *Tsui-weng t'an-lu* (A record of the remarks of the drunken old man), and other works from the Sung attempt to come to terms with the many forms of "storytelling" (*shuo-hua, hua-pen, hsiao-shuo*) by classifying the various genres and types of popular stories.

Four major genres of popular storytelling (*shuo-hua*) are listed in the *Tu-ch'eng chi-sheng* and *Meng-liang lu*: "story" (*hsiao-shuo*), "narration of Buddhist scriptures" (*t'an-ching*), "narration of histories" (*chiang-shih*), and "improvisation" (*ho-sheng*). The category "story" has many subgenres; the *Tsui-weng t'an-lu* mentions stories about the supernatural (*ling-kuai*), love (*yen-fen*), the extraordinary (*ch'uan-ch'i*), crime, (*kung-an*), chivalry (*p'u-tao, kan-pang*), magic (*yao-shu*), and immortals (*shen-hsien*) and lists more than a hundred titles in these subgenres (Huang Lin and Han, 80, 88–89).

Particularly noteworthy is a discussion on the nature of *hsiao-shuo* in the *Tu-ch'eng chi-sheng*. *Hsiao-shuo* is said to be a mixture of *hsü* (imaginary) and *shih* (real), and *chen* (true) and *chia* (false).

"The narrators of history fear most the narrators of *hsiao-shuo*, for these can resolve the events of a whole dynasty or a generation in an instant" (Nai, 82; trans. Bishop, *Colloquial Short Story*, 8). Observations such as this go beyond purely moral, social, and institutional considerations to touch on the nature of fictional representation.

From Historicity to Fictionality in the Ming and Ch'ing

In the Ming and Ch'ing periods, people increasingly realized that much of fictional narrative is self-consciously non-historical and ostensively creative and that fiction ought not to be judged and read as defective history and quasi-history but to be understood on its own terms. Many commentators no longer regarded *hsiao-shuo* as something that needs to be faithful to history. The truth content of a work does not lie in its adherence to the specific details of past history. Fabrication, creation, and invention belong to the very nature of this type of work. Truth means different things in fiction and history. The fiction writer configures events, characters, emotions, and "truth" in a new fashion. Verisimilitude—a resemblance to the real world or an internal psychological truthfulness—becomes the new criterion for fiction among many critics. I am not arguing that verisimilitude was absent in historical discourse. As I have shown in previous chapters, the claim to historicity is merely another form of verisimilitude.[12] Rather, the point is that the historians and many early fiction critics did not rationalize verisimilitude as such. The critical scene visibly changes in the late imperial period. As Andrew Plaks points out, the Ming-Ch'ing commentators felt an "obvious fascination . . . for the maintenance of an impression of convincing verisimilitude within the unabashed fabrication of a fictional mode" ("Terminology and Central Concepts," 112).

Among the new terms used to describe the artistic quality of fictional writings are *pi-chen* (realistic), *hsiao-hsiang* (exact picture), *hsiao-wu* (exact image of the thing), *ch'uan-shen* (spiritual resemblance), *hua-kung* (natural craftsmanship), *hua-kung* (artifice), *pai-miao* (sketch), *hua* (draw), *mo-hua* (pictorial), *mo-hsieh* (descriptive), and *ju-hua* (picture-like). These concepts acknowledge the fictionality of literary texts and point to their artistry and artifice. The writers are free to compose events that are historically untrue.

Thanks to Andrew H. Plaks's studies, Yeh Lang's *Chung-kuo hsiao-shuo mei-hsüeh* (The aesthetics of Chinese fiction), and David Rolston's recent *How to Read the Chinese Novel*, we know more about the details of Ming and Ch'ing criticism of fiction. Ming and early Ch'ing critics such as Hsieh Chao-che (1567–1624), Feng Meng-lung (1574–1646), Li Chih (1527–1602), Yeh Chou (fl. 1610), Chin Sheng-t'an (1608–61), and Chang Chu-p'o (1670–98) become spokesmen for the change in the aesthetics of Chinese narrative.

In *Wu tsa tsu* (Five miscellanies), Hsieh notes the necessity of mixing real and fictive events in literary works: "In regard to fiction [*hsiao-shuo*] and dramatic compositions [*tsa-ch'ü hsi-wen*], there should be a mixture of the fictive [*hsü*] and the real [*shih*]. Then they become writings that capture the essence of literary games. One should make sure that the feelings and scenes are extremely well constructed without asking whether they really exist or not" (Hsieh, 1287). For Hsieh, what matters in literary composition is apparently not the historicity and factuality of the story. The point is that events should appear real and factual. As long as a story is realistically narrated, as long as it conveys *li* (principle, truth), it does not matter if the events (*shih*) are historically verifiable. Works such as the *Shui-hu chuan* and the *Hsi-yu chi* (Journey to the west), even though the latter is full of fantastic and supernatural happenings, exhibit the "uttermost truth" (*chih-li*). Hsieh deprecates works such as the *San-kuo yen-i* (Romance of the Three Kingdoms) and the *Hsüan-ho i-shih* (Events of the Hsüan-ho period) for their "bookish fidelity to the events of the past" (1287). For Hsieh, many of his contemporaries have the unfortunate habit of applying the criterion of historical verifiability to fiction. "If the dates, years, and characters' names must correspond to those in standard history, who would dare write? If this is the case, it would be enough to read history. What is the point of calling it a game?" (1287)

Feng Meng-lung also discusses the dialectic of *li* and *shih*, and of real (*chen*) and fictive (*yen*) in history and fiction. In the Preface to the *Ching-shih t'ung-yen* (Words to warn the world), he states that events in fiction do not have to be completely real or completely fictive. The story need not be based on real events if it performs a positive social function and conveys some ultimate principle. "The characters may not have done the things, and the things may not belong to the characters" (Tseng Tsu-yin et al., 97). The truthfulness of a story does not depend on whether the depicted events are historically real. What matters is its "principle" (*li*). Feng also points out a central difference between historical writing and fictional writing in discussing the relationship between *shih* and *li*. In history, both events and principles have to be true. In fiction, however, the writer does not have to follow the particulars of past events if the story points to some universal truth.

Another important term in Feng Meng-lung's conception of *hsiao-shuo* is the idea of *ch'ing* (love, emotion, feelings), an idea that evokes rich connotations. He compiled a comprehensive work on the subject, the *Ch'ing-shih* or *Ch'ing-shih lei-lüeh* (History of love, by categories), from various sources. The book classifies over 870 titles involving *ch'ing* into 24 categories of stories. In the two prefaces to the work and in the comments by the "Historian of Love" (*ch'ing-shih shih*) concluding many of the stories, Feng makes *ch'ing* into an eternal, all-generating, and all-embracing force in the universe. As an "unofficial historian" of *ch'ing*, his purpose is to perpetuate the "teaching of *ch'ing*" (*ch'ing-chiao*). As he claims, "All the Six Classics teach *ch'ing*." *Ch'ing* was taken as the underlying force in nature and social life.

Ch'ing is an important term in the criticism of poetry and rhymeprose (*fu*). What we are witnessing here is the growth of a lyrical, subjective vision in Chinese narrative in late imperial China and the transference of the concept of *ch'ing* to the criticism of narrative fiction. In this process of "dehistoricization" and "lyricization," subjective vision and emotional appeal take precedence over the hard facts (*shih*) of history.[13] As we will see, commentators on works like *Chin P'ing Mei* and *Hung-lou Meng* would soon elaborate the concept of *ch'ing* in the analysis of fiction. Critical discussions of fiction often involve the triad of *li*, *shih*, and *ch'ing*.[14]

Perhaps one of the most decisive steps in moving toward a poetics of fiction centered around the extensive commentaries on the *Shui-hu chuan*. Most significant in terms of fictional criticism are several late Ming and early Ch'ing editions of the novel. The Jung-yü T'ang 100-chapter edition (1610)—*Li Cho-wu hsien-sheng p'i-p'ing chung-i Shui-hu chuan* (The *Shui-hu chuan* of loyalty and righteousness with commentary by Mr. Li Cho-wu); the Yüan Wu-ya 120-chapter edition (ca. 1611)—*Li Chih p'ing chung-i Shui-hu ch'üan-chuan* (The complete *Shui-hu chuan* with commentary by Li Chih); and Chin Sheng-t'an's 70-chapter edition fully reveal the commentators' conception of fiction. The criticisms and commentaries of Li Chih, Yeh Chou (arguably the real commentator of the Jung-yü T'ang edition of the novel),[15] and later Chin Sheng-t'an are the high point of this new poetics of narrative. A remarkable feature of their commentaries is that they highlight the fictionality of the novel and are therefore able to appreciate its psychological, descriptive truthfulness all the more. Their positions are repeatedly expressed in the prefaces, general comments on each chapter, and interlinear and marginal comments. Several comments on the veracity of the novel in the Jung-yü T'ang version can serve as examples.

The events and episodes in the *Shui-hu chuan* are all fictive, but they look real [*pi-chen*]. This is why it is marvelous. (*Shui-hu chuan*, 53)

The words of the *Shui-hu chuan* are originally fabricated [*chia*]. But because he [the author] is able to describe real situations [*chen-ch'ing*], it becomes immortal with heaven and earth. (218)

The writing in this chapter is vivid [*pi-chen*], natural [*hua-kung*], and lifelike [*hsiao-wu*]. (398)

In the essay "The Literary Merits and Demerits of the 100 Chapters of the *Shui-hu chuan*" ("*Shui-hu chuan* i-pai hui wen-tzu yu-lüeh"), the commentator marvels at how lifelike and vivid the characters are. Although the characters were all "airy inventions" (*p'i-k'ung nieh-tsao*) of the author, they "resemble real people and are full of life" (*Shui-hu chuan*, 26). This depiction of lively figures makes the novel appealing to the readers.

This aspect of Li Chih's and Yeh Chou's criticism is developed further in Chin Sheng-t'an's commentary. Chin formulated the famous distinction between historical discourse and fictional discourse in his seminal essay "How to Read the Fifth Book of Genius." The difference between the *Shih-chi* and the *Shui-hu chuan* is one between the principle of *i-wen yün-shih* (to use writing to transmit events) and that of *yin-wen sheng-shih* (to give birth to events through writing). Whereas historical writing aims at recording past events, fiction makes up non-existent events because of the exigencies of its own narration. A novel is necessarily composed of fictive elements.

In terms of this new aesthetics, Chin finds the *Shui-hu chuan* superior to both the *Hsi-yu chi* and the *San-kuo yen-i*. Events in the *Hsi-yu chi* are too fantastic to be true, and those in the *San-kuo yen-i* are too faithful to historical details to be enjoyable reading. The *Shui-hu chuan* strikes a balance between the two. In the *San-kuo yen-i*, "the author's pen cannot move or turn at will. It is just like an official sending a message through his attendant. The latter can use his voice only to transmit what he has been told. Indeed, how dare he add or subtract a word" (Rolston, 132)? Moreover, "the *Shui-hu chuan* does not talk about ghosts, spirits, or other strange and exotic matters. This is where its power surpasses other books. In the *Hsi-yu chi*, whenever the author is at a loss as to what to do, the Bodhisattva Kuan-yin of the Southern Seas comes to the rescue" (Rolston, 134).

For Chin, the *Shui-hu chuan* is also superior to other novels because of its colloquial, everyday language. Such language conveys an immediacy and verisimilitude lacking in popular novels written in the literary language. "The *Shui-hu chuan* does not contain literary language particles like *chih, hu, che, yeh*. Each individual character is made to speak in his own way" (Rolston, 134). The novel is itself a storehouse of dialects, slang, and idiolects of the Sung and Yuan periods. Its language conveys a degree of truthfulness and authenticity unparalleled by the language used in other novels.

What Anthony C. Yu calls the revolutionary moment in the Chinese narrative tradition is the self-reflexivity of the *Hung-lou Meng*.[16] Unlike previous novels, it calls attention to its own fictionality, undatability, absurdity, illusoriness, and unreality. Yet both the nameless narrator and the commentator Chih-yen Chai (Red Inkstone Studio) insist on the extreme truthfulness of the novel even as they assert its fictionality. Much of Chih-yen Chai's commentary is a reflection on the interrelations of *li, shih*, and *ch'ing* in the novel. He is fascinated with the interplay of fictive and real events in the story. There are fictive events that did not exist historically but could exist according to probability and necessity. Such factually non-existent things are narrated with high credibility in the novel. The following comments are taken from the *chia-hsü* (1754) edition of the *Hung-lou Meng*:

It is also a good idea to follow the ancient names of government offices. I like this sort of absurd thing the most, things that are half real and half fictive, half ancient and half contemporary. They are non-existent as things, but their principle necessarily exists. They are extremely illusory and mysterious. (Ts'ao, chap. 2, 24a)

Such a narrative method is the marvelous writing of most truthful feelings and principles. (chap. 2, 24b)

The writing is excellent, the principle is what must exist, and the words are those that are the most painful and the saddest. (chap. 2, 27a)

Readers should not ask whether there is or isn't such an event. We should cheer ourselves up with wine simply because our minds and eyes are entertained by this sort of fresh and marvelous writing. (chap. 7, 99b)

This seems to be extremely absurd, but something that necessarily exists in the world. (chap. 7, 100b)

Throughout the *keng-ch'en* (1760) edition, there are also extensive comments on the question of truth and falsehood, on what is real and what is fictive.

These are naturally the uttermost feelings and principles, things that necessarily exist. (Yü P'ing-po, chap. 29, 471)

A piece of absurd talk of a stupid woman, but really something that necessarily exists in the world. (chap. 42, 503)

The Story of the Stone contains real-life feelings and situations, events and words that necessarily exist. (chap. 16, 252)

It matters little if events (*shih*) are not historically verifiable; the story is a truthful story if its *li* (principles, reasons, laws) and what is called the idea of *ch'ing* (feelings, emotions, situations, descriptions) are real.[17] Events may not be factually true so long as they produce an effect of truth in the mind of the reader.[18]

Even more important than *shih* and *li* in the *Hung-lou Meng* is *ch'ing*.[19] Within the novel and throughout the Chih-yen Chai commentary, *ch'ing* becomes the key and unifying theme. The meaning of the word ranges from feelings to emotions, attachments, love, passion, sentience, and human nature in the novel. In the first chapter, the narrator proclaims that "the general purpose of the novel is to talk about *ch'ing*" (Ts'ao, 9a). In Chapter 8 of the *chia-hsü* edition, Chih-yen Chai states: "The author wished all the people in the world to cry for this word *ch'ing*" (126a).

Even this brief sketch of the emergence of a poetics of Chinese fiction should make it apparent that many critics have removed fiction from its dependence on fidelity to "events" (*shih*) in the historical past. Fictional texts are now judged on the degree of the truthfulness of their internal principles and feelings, or *li* and *ch'ing*, which are among the most polysemous of Chinese critical terms.

Another noteworthy development in the poetics of Chinese narrative at this juncture is that the manner of reading popular novels was often carried over into reading historical writings. *Hsiao-shuo* critics are inclined to make comparisons between the *Shih-chi* and vernacular novels. Novelists are said to be indebted to the *Shih-chi* for their compositional methods, but the novels surpass the *Shih-chi* in powers of description. Ming readers sometimes use the same terms to describe the *Shih-chi* as they do the popular novels—expressions such as *mo-hua* (pictorial), *mo-hsieh* (descriptive), and *pi-chen* (realistic). This is perhaps evidence for the reverse influence of the poetics of fiction on the appreciation of historical writing. For instance, Mao K'un said of the *Shih-chi*: "The grand historian's description [*mo-hua*] is superb." And "the elegance of its tone, the exquisiteness of its description [*mo-hua*], the moving power of its spirit, and the sadness and resentment of the feelings and events are all unparalleled in a thousand years" (Arii, 1: 51a, 52a). Wang Shih-chen (1526–90) wrote that "its narration [*hsü-shih*] is vivid [*hsiao-wu*] as a result of natural transformation [*hua-kung*]" (Arii, 1: 52b). Commenting on the scene of the death of Hsiang Yü in the "Basic Annals of Hsiang Yü," T'ien Ju-ch'eng (fl. 1526) wrote that "the historian's description [*mo-hsieh*] is true to life [*pi-chen*] and picture-like [*ju-hua*]"; "its narration captures the manners of people [*jen-ch'ing*] and touches people" (Arii, 1: *chüan* 7, 19b, 20a). Chung Hsing (1574–1625) remarked of a scene in the annals that it was "as if what was described [*mo-hsieh*] were before my eyes" (Arii, 1: *chüan* 7, 21b). These statements seem to indicate that the commentators were highly aware of the artistic reshaping of historical materials. History writing is a craft, and the historian re-presents the past with a vivid, effective manner of narration. Fictional texts have opened readers' eyes to the nature of historical writings.

Not all commentators welcomed the superseding of historicity by verisimilitude as a critical criterion. Some critics still judged the Chinese novel by the standards of historical writings. Lovers of historical romances like the *San-kuo yen-i* praised certain novels because of their historical character. The strength of a novel lay in its presentation of real historical events rather than fabricated incidents. In his "Preface to the Popular Novel *San-kuo yen-i*" ("*San-kuo chih t'ung-su yen-i* hsü"), Chiang Ta-ch'i (fl. 1494) takes the work as a successful popular history. It is a book that commoners could enjoy. Its simple language and its presentation of "real events" make it "almost a history" (Chu I-hsüan and Liu Yü-ch'en *San-kuo yen-i*, 270). Chang Shang-te (fl. 1522), another Ming critic, makes a similar point in his preface to the novel, "*San-kuo chih t'ung-su yen-i* yin." The popular novel is a "wing" or a supplement to "authentic history" (Chu I-hsüan and Liu Yü-ch'en, *San-kuo yen-i*, 271).

Mao Tsung-kang follows the path of Chin Sheng-t'an in his commentary on the *San-kuo yen-i*, but reverses Chin's evaluation of the relative strengths of the major novels. He finds the *San-kuo yen-i* better than the *Shui-hu chuan* and *Hsi-yu chi* not because of its lifelike, "verisimilar" portrayal of fictive characters but because of its faithfulness to the historical past. He repeatedly emphasizes the factuality (*shih*) of the novel in comparison to other works of fiction.

The *Hsi-yu chi* creates ex nihilo a world of monsters and magic that is fantastic and uncanonical, but this feat is not as impressive as that of *The Romance of the Three Kingdoms*, which faithfully relates [*shih-hsü*] a tale of emperors and kings that is true and verifiable. . . .

The realism of the *Shui-hu chuan* is to be preferred to the fantasy of the *Hsi-yu chi*. Nevertheless, because the author was free to create his material ex nihilo and to manipulate his plot at will, as a feat of literary craftsmanship his achievement was not as difficult as that of the author of *The Romance of the Three Kingdoms*, who succeeded in giving artistic form to predetermined material that would not admit of alteration. (Chu I-hsüan and Liu Yü-ch'en, *San-kuo yen-i*, 309; Rolston, 193–95)

Mao is one of the most eloquent spokesmen for *shih* (real, substantive) as opposed to *hsü* (fictive, empty) in Chinese narrative. Although he emerged on the critical scene after Chin Sheng-t'an, his views followed earlier notions about narration. His ideas come close to the position of historians in regard to fictional narrative.[20]

Depiction of Lifelike Characters in the Novel

The depiction of characters in the novel is another area deserving attention in terms of the evolution of the poetics of Chinese narrative. In historical writing, the biography (*lieh-chuan*) is the place where individual characters are delineated. The portrayal of distinct personalities and the depiction of extraordinary, fascinating characters in Ssu-ma Ch'ien's *Shih-chi* have left an enduring impression on readers. Later dynastic histories rarely have as strong an appeal as the *Shih-chi* in terms of character portrayal. The historical biography seemed to become more and more schematized and rigid as historians conformed to orthodox Confucian principles in writing about the past. As I mentioned earlier, Ssu-ma Ch'ien himself was occasionally criticized for failing to adhere strictly to orthodox views of certain historical personages.

The T'ang fictional biography opened a new field in the Chinese narrative tradition. The presence of supernatural beings and the portrayal of love and passion deviated from the standards of historical narrative. However, contemporary writers and critics never theorized their tales as anything radically new or fictive. The form of the fictional biography derived from the historical biography, and the storyteller took pains to point out the historicity and credibility of his story. It is usual for authors to specify "reliable" sources for the story and comment appropriately on the morality of the events.

There were new developments in character portrayal in Ming and Ch'ing novels. Among the commentaries on the great Ming novels, Mao Tsung-kang's on the *San-kuo yen-i* stands out for its traditional, orthodox moral judgments of the characters. Mao thinks that the novel is successful in creating three types of people: worthy ministers, famous generals, and unscrupulous heroes (*chien-hsiung*). Chu-ko Liang, Kuan Yü, and Ts'ao Ts'ao are, respectively, the supreme example of each. Whereas Chu-ko Liang and Kuan Yü are the paragons of loyalty, wisdom, righteousness, and bravery, Ts'ao Ts'ao typifies the kind of people who "seem to be loyal," "seem to show proper allegiance," and "seem to be chivalrous." Mao views the characters in terms of absolute types, exemplary heroes, and models and gives a moral-historical reading of the novel. The characters are clear-cut types to be emulated or despised by posterity. In this respect, his interpretation comes close to the orthodox historical conception of personages from the past.

Mao's view of character portrayal in the novel is not shared by other important critics. They have a great awareness of the complexity and multifacetedness of individual figures. Their readings of novels are much less based on preconceived moral standards. The point of departure in their discussion is not abstract moral types but the individuality of each person. The general comment at the end of Chapter 3 of the Jung-yü Tang edition of the *Shui-hu chuan* is an example of how Li Chih or Yeh Chou understood the Liang-shan heroes:

> The depiction of Lu Chih-shen remains alive in all times. This is truly marvelous writing in terms of truthfulness and inspiration. The enduring appeal of the *Shui-hu chuan* lies in the fact that there is still further distinction within what is the same and what is different. For example, Lu Chih-shen, Li K'uei, Wu Sung, Juan the Seventh, Shih Hsiu, Hu-yen Cho, Liu T'ang, and so on are all men of quick temperament. But because of [the author's] description and carving, each person has his own character, his own appearance, his own ability, and his own status. Without a tiny bit of blurring, each distinguishes himself. The reader does not need to know their names. He knows who is who just by looking at the events and actions. (*Shui-hu chuan*, 97)

Chin Sheng-t'an follows Li Chih and Yeh Chou in his analysis of the characters. For him, the main strength of the *Shui-hu chuan* lies in the author's ability to create 108 distinct personalities.[21] Many of the characters and events are historically nonexistent and therefore necessarily were invented by the author. Yet the author created these lifelike, memorable characters. "Other books you read through once and stop, but one never tires of reading the *Shui-hu chuan* because it succeeds completely in describing the different personalities [*hsing-ko*] of all 108 people" (*Shui-hu chuan*, 17; Rolston, 135). The author truly possesses "a most natural [*hua-kung*] and lifelike [*hsiao-wu*] style" (*Shui-hu chuan*, 18; Rolston, 137). Each character is made to speak his own idiom and act in his own manner. Speaking of "rough men" (*ts'u-lu*) alone, for example, Chin finds tremendous further differences among these people.

Just in the description of rough men alone, the *Shui-hu chuan* uses many methods of description. For example, the roughness of Lu Chih-shen is that of a man of hasty temperament, that of Shih Chin the impulsiveness of youth, that of Li K'uei wildness; the roughness of Wu Sung is that of an untrammeled hero; the roughness of Juan the Seventh comes from his pent-up sorrow and anger; and the roughness of Chiao T'ing is simply his bad temper.   (*Shui-hu chuan*, 18; Rolston, 136)

Similar attention to the subtleties and nuances of character portrayal is evident throughout Chin's commentary.

The possibility of inventing 108 distinct personalities in the novel is accounted for by Neo-Confucian epistemology. Chin Sheng-t'an asked how the author Shih Nai-an could create vivid pictures of "adulteresses," "thieves," and so many other characters if he himself had never been an adulteress or thief. His answer is that Shih Nai-an had investigated things (*ko-wu*) and studied the causes and conditions (*yin-yüan*) of the phenomenal world for as long as "ten years." In this manner, the author was able to grasp the laws (*fa*) of the universe and of writing and to bridge the gap between the truth of fiction and life in the real world.

If the *Shui-hu chuan* describes the world of heroes and heroic actions, the *Chin P'ing Mei* presents familiar scenes of everyday life and ordinary people. Commentators focus on an aspect of humanity they commonly refer to as *ch'ing* or its various compounds such as *jen-ch'ing* and *shih-ch'ing*. The connotations of these terms range from the inner nature of human beings to their behavior, appearance, relationships, feelings, and emotions. It is an area that is rarely explored in Mao Tsung-kang's moral interpretation or even in Chin Sheng-t'an's brilliant character analysis.

In the opening line of "How to Read the *Chin P'ing Mei*" ("*Chin Ping Mei* tu-fa"), Chang Chu-p'o reminds the reader of the fictionality of the novel. "The author has invented [*p'i-k'ung chuan-ch'u*] the three characters [whose names make up the title], P'an *Chin*-lien, Li *P'ing*-erh, and Ch'un-*mei*" (Huang Lin, 65; Rolston, 202). Because of the creative skills of the author, the reader is allowed to vicariously enjoy a truthful and realistic story. The author managed to create vivid, lifelike characters.[22] The protagonists in the novel are unmistakably far removed from the realm of heroes. The novel is inhabited by a multitude of anti-heroes, negative characters, lowlifes, adulterers, and upstarts. The world of the novel is one of lust, passion, scheming, jealousy, money-grubbing, and moral depravity. Chang's comments on the characters are hardly complimentary.

Hsi-men Ch'ing is an undiscerning scoundrel, Wu Yüeh-niang is an artful hypocrite, Meng Yü-lou is endearing, P'an Chin-lien is inhuman, Li P'ing-erh is infatuated, Ch'un-mei is unruly, Ch'en Ching-chi is a frivolous non-entity, Li Chiao-erh is lifeless, Sun Hsüeh-o is stupid, Sung Hui-lien does not know her place, and Ju-i is a mere surrogate. As for the rest, Wang Liu-erh, Lady Lin, Li Kuei-chieh, and the like can scarcely be considered human. Ying Po-chüeh, Hsieh Hsi-ta, and company are utterly unconscionable, and Grand Preceptor Ts'ai and the censors, Ts'ai and Sung, might just as well never have been born.   (Huang Lin, 74; Rolston, 220)

Little in the story is morally edifying. The author wrote a book not about "loyal ministers and filial sons" but about "adulterous men and lascivious women." Herein lies the greatness of the novel for Chang, namely, in its penetration of human nature, human relations, and the world as it is. The author "must have been thoroughly acquainted with the ways of the world [*jen-ch'ing shih-ku*] in order to be able to depict the inner spirit of his characters with such verisimilitude [*mo-shen*]. . . . The author succeeds in portraying each of the characters in his book with utter fidelity to human nature [*jen-ch'ing*]. He transforms himself [*hua-shen*] into a multitude of guises, representing all sorts of people" (Huang, 81; Rolston, 233).

Chang foregrounds the importance of *ch'ing* (feeling, emotion, human nature) and *li* (principle, reason) in the writing of the novel.

The prerequisite for a successful literary creation can be summed up in two words: emotion [*ch'ing*] and reason [*li*]. The key to this long work of a hundred chapters is also only these two words, emotion and reason. If you can determine the particular mixture of emotion and reason in a character's heart, you have captured the character. Though this character's speech may be mixed in with those of many others, whenever he opens his mouth, what he says will express his particular balance of emotion and reason.   (Huang Lin, 77; Rolston, 224–25)

The distinctiveness of the speech and appearance of a character is the result of the author's penetration into that character's inner nature, its "emotion" and "reason." It is the "utter fidelity to human nature" and "the ways of the world" that accounts for the power, realism, and truthfulness of the novel. Chang Chu-p'o's analysis of the characters in the *Chin P'ing Mei* has gone further than Mao's interpretation of *San-kuo yen-i*, or even Chin's reading of the *Shui-hu chuan*. The basis of his analysis is not absolute moral categories; it is also more than the individuality of the heroes. Chang uses terms such as *ch'ing-li* and *jen-ch'ing* to refer to human nature, in all its naked ugliness, its contradictoriness, and its complexity. Later in the *Hung-lou Meng* and the Chih-yen Chai commentary, stereotypical portrayals of characters and worn-out literary conventions are severely criticized. The novel is said to rise above all the clichés of popular fiction and drama.

These commentators' discussions of fictional characters are far removed from the portrayal of human beings in the standard histories. Perhaps one can discover a parallel among the standard histories only in the unconventional and rather subjective portrayals of certain extraordinary individuals in Ssu-ma Ch'ien's *Shih-chi*. To the extent that the *hsiao-shuo* commentators focus on areas of character portrayal that were largely neglected and unexplored by historical writers after the *Shih-chi*, one can speak of a distinct development in the poetics of Chinese narrative in the Ming and Ch'ing.

Form and Structure in the Novel

The commentators were struck by the formal innovations of the novel and clearly felt that there had been a breakthrough in narrative. The narration of events (*hsü-shih*) in the new novel had accomplished things that historical narrative could not. They acclaimed the form and structure of the novel significantly different from and even better than those of historical writings.

Commentators such as Chin Sheng-t'an, Mao Tsung-kang, and Chang Chu-p'o are unanimous in stating that the new novel is more effective in vividly describing characters than the historical biography. Although Ssu-ma Ch'ien's biographies presented memorable characters, the connections between the biographies themselves are tenuous and unclear. The annals-biography (*chi-chuan*) form created by Ssu-ma Ch'ien fails to render a continuous, organic story. The genre of the novel achieves much more flexibility in the manner of narration by stepping out of the straitjacket of historiography. Thus, Chin writes about narrative units in the *Shui-*

hu chuan: "For every character who appears in the *Shui-hu chuan* a clear-cut biography [*lieh-chuan*] is provided. As for the events contained within them, each section further forms an independent unit in itself. Sometimes two or three chapters will form such a unit. Sometimes it takes five or six sentences" (*Shui-hu chuan*, 17; Rolston, 135).

Mao Tsung-kang basically follows Chin Sheng-t'an in discussing the narrative structure of the *San-kuo yen-i*:

The narrative [*hsü-shih*] artistry of *The Romance of the Three Kingdoms* is comparable to that of the *Shih-chi*, but the difficulties involved in composing its narrative [*hsü-shih*] were twice as difficult as those involved in the case of the *Shih-chi*.

In the *Shih-chi* each state and each individual is given separate treatment, with the result that the material is divided up into separate categories of basic annals [*pen-chi*], hereditary houses [*shih-chia*], and biographies [*lieh-chuan*]. This is not so in the case of *The Romance of the Three Kingdoms*, where the basic annals, hereditary houses, and biographies are combined to form a single composite work. When things are treated separately, the text of each section is short and it is easy to exercise artistic control, whereas when things are combined, the text becomes long and artistic success is more difficult to achieve.   (Chu I-hsüan and Liu Yü-ch'en, *San-kuo yen-i*, 308; Rolston, 193)

Mao here speaks of the formal and structural innovations of the novel. The novel is able to weave a coherent whole out of various units that would remain separate in historical narrative.

In his discussion of the *Chin P'ing Mei*, Chang Chu-p'o expresses a similar view in regard to differences in the manner of narration between fiction and history.

The *Chin P'ing Mei* is a veritable *Shih-chi*, but the *Shih-chi*, though it contains both individual biographies [*tu-chuan*] and collective biographies [*ho-chuan*], treats each biography separately. The hundred chapters of the *Chin P'ing Mei*, on the other hand, constitute a single biography [*chuan*] in which hundreds of characters are treated. Though the presentation is discontinuous, each character has a biography of its own.   (Huang Lin, 75; Rolston, 221)

With its new narrative structure, the novel surpasses history. Its narration constitutes a continuous flow rather than a segmented portrayal of separate events and characters.

The commentators also discovered new structural devices in the novels.[23] Each text has its own distinct units and divisions. Yet, all segments are ultimately related. The beginning of a novel is necessarily related to the conclusion. In Chin Sheng-t'an's analysis, the *Shui-hu chuan* "begins with peace in the empire and ends with peace in the empire." Within the novel, the several major divisions are marked by the appearances of the words "stone tablet" (*shih-chieh*). The fine artistry of the work is analogous to the structure of a well-wrought examination essay. "The various events and devices in those pages are used as methods to begin [*ch'i*], continue [*ch'eng*], change direction [*chuan*], and sum up [*ho*] the composition" (*Shui-hu chuan*, 16; Rolston, 133). Chin Sheng-t'an identifies many structural principles and rhetorical devices in the *Shui-hu chuan*. He coined his own terminology for the various devices of contrast, comparison, indirect description, repetition, foregrounding, and backgrounding. (In his own terms, they are *ts'ao-she hui-hsien fa* [snake in the grass and the chalk line], *mien-chen ni-tz'u fa* [needles wrapped in cotton and thorns hidden in the mud], *pei-mien p'u-fen fa* [whitening the background to bring out the foreground], *cheng-fan fa* [full repetition], *lüeh-fan fa* [partial repetition], and so forth.) These structural configurations bring out hidden dimensions of meaning that would escape the notice of the ordinary reader.

Mao Tsung-kang, Chang Chu-p'o, and other commentators also outlined the basic structure and compositional principles of the major novels in the wake of Chin's reading of the *Shui-hu chuan*. Mao, for example, argues that there are six significant beginnings and conclusions between the initial beginning and the final conclusion in the *San-kuo yen-i*. Moreover, the novel follows twelve "structural principles" (*chang-fa*). Some of these principles are variations or further elaborations of those of Chin's.

Chang Chu-p'o is also in the habit of talking about the overall structural design as well as "regular structural devices" (*pan-ting ta chang-fa*). There are many moments of interweaving, insertion, dovetailing, direct and indirect description, repetition, and juxtaposition in the narration of the *Chin P'ing Mei*. There are "places of pivotal importance" (*kuan-chien ch'u*) and "great spatial settings" (*ta chien-chia ch'u*), as well as many "rules of literary composition" (*wen-chia chih fa-lü*).

In terms of the overall structure of the novel, Chang tells that it "consists of two halves. The first half is 'hot' and the second half is 'cold,' but in the first half there is 'cold' in 'heat' and in the second half there is 'heat' in 'cold'" (Huang Lin, 85; Rolston, 239). All the minute details and individual units of the novel are subsumed under a great design. The beginning of the novel and the hundred chapters are made to dovetail with the grand conclusion. All the sections and episodes move toward, after all, a final end, a "telos." Commenting upon the last chapter, Chang says that "this chapter is the ocean to which the myriad rivers return" (Huang Lin, 224). The entirety of previous events and incidents is oriented toward this final destiny.

The first chapter relates brothers and in-laws, and it begins with the word *ti* [brother]; the last chapter relates the spiritual transformation of Hsiao-ko, and it concludes with the word *hsiao* [filial piety]. Thus we come to understand that this book about adulterous affairs is really a book about filial sons and loving brothers [*hsiao-tzu t'i-ti*], and about tears shed at the end of one's career. The book begins and concludes with filial piety and brotherly love. Whoever calls it a "pornographic book" is without filial piety and brotherly love. . . . I wish to let all sons and brothers know that the author wanted to advance the teaching of filial piety and brotherly love in a fallen world. (Huang Lin, 226)

The final grand import is inseparable from the structural devices of the novel. By now, the art of narration has indeed traveled a long way from that of historical writing. The popular novel has perfected a narrative form beyond the previous major narrative forms— the biography (*chuan*), the annals-biography (*chi-chuan*), and the chronology (*pien-nien*). Due to its formal innovations, the novel has developed a distinct "poetics" of its own, one with more narrative potential and elasticity than the poetics of historiography.

I hope by now that the contours and outlines of the long and steady development of the Chinese poetics of narrative are clearer. The process is characterized by both surprising changes and the resilience of time-honored beliefs. The Chinese historical approach to narrative is certainly an interesting phenomenon among the various literary systems in the world. As I have argued in this study, following previous scholars, the Chinese tradition tends to comprehend the vast output of heterogeneous narrative materials within the all-encompassing notion of history. Such an attitude to the variety of narrative discourse has its moments of critical acumen and disciplinary rigor. The great bibliographic, classificatory systems devised by the rational-minded, all-discerning historians left no form of writing and no type of discourse outside their scope. Both the procedures of "transcribing" or "representing" the reality of the past and the conventions of historical interpretation in Chinese historiography seem perfectly developed and well suited to their ends.

It is also true, however, that this resolute historical disposition fails to do justice to many forms and genres of narratives, especially what is called *hsiao-shuo* in Chinese terminology. For most of Chinese critical history, institutional, moral, and social considerations have relegated the discourse of *hsiao-shuo* to marginal status. As a result, the nature of fictional narrative was not fully comprehended, and Chinese narrative theory remained a lopsided, history-centered narrative theory for a long time. It was not until the flourishing of popular storytelling in late imperial China that critics of *hsiao-shuo* were able to explore its aesthetic, literary, and "poetic" features fully. Only then was *hsiao-shuo* understood as something quite distinct from history.

From the point of view of comparative, cross-cultural poetics, I hope my research has also given a more balanced and precise discussion, however sketchy and hasty it may be, of the origins and transformations of a few key terms in narrative studies. Western concepts of "narrative," "history," and "fiction" sometimes do and sometimes do not correspond to the lexical Chinese counterparts. China and the West share some premises about the nature of narrative discourse, but differ over others. The bulk of this study deals with the Chinese critical scene. Nevertheless, it may help clarify a few points in the comparative poetics of narrative and thus benefit those who share these scholarly interests.

Storytelling and Critical Paradigms
in the Study of Chinese Narrative

If you parade your little theories [*hsiao-shuo*] to fish for
renown, you will be far from the Great Paradigm [*ta-ta*].
—"External Things," *Chuang Tzu*

In retrospect, an important methodological change in the study
of Chinese narrative occurred in the mid-1970's. This change
may briefly be characterized as the replacement of the traditional
historical/historicist approach by a formalist-structuralist orientation. As students of Chinese literature well know, the traditional
prestige of historical studies in China continued into the twentieth
century. The turn away from historical studies proved to be a major event in Chinese literary studies.

My intentions here are first to characterize the assumptions and
problems involved in this "paradigm change" and then to suggest
ways to rehabilitate the historical approach in Chinese literary
scholarship without returning to the historicist orientation. A new
awareness of the importance of history may allow us to chart some
alternatives for comprehending the problematic of narrative/his-
tory in Chinese literature. In the final section, I reflect upon the idea
of "paradigm" itself in literary studies, particularly the problem of
the co-existence of several competing paradigms and theories. By
proposing a new way of looking at critical paradigms, I hope to
arrive at a better understanding of the methodological issues in the
study of Chinese narrative.

Displacing History in Literary Scholarship

In the wake of Thomas S. Kuhn's *Structure of Scientific Revolutions*, literary critics began to discuss the question of "paradigm change" in literary studies. In his 1969 essay "Paradigmawechsel in der Literaturwissenschaft," Hans Robert Jauss outlined three major paradigms of literary studies in the West: the classical-humanist, the historical-positivistic, and the aesthetic-formalist. The aesthetic-formalist approach, as a "werkimmanente Ästhetik" (work-oriented aesthetics; 49), pays more attention to intra-literary factors than to extra-literary facts. Jauss saw it as replacing the previous historical approach. These changes in Western literary studies inevitably exerted an impact upon sinology.

Around 1974, Yu Ying-shih spoke of the need for a "paradigm change" in *Hung-lou Meng* scholarship, also borrowing the term from Kuhn's *Structure of Scientific Revolutions*. In reviewing the history, exhaustion, and pitfalls of previous critical paradigms, he called for a radical new orientation in the study of the novel. In a sweeping statement on the history of research on *Hung-lou Meng*, Yu wrote:

For the past fifty years, the nature of "Redology" has been such that its chief efforts have been devoted to research on the historical aspect of the novel. Our Redologists, being mostly historians or adherents to the historical method, have naturally focused their attention on the world of reality the novel described, so much so that the other world in the novel—the ideal world, the castle in the air, that the author "labored ten years" to create—was utterly neglected. (*"Hung-lou Meng,"* 237)

According to Yu, the fallacy of the "historical" and "autobiographical" approaches arises from their neglect of the literary aspects of the work. The *Hung-lou Meng* had been studied more as a historical and sociological document than as a work of literature.

In fact, what has for half a century been called Redology, or *Hung-lou meng* scholarship, was nothing other than Ts'ao Hsüeh-ch'in scholarship, or the study of the man Ts'ao Hsüeh-ch'in and his family history. This substitution of Ts'ao Hsüeh-ch'in scholarship for *Hung-lou Meng* scholarship necessarily involved certain sacrifices, one of the greatest of which, as I see it, is the obscuring of the line of division between the two worlds of the novel. (238)

Hung-lou Meng scholars devoted themselves to the historical aspects of the novel, such as the social and political circumstances that gave rise to the writing of the work or the family history of the author. The most misleading aspect of their approach is the reading of the novel as the author's autobiography and as a social history of the times. Their chief interest is the relationship between the author and the work.

Yu's pungent critique had implications for the entire field of Chinese literary studies at the time. Sinology in the West and traditional Chinese "literary" studies had been concerned mostly with textual scholarship—matters of editions and emendations, the search for sources and adaptations, and the identification and verification of authorship. As the modern scholar Karl K. S. Kao states the case, "It comes as no surprise that modern studies of Chinese fiction are almost always bound up with attempts at identifying sources and tracing influences. It will be no exaggeration to say that source identification lies at the very center of modern research in the field" (Kao, "Aspects of Derivation," 2). When scholars did venture beyond questions of sources and authorship, such as in mainland China where a crude Marxist theory of literature reigned, the literary work was seen as a sociological reflection of patterns of "class struggle" and the decay of the feudal society.

With great enthusiasm, Yu Ying-shih envisioned the coming of a "new paradigm" in *Hung-lou Meng* scholarship, no less than a "revolution in Redology."

The new "paradigm" strives to break away from the cage of the "autobiographical approach" in order to enter the spiritual realm and the ideal world. Therefore, it also transcends the tradition of historical scholarship in Redology. Seen from this perspective, there exists not only the division of the real world and the ideal world in the *Hung-lou Meng*, but also two different worlds in *Hung-lou Meng* scholarship. The "autobiographical approach" deals only with the world of reality or the world of history that the author lived and experienced. But the new "paradigm" will tread on this world to climb onto the world fabricated by the author or the artistic world. Therefore, the new "paradigm" has one whole more world than the "autobiographical approach." (*"Hung-lou Meng,"* 28)

In this brave new world to be won by the revolutionary new paradigm, the critic is to take account of the artistry and *literariness* of the artwork. Previous approaches erred in equating the extrinsic questions of author and history with the intrinsic concerns of literary creativity. The new approach shifts the focus from the world of history and reality to the world of art and imagination.

This position is echoed in Lucien Miller's study *Masks of Fiction in "Dream of the Red Chamber": Allegory, Mimesis, and Persona*, which was published in 1975. Miller, too, points out that the ostensively allegorical level of the novel had been largely eclipsed by historical scholarship. Many critics unduly overemphasize the realistic, mimetic dimension at the expense of the mythic, allegorical dimension. "The problem of nearly all of the interpreters of *Dream of the Red Chamber* is their tendency to seek the significance of the novel in Ming dynastic history, Ch'ing politics, Ts'ao clan documents, or a Chinese 'feudal' society, rather than in the text of the novel itself" (Miller, 15). For Miller, the meaning of the novel is to be sought not in extra-literary facts but within the textual structure that the author builds.

The publication of Andrew H. Plaks's *Archetype and Allegory in the "Dream of the Red Chamber"* in 1976 was another major step in the development of the new paradigm. Plaks's research is an integrative study of Chinese literary, cultural, and philosophical systems. It pays more attention to the "mythic" structure embedded in the novel than to the "mimetic" structure. The advantage of Plaks's approach over previous ones is its serious and comprehensive treatment of the novel as a work of literature rather than as a historical document.

Plaks's endeavor to investigate the literary aspects of the narrative was not without methodological underpinnings. His innovative study of what is considered the greatest narrative in the Chinese tradition relies heavily on then-popular Western methodology and concepts. The study speaks of recurrent literary structures: archetypes, themes, motifs, and topoi. As Plaks writes, "What we are really concerned with here in connection with the notion of archetype are patterns of more generalized structure, since it is only on this subsurface level that we can perceive a common ground within the widely varying details of religious belief, historical event, social milieu, and natural environment . . . that occur over a span of millennia" (12–13). The methodology that informs the study is a structuralist search for a pristine deep structure governing the

Chinese literary system. The reconstructed archetypal patterns are a coherent, totalized, and self-enclosed cultural infrastructure. Plaks's critical paradigm is a structuralist synchronic model aiming at textual homology and homogeneity rather than discrepancy and indeterminacy. As one critic recently commented in retrospect, perhaps with a little exaggeration, "He is more concerned with the issue of formal continuity and ideological unity than with 'disruptions' and 'discontinuities' in a text" (Wang Jing, 264).

Under the influence of New Criticism and especially archetypal criticism and structuralism, a new set of premises began to take root in the study of Chinese narrative. Critics became less interested in the interrelations of the author, the work, and history. The new assumption was that a text functions within a self-contained literary system. It can only be meaningfully understood within a universe of recurrent themes and deep structures. There exists a structural unity within each and every narrative and a relationship of homology among the narratives of a given literary system. These presuppositions about the nature of the literary text are readily apparent in the multitude of archetypal studies of Chinese narrative from the 1970's to today.[1]

The notion that a narrative text is an artistic unity carefully conceived by the author is pervasive in critical circles. As noted by Liao Chaoyang, critical interpretation of another major Chinese narrative, the *Chin P'ing Mei*, has often revolved around two tasks: "the decipherment of a conceptual unity invested with moral seriousness and human significance, and the elucidation of meaningful relations through which details are subsumed within an artistically satisfying formal coherence" (77). Their implications for literary analysis aside, these assumptions about the nature of the text can be crucial to the fate of a work in textual scholarship. The genesis of a Chinese story, especially of a vernacular story, is complex enough. The textual scholar faces such thorny problems as the existence of several variant texts, uncertain and multiple authorship, and traces of both oral storytelling and literary composition. In choosing the "best" edition out of several extant editions of a work, scholars can argue, as they usually do, that one edition is superior and must have been the "original" version created by the author because it exhibits formal unity and homogeneity of material. Obviously the idea of formal coherence can be both helpful and extremely misleading in making decisions about authorship, edition, and emendation.

As far as literary analysis is concerned, it is evident that the idea of formal unity is not without its faults. At times it restricts rather than enhances our understanding of the literary work. Liao Chaoyang has astutely identified "the crux of the matter":

A work of literature, under the accepted paradigm, has to be shown to be coherent and unified in design, evidencing an author in full control of the representation; in determining whether this is the case one may regard deviant details as indications of artistic incompetency, or one may employ procedures that would construe meaning outside the literal sense of the text, reconstituting continuity on the thematic level of understanding, where a larger context would affirm the presence of a certain true meaning informing the details.   (80)

At its worst, the criterion of formal unity is mistaken in conception and facile in actual literary analysis. The interpreter infuses a sense of wholeness into the text and explicates the details by reference to a central conceptual unity. Segments of the text that resist the coherence of the artistic design are either dismissed as technically immature or made meaningful through correlations to a higher and larger level of understanding.

In his programmatic essay "Three Readings in the *Jinpingmei cihua*," Liao advocates a deconstructive mode of reading Chinese narrative. This essay, appealing for another change in critical perspective, appeared in 1984, a decade after Yu Ying-shih's call for a "paradigm change." In the deconstructive paradigm, interpretation is a "negative hermeneutics, with principles of indeterminacy and the open text" (Liao, 81). Reading is a "process of both deconstruction of theme and voice, and reinscription of a plurality of authorial voices" (81). The text is "the intersection of complex cultural and textual determinations" (82). It is "no longer an organism, but a network" (82). For Liao and other deconstructionist critics, a taste for meaning or a desire to make sense out of the novel on the part of the reader is doomed to failure, for the novel shows the "essential non-meaning of worldliness" (99).

In giving this brief account of the history of a decade of paradigm changes, I do not mean to imply that there were no self-conscious reflections on methodology in the study of Chinese narrative before or after that period. C. T. Hsia's humanist and New Critical reading of the classical Chinese novel, for example, was an innovation in the field in the 1960's.[2] Jaroslav Průšek's research in Chinese literature was guided to a certain extent by Russian Formalism and Prague Structuralism. Neither of them, however, advertised his studies as being in the nature of a revolutionary paradigm change. As a matter of fact, every individual study either explicitly argues for or implicitly presupposes the validity and fruitfulness of its own approach. For a study to have no methodological assumptions whatsoever is an illusion.

My purpose here is, rather, to trace the emergence, the ascendancy, and finally the crisis of the "formal approach" in the field. The formal approach, borrowing concepts and terms from formalism, New Criticism, archetypal criticism, and structuralism, set out to redress the errors of traditional historical studies by examining the literariness of Chinese narrative works. Formalists pointed out that the investigation of Chinese literature should not be a historical discipline but is properly the domain of literary studies. As time passed, some of the assumptions underlying "literary" studies were questioned, for example, their reductionism, their quest for immutable forms and structures, and their notion of unity and homology.

Liao's deconstructive reading of the *Chin P'ing Mei* represents a self-critique of the excesses as well as the methodological foundations of the formal approach. What were formerly characterized as the unities of the text are now replaced by signs of indeterminacy, decentering, and displacement. In his lavish deconstructive rhetoric, narrative becomes the playground of the weaving and unweaving of meaning. In the end, however, Liao's approach to Chinese narrative seems to amount to nothing more than a mutation of the formal paradigm. He and his "formalist" predecessors alike remain silent on the issues of history and ideology in Chinese narrative.

History/Story in the Chinese Narrative Tradition

To paraphrase Yu Ying-shih, the substitution of literary scholarship for historical scholarship necessarily involves certain sacrifices, one of the greatest of which is the neglect of ideology and the divorce of literature from history. For critics like Liao Chaoyang, a text from the past reveals no definite meaning to the present, for history itself exhibits no meaningful pattern. Formalism as such has little to tell us about historical reality. However, formalism is not always incompatible with the raising of ideological and social issues. To give a good example, in his staunchly Russian-Formalist approach to traditional and modern Chinese literature, Průšek repeatedly demonstrated the significant role of form and formal innovation in creating a new vision of the world, a vision denied some traditional forms of literati writing. The prose writing of the literati "could serve only to communicate reality at second-hand, reality already expressed and formulated," and remained a "system of ready-made formulas." The language of vernacular fiction is the "living language of everyday speech, which continually adapts itself to every new reality, never remains quiescent, but is constantly undergoing change and rejuvenation." With the ever-present tendency toward deformation, exaggeration, and inventiveness in vernacular fiction, "we see traits scarcely perceptible in reality. . . . A certain shift in the angle of observation can throw new light on a relation which we had always considered perfectly natural, but which now appears grotesque, stupid or whatever" ("Reality and Art," 96–97). Průšek's classic formalist approach posits not a separation but a close bond between literary form and historical reality.

The necessity for a change, perhaps not so grand as something on the order of a revolutionary paradigm change, is certainly felt in the study of Chinese narrative. "It is high time to search for a different mode of reading Chinese narrative, whether historical or fictive" (Anthony C. Yu, 19). Our theoretical practice has become more self-reflexive and self-critical, conscious of its own crisis. To me, a new form of inquiry in the study of Chinese narrative should address issues neglected by previous approaches. The formal paradigm is basically interested in abstract, atemporal structures detached from historical, ideological, and discursive contexts. What need to be addressed now are the questions of ideology and history largely eclipsed in both traditional textual scholarship and modern formalist criticism. This view certainly does not imply a return to the kind of historical scholarship interested only in the relationship of the text to the life and thought of its author. Nor does it endorse a simplistic mimetic view that regards the literary text as a "reflection" or "mirroring" of historical reality.

One recent attempt to return to history is Andrew H. Plaks's magisterial *Four Masterworks of the Ming Novel*, published in 1987. The orientation of the new book differs markedly from his synchronic approach to the *Hung-lou Meng* in the 1970's. This time, Plaks takes history in the study of Chinese narrative seriously. He claims that the "four extraordinary works"—*ssu ta ch'i-shu* (*San-kuo chih t'ung-su yen-i, Chung-i Shui-hu chuan, Hsi-yu chi,* and *Chin P'ing Mei tz'u-hua*)—should be viewed as the products of a specific historical period (roughly corresponding to the sixteenth century by Western reckoning). The final editions of these texts are self-conscious, artistic products, "reflections of the cultural values and intellectual concerns of the sophisticated literary circles of the late Ming period" (ix). Critical interpretation of these works must begin with the historical milieu of sixteenth-century China and recognize, more specifically, that all four novels subscribe to an essentially Neo-Confucian outlook.

Having acknowledged history as the ground of narrative, Plaks takes another major step. He assumes that underlying the Chinese novel is the rhetorical figure of irony. For him, irony is crucially present in the Ming novel as well as in the European novel, which emerged slightly later. In revealing his critical stance, he admits: "My insistence on an ironic reading of these books betrays the fact that I come from the perspective of comparative literature methodology, and in particular from recent theories of the novel in Western criticism" (xi). Yet, Plaks is reluctant to engage in a discussion of Western scholarship of irony and how irony might be crucial in understanding the novel in general. He takes it for granted that irony is central in both the Chinese and the European novel.

Plaks's study seems caught in a basic dilemma that arises from a contradiction between his two main assumptions. On the one hand, he claims that the Chinese novel can be thoroughly understood only in its specific historical context; on the other hand, he assumes that the Chinese novel is, like the European novel, governed by the principle of irony. Plaks simultaneously historicizes and dehistoricizes Chinese narrative. The historicity of particular literary works is opposed to an ahistorical and transhistorical analytical concept. This self-contradictory orientation accounts for both the insights and the misprisions of his monumental study. He masterfully and with profound insight demonstrates ironic readings of the four novels. He also presents an overview of the effects on the novel of aspects of sixteenth-century Chinese thought, especially Neo-Confucianism. Yet, it remains uncertain whether the systematic irony he finds in the Chinese novel is the result of his own ingenuity or that of the sixteenth-century Neo-Confucian readers. Perhaps one indication of his analytical strategy is his treatment of the four novels in reverse chronological order. He chooses to begin his analysis of the Ming novel with the *Chin P'ing Mei*, the last of the four to appear, to highlight the ironic inversion of Neo-Confucian self-cultivation. For convenience' sake in illustrating the predominance of irony, he changes the temporal sequence of the novels, an aspect of analysis he himself emphasizes repeatedly.

The dilemma of balancing respect for the historical character of literary texts and the desire to appropriate cross-cultural and trans-historical methodologies is not a problem of Plaks's brilliant study alone but confronts all researchers. The tension between the historicity of narrative and the ahistoricity of critical paradigms seems irreconcilable at times. In the following, I briefly point to some directions that might allow us to bypass this problem.

To rehabilitate the uses of history in critical discourse, what is needed is another sense of history. In particular, the relationship between history and narrative needs to be clarified in several ways. First, the return to history is possible only if one fully understands its essentially *narrative* quality. Direct knowledge of "history" as an objective social process is denied to us. It can be comprehended only insofar as it functions as *story* or *narrative*. For me, "historicity" and "narrativity" are inextricably linked. Even someone like Fredric Jameson, who is otherwise interested in a Marxist reconstruction of History, is willing to admit that history is an "absent cause," no longer directly accessible, and largely a "narrative category." History is "fundamentally non-narrative and non-representational; what can be added, however, is the proviso that history is inaccessible to us except in textual form, or in other words, that it can be approached only by way of prior (re)textualization" (Jameson, 102, 82). Or as a "new historicist" states, one should have a "reciprocal concern with the historicity of texts and the textuality of history" (Montrose, 20). On the one hand, literary texts are necessarily embedded in their social, historical, and institutional provenance. There is no text apart from its historical context. Yet, on the other hand, one can never have any direct access to the historical past except through surviving textual traces. History can reveal itself only through narrativization and textualization.

Second, one should dispense with the notion of the totality of history, of one master narrative, or of one grand story. Rather, one should allow for the coexistence of multiple, competing, and conflicting hi/stories. This view differs fundamentally from the previous understanding of history. "The earlier historicism tends to be monological; that is, it is concerned with discovering a single political vision" (Greenblatt, 5). The new historical orientation features not History, a single gigantic totality, but histories, full of the forces of heterogeneity, fragmentation, contradiction, and difference. In his multivolume study *Time and Narrative*, Paul Ricoeur, a committed hermeneutician, dismisses the Hegelian notion of the *totality* of history but suggests the necessity of *totalization* as an "imperfect mediation." The new historical hermeneutics is "an open-ended, incomplete, imperfect mediation, namely, the network of interweaving perspectives of the expectation of the future, the reception of the past, and the experience of the present, with no *Aufhebung* into a totality where reason in history and its reality would coincide" (3: 207). Given the abolition of the totality of history, I would differ from Ricoeur by adding that "totalization" is only one, and certainly not the most important one, of several possible strategies of (re)constructing history. As I explain in the following, "decentering" or delegitimation is a more urgent task in the study of Chinese narrative.

Third, the return to history should pay special attention to the ideological and political implications inherent in hi/storytelling. Narrative discourse is invested with ideological functions. In the Chinese narrative tradition, one may postulate that histories, stories, and fictional works perform two major political functions. To borrow Jean-François Lyotard's terms, the two functional polarities of traditional Chinese narrative are "legitimation" and "delegitimation." At one extreme of the wide spectrum of Chinese narratives, official historiography is the grand master metanarrative that legitimizes itself and the political order. At the other extreme, "small stories" (*hsiao-shuo*) are suppressed, marginalized narratives that delegitimize the existing social structure and undermine official discourse. "The little narrative [*petit récit*] remains the quintessential form of imaginative invention" (Lyotard, 60). "Official dynastic histories" (*cheng-shih*), on the one hand, and what have been derogatively called "unofficial histories" (*pai-shih*, *yeh-shih*) and "supplemental histories" (*pu-shih*), on the other hand, are rival stories competing for readers and the stamp of authenticity. In each of the diverse types of Chinese histories or stories, a notion of the legal subject that can serve as the agent or agency of narrative is presupposed or implied. Historicity/narrativity as a "distinct mode of human existence is unthinkable without the presupposition of a system of law in relation to which a specifically legal subject could be constituted" (White, *Content of the Form*, 13–14). Historical/fictional representation is conceivable only in terms of its interest in law, legality, and legitimacy. Hence, the new historical orientation has a profound interest in the issue of legitimacy and the decentering of the loci of legitimacy and power in Chinese narrative discourse.

To pursue Chinese literary studies along the lines just outlined would reveal aspects of Chinese narrative discourse ignored by the previous historical and formalist approaches. The "literary" text is here seen as historically and ideologically constituted in its very fabric and texture. Upon close scrutiny, Chinese fictional narratives do appear to be historically, ideologically, and formally "overdetermined" texts. One notices in a Chinese story, to a greater or lesser extent, an incongruity between the storytelling frame and the main story, the co-presence of several languages (literary, colloquial, dialectal), the episodic construction of plot, the mingling of different religious and ideological persuasions, and marks of linguistic and literary disparity as a result of redaction, adaptation, and interpolation over various historical periods. These discrepancies within a Chinese narrative, be it a T'ang tale, a *pien-wen* text, a vernacular story, or an extended novel, are not indications of the "limitations of Chinese fiction" in comparison to Western fiction. As Eugene Eoyang notes in his study of *pien-wen* texts, they reveal the very nature of Chinese fictional discourse in a positive way.[3] The lack of internal coherence signals another kind of organizational principle, a "dialogic" principle. Despite the storytellers' obtrusive moralization, the stories themselves are replete with generic mixture, textual indeterminacy, contending ideological voices, and contradictory historical realities. The absence of stylistic rigidity and philosophical fixity is an indication of the historical, social, and literary overdetermination of the "heteroglossia" of the narrative text.

The Chinese narrative text as a historically overdetermined discourse has a specific place and performs a specific function in the hierarchy of discourses and the universe of literary genres. In Confucian society, *hsiao-shuo* or fiction has a distinct position in relation to other discourses, say, the Classics, historiography, and classical poetry. It is received, read, and evaluated by the public according to predetermined or variable sets of literary and cultural expectations. From the vantage point of narrative, Chinese historical writings and fictional writings may be seen as two different kinds of narrative discourse. To be sure, the line separating the two is difficult to draw at times. An unofficial account of events may appear to be so "true" and so morally edifying that it is assimilated to the rank of official history. Conversely, figures and events recorded in official history often become the stuff and material of fictionalized popular narratives.

Yet, it seems meaningful to posit certain differences in terms of social function, the nature of discourse, and the mode of representation between historical and fictional discourse. Historical narrative, especially "official history" (*cheng-shih*), is the valorized discourse. It tends to be a monologic, cohesive, and centripetal form of narrative. In contrast to the generic and ideological purity of historical discourse, fictional narrative can be said to be a "dialogic" discourse. In terms of mode of representation, Chinese dynastic histories strive for the illusion of naturalness, authenticity, factuality, *vraisemblance*, or simply "reality." In contrast, Chinese fiction often involves the fantastic, the irrational, and the unreal. Fiction unleashes an interminable process of genesis, dissemination, and grafting of texts, short stories, small narratives, minor discourses, and unorthodox versions of history. In regard to the social function of storytelling, official historiography is the grand Chinese narrative of legitimation, and *hsiao-shuo* serves to delegitimate the master codes of the grand stories.

It is also a timely task to look at Chinese narratives as both social institutions and discursive activities. The tension between a totalizing and stabilizing tendency and a decentering and disruptive tendency in the dynamism of the literary system appears to be constant. On the one hand we find the institutionalization, regulation, and ordering of writings and discourses, and on the other the eruption, formation, and proliferation of new writings and discourses. The institutional and discursive constraints establish generic boundaries and social functions for the varieties of writings. Certain modes of reading and writing are encouraged and others are discouraged in order to consolidate existing literary conventions and the orthodox views of things. For instance, traditional historical interpretation, or Confucian historical hermeneutics, is one very important way of controlling and regulating the reception of narrative, both historical and fictional.[4] Relations of domination and power struggles do not necessarily come from sources outside the discursive system; they may well originate in the system itself. The mechanism of textual domination operates within the system. There exists a hierarchical discursive universe in which certain types of writing, such as "official history," have priority over other types such as "miscellaneous narratives" and "miscellaneous histories" (*tsa-shu, tsa-shih*). Some narrative forms are considered more true, more real, and more credible than others.

It is equally important to observe the patterns of textual dissemination, discursive dissension, and ideological subversion in a controlled and institutionalized literary universe. One could, for example, inquire how and to what extent a Chinese short story complies with, or resists, or even delegitimizes the dominant grand historical discourse. How might Chinese fictional narrative be meaningfully construed within the horizon of aesthetic and ideological expectations of historical narrative, or how might it have to be read against that very horizon? In what way could a *hsiao-shuo* create a literary structure that appears aesthetically "unnatural" and ideologically "heretical" to the reader and thus cause a hesitation in its reception? A story that does so has already effected a slight but significant structural change in the order of narrative discourse. Accounting for the equilibrium and disequilibrium between a total and totalizing system of discursive orders and the individual acts of storytelling as decentering discursive activities seems a paramount task.

Conclusion: From the "Great Paradigm" to "Small Stories" in Literary Studies

So far I have discussed certain questions relating to the succession of critical paradigms in the study of Chinese narrative in the past two decades. In the following, I address the problem of the simultaneous existence of different and competing paradigms in literary studies. How does one respond to a multiplicity of paradigms and theories?

In *The Structure of Scientific Revolutions*, Thomas S. Kuhn elaborated two aspects of paradigm. First, Kuhn emphasizes the communal character of paradigm. "A paradigm is what the members of a scientific community share, *and*, conversely, a scientific community consists of men who share a paradigm" (176). A paradigm "stands for the entire constellation of beliefs, values, techniques, and so on shared by the members of a given community" (175). Second, a paradigm also serves as a model or exemplar for solving puzzles and problems. A new paradigm emerges in response to a crisis in scientific studies. A revolution in science occurs when a great new paradigm replaces an old one because it better explains the phenomena under investigation. Kuhn's formulation of the idea of paradigm is deliberately circular. A paradigm is what a community believes, and a community is that which shares a paradigm.

The further question is What happens when there are different interpretive communities? What should one do when incommensurable opinions co-exist? Kuhn, in attempting to solve the problem of rival paradigms and theories, suggests that people of different viewpoints be understood as "members of different language-culture communities" (205). A communication breakdown thus becomes a problem of translation. Each language community has to learn to translate the other's theory and its consequences into its own language. "Since translation, if pursued, allows the participants in a communication breakdown to experience vicariously something of the merits and defects of each other's points of view, it is a potent tool both for persuasion and for conversion. But even persuasion need not succeed, and, if it does, it need not be accompanied or followed by conversion" (202–3).

The challenge is to translate, understand, and imagine the viewpoints of others. Only then one can become aware of the insights and limitations of his or her own system of thought. In literary criticism just as in scientific investigation, the danger lies in converting/coercing different language communities to accept one single theory or paradigm. As the anthropologist Clifford Geertz states the problem, "the hallmark of modern consciousness . . . is its enormous multiplicity. For our time and forward, the image of a general orientation, perspective, *Weltanschauung*, growing out of humanistic studies (or, for that matter, out of scientific ones) and shaping the direction of culture is a chimera" (161). It seems that the task of criticism in the modern and post-modern age is to forestall the hegemony of any single great paradigm or a grand metanarrative claiming a transcultural and transhistorical significance.

Today, the issue is perhaps not the succession but the co-extension of paradigms and theories. The paradigms are languages or Wittgensteinian language games, each with its own rules. These language games are in a sense relative or "relativistic."[5] First, they can be validated or invalidated only according to their own rules. The games operate within the rules of their own discourse rather than according to some external standard. As Lyotard puts it, "the striking feature of post-modern scientific knowledge is that the discourse on the rules that validate it is (explicitly) immanent to it" (54). Second, the individual games become doubly relative once they are situated in the broad global context of multilingualism or "polyglossia," for there appears to be another frame of reference external to the rules of the games. In the cross-cultural, multilingual, and interdisciplinary scene, "we are all natives" (Geertz, 151), and all knowledge is "local knowledge."

Now, one may argue that all critical paradigms in literary studies are necessarily "small stories" and little narratives (like traditional Chinese fiction, they are *hsiao-shuo*), which sometimes pretend to possess the global significance of a grand master narrative. A theory is inescapably a "metastory," a story about a story. It has to resort to the power of narrativity for its interpretive and explanatory pretensions. Theories themselves are but accounts, histories, stories, or narratives that propose new rules and new moves for the games. The worst scenario that could happen is the formation of one monolithic, monologic PARADIGM in critical discourse. The rules, old or new, in each game have only limited, contingent, and local values. In fact, the proliferation of many languages and discourses makes one universal metalanguage impossible today.

At this point, the notion of critical paradigms overlaps with my previous description of Chinese narrative discourse. The function of paradigms and that of narrative discourse are one and the same. The dissemination of multiple and heterogeneous paradigms and language games is analogous to the spread of "fiction" (*hsiao-shuo*) in Chinese society. Paradoxically, the state of *post*-modern science, as stated by Lyotard, is not unlike the functioning of *pre*-modern Chinese narrative. Both are concerned with "such things as undecidables, the limits of precise control, conflicts characterized by incomplete information, '*fracta*', catastrophes, and pragmatic paradoxes" (Lyotard, 60). Literary theories or critical paradigms amount to "incomplete information," new versions of "unofficial histories," "supplemental histories," and "small stories." The circulation and functioning of these polymorphous and at times subversive little theories and narratives discredit the view that there is a single grand master narrative. Both a critical paradigm as a special form of storytelling and storytelling as creating a new "paradigm" or worldview are engaged in the ceaseless, circular process of generating new and alternative accounts of events and actions past, present, and future.

Given the "relativity" of the individual stories, paradigms, and theories, "translation" becomes doubly important. What we have figuratively understood as translation is the process of entering the mindset of others, grasping the positions and internal coherence of other theories and narratives, and seeing ourselves as others see us. When translation happens, the different paradigms become less relative and not wholly incommensurable, for genuine mutual understanding has just occurred.[6] Once the differences among the various theories and stories are recognized, one has come a step closer to establishing the ground for the interplay of diverse cultural forms. As Geertz so elegantly puts it, the final step toward a general consciousness amid diversity is to "construct some sort of vocabulary in which [the differences] can be publicly formulated— one in which econometricians, epigraphers, cytochemists, and iconologists can give a credible account of themselves to one another" (161).

I conclude by invoking a little story about stories by the late Ming scholar Feng Meng-lung to further illustrate my previous arguments. Feng's preface to his collection of short stories, *Ku-chin hsiao-shuo* (Stories old and new), is, in my opinion, one of the best accounts of narrative discourse of all times. He celebrates the proliferation of hi/stories at the death of the reign of History. According to him, stories (*hsiao-shuo*) have existed from the beginning of Chinese history, along with other official genres. Fictional writings are produced by non-Confucian, unorthodox philosophers, and humble streetside storytellers. Although given only marginal value by society, they have a greater power to affect and transform the readers than do such Confucian classics as the *Hsiao-ching* (Classic of filial piety) and the *Lun-yü* (Analects).

More important, the stories themselves differ from each other. For Feng Meng-lung, one cannot apply the same measure in judging the worth of all stories. It would be inappropriate to evaluate a T'ang tale by the same standard as a Sung story, and vice versa. Narratives from the Chou, the Han, the T'ang, and the Sung have their own distinctive features. In his characteristically earthy, figurative, and incisive expression, Feng compares the situation to the necessity of not wearing the same clothes for all the seasons. There is no one standard that fits all. "The pear eater has a taste for apricots" (Feng, 1).[7] For Feng, a taste for one does not preclude a taste for the other; no single story or theory will please all audiences. For us, the point is that there is not one Great Paradigm (in Chuang Tzu's vocabulary, *ta-ta*). The Great Understanding, the Way, or the Paradigm becomes accessible to us when we have truly recognized not only the relativity of each and every little narrative (*hsiao-shuo*) but also the value and worth inherent in each narrative's partial truth and local knowledge.

Notes

For complete author names, titles, and publication data for the works cited here in short form, see the Works Cited, pp. 183–96.

Introduction

1. The Western reader may be as bewildered by this real Chinese catalogue of histories as by Jose Luis Borges's imaginary story about the listing of animals in a "certain Chinese encyclopedia." This story about "a certain Chinese encyclopedia entitled *Celestial Emporium of Benevolent Knowledge*" may be found in "The Analytic Language of John Wilkins." The passage reads as follows: "Animals are divided into: (a) belonging to the Emperor, (b) embalmed, (c) tame, (d) sucking pigs, (e) sirens, (f) fabulous, (g) stray dogs, (h) included in the present classification, (i) frenzied, (j) innumerable, (k) drawn with a very fine camelhair brush, (l) *et cetera*, (m) having just broken the water pitcher, (n) that from a long way off look like flies" (Borges, 101). This fable has elicited laughter and puzzlement, as well as critical reflection among scholars. Eric S. Rabkin, for example, begins his definition of the fantastic with a consideration of Borges's passage in *The Fantastic in Literature*, 3–41. In the "Preface" to *The Order of Things*, Foucault wrote that his work first arose out of this passage in Borges. In yet another metacommentary, Zhang Longxi ("The Myth of the Other") reconsiders the theme of the other in cross-cultural studies first through a discussion of Foucault's appropriation of Borges.

2. Poetics here means, in the words of the modern critic Jonathan Culler (*Pursuit*, 37), the "semiotics of literature, which does not interpret works but tries to discover conventions which make meaning possible. Here the goal is to develop a poetics which would stand to literature as linguistics stands to language. Just as the task of linguists is not to tell us what individual sentences mean but to explain according to what rules their elements combine and contrast to produce the meanings sentences have

for speakers of a language, so the semiotician attempts to discover the nature of the codes which make literary communication possible."

3. A survey of Chinese theories of literature would be incomplete if it did not cover Chinese conceptions of various forms of narrative. Existing full-length studies of Chinese literary theories such as James J. Y. Liu's *Chinese Theories of Literature* are based mostly on Chinese theories of poetry. Chinese "narrative theory" should not be ignored but become an integral part of future discussions of Chinese literary theory.

4. For a recent study of the list of genres in a Chinese literary anthology such as the *Wen hsüan*, see Knechtges's Introduction in Xiao, 1–70. For a study of the typology of Chinese historical writings, see Pritchard, 187–219; see also Han. On the development of literary canons and literary anthologies, see Wang Yao.

5. For a representative example of such an argument, see Mair.

6. At this point, I simply note that it would be anachronistic to equate *hsiao-shuo* with "fiction." As I will try to demonstrate throughout the study, *hsiao-shuo* has more connotations than the English "fiction" can imply. *Hsiao-shuo* has been classified under the category of *tzu-pu* in bibliographic treatises since the *Sui-shu*. *Tzu-pu* is itself a nebulous term. The editors of the *Ssu-k'u*, for example, defined it as "works that advance ideas [*shuo*] are in the *tzu* category." *Shuo* can imply ideas, theories, talks, persuasions, arguments, stories, and a number of other things. See Morohashi, 3: 777.

Despite the rigidity and stability of the definition and classification of the term in official discourse, the meaning of *hsiao-shuo* undergoes change in the hands of practicing commentators and critics. Gradually the term comes to imply works that are feigned, fabricated, imagined. In historical retrospect, a work can be called a fiction only when readers treat it as an invention meant to be read as an invention and not as an attempt to deceive readers into thinking it is a description of actual events. It seems that it is only then that a reader would approach a fiction as a possible comment on its own mode of discourse and read its fictionality as part of its meaning.

Chapter 1

1. For examples of the application of Western critical standards to Chinese fiction, see Bishop, *Studies in Chinese Literature*, 237–45; and Hsia, 6 and *passim*. For a critique of this trend, see Eoyang.

2. Genre study is more an enterprise of the Renaissance and thereafter than of Greek and Roman antiquity. The ancients' classification of kinds of literature was less systematic than has been thought by many. Thomas

G. Rosenmeyer (78) asserts that literary criticism in antiquity "does not, in the end, result in a systematic genre classification, let alone the setting up of a triad." See also Russell; and Guillén, esp. chap. 4, "On the Uses of Literary Genre," 107–34.

3. In an effort to develop a comprehensive theory of discourse, Barbara Herrnstein Smith distinguishes between "natural discourse" and "fictive discourse" in *On the Margins of Discourse*. By natural discourse she means the utterances "that can be taken as someone saying something, somewhere, sometime, that is, as the verbal acts of real persons on particular occasions in response to particular sets of circumstances" (15). She emphasizes that "a natural utterance is a historical *event*: like any other event, it occupies a specific and unique point in time and space" (15). Fictive or mimetic discourse is then, as she defines it, the representation of natural discourse. Fictive works are not historical events but rather the "*representations* (simulacra, images, quasi-instances) of natural 'phenomena'" (xi). In her approach, fictive discourse is not a representation of Platonic Forms or some ultimate reality. Rather, it is a representation of a discourse, a language-context. There is, however, a lingering strain of Platonism in defining discourse as *mimesis* and *representation*. Smith's approach is characteristically Western. The idea that fictive discourse is a representation of natural discourse recalls similar statements by Plato and Augustine.

4. On the etymology of the term "history" and the idea of history in antiquity, see Press.

5. See, e.g., Cornford; K. Egan; and Boer.

6. See Spiegel.

7. See Jauss, "Chanson de geste"; and idem, "Theory of Genres and Medieval Literature," in *Aesthetic of Reception*, 76–109.

8. See Gossman.

Chapter 2

1. See Twitchett.

2. See Wang Kuo-wei, 263–74; see also Chang T'ai-yen, 212–13.

3. See Pai Shou-i, 3–7.

4. For a critical assessment of Mair's claims, see DeWoskin.

5. An indication of the persistence of certain literary presuppositions in the Chinese tradition may well be the flourishing of reportage in the People's Republic of China. Reportage, which is said to fall between fiction and journalism, presents a problem that is typically Chinese. The assumption is that the truthfulness of the reportage is grounded in historicity and factuality. Although his is never the officially authorized version of the

story, the narrator pretends that he has gathered secret information and is telling an inside story otherwise inaccessible to the populace. For a reception study of reportage in China, see Chen Xiao-mei.

6. The existence of *hsiao-shuo* as a counter-discourse to the ideology of the official literary canon is not confined to China but extends to other parts of East Asia. Compare this passage from the article "Ideology and Korean Literary History" by Peter H. Lee, a Koreanist:

Three unofficial genres in Korea (as in China) include prose fiction, random jottings, and drama. The East Asian term for fiction (*hsiao-shuo*, *shōsetsu*, or *sosŏl*) does not denote the western novel. The East Asian term was used derogatively to designate all traditional prose fiction, because it created a world other than that sanctioned by the establishment and offered alternative views of reality. The tyranny of historiography and the Confucian insistence on historicity exercised considerable influence in the development of fiction. Viewed with suspicion and contempt by the authorities, fiction was considered as outside the literary canon. Some encyclopedias may include some fictional works under various headings, but such compilations, often undertaken for political reasons to keep the literati out of trouble, were regarded as miscellaneous compendia. The literary miscellany, or random jottings (*pi-chi*, *zuihitsu*, or *chapki*) is an anti-genre that flaunts [*sic*] the prescriptive conventions of the formal prose genres, with their stilted rhetoric. It attempts to disregard the hierarchy of relative importance among the subjects but values the activity of the author's inquiring mind. The form allows the writer to view his tradition critically, question the official view of experience, and adopt an open stance that allows a wider horizon of inquiry and a hermeneutic expansion of consciousness. It includes the reportorial, biographical, autobiographical (and sometimes fictional) narrative and poetry criticism. The fact that the literary miscellany was excluded from a given writer's collected works, even in the case of a high state minister, demonstrates its relative low place in the hierarchy of prose genres.   (Yang Zhouhan and Yue, 107–8)

7. See Derrida, *Of Grammatology*, 141–64, 269–316.

8. On censorship and the banning of *hsiao-shuo*, see Wang Li-ch'i; André Lévy, 1–13; and Tai-loi Ma.

Chapter 3

1. For the differences between these two traditions and more specifically between Liu and Chang, see the extensive discussion in Hsü, esp. chap. 7, "Liu Chang shih-hsüeh chih i-t'ung" (Differences and similarities

between Liu Chih-chi's and Chang Hsüeh-ch'eng's historiography), 163–201.

2. It has been theorized that the narratives in the *Tso chuan* existed first as complete stories and were later broken up and placed under the corresponding year in the *Ch'un-ch'iu*. For a recent study and translation of the *Tso chuan* by Burton Watson, see under Tso-ch'iu Ming.

3. For this basic contradiction, namely, the "incompatibility of the principles of truthful recording and of appropriate concealment" in Chinese official historiography, see Yang Lien-sheng.

4. My analysis is limited to the narrative tradition. For a self-proclaimed application of the principles of the *Ch'un-ch'iu* to the writing of historical drama, see the "Introductory Remarks" and the first scene in K'ung Shang-jen. See also Struve.

5. On the date and authenticity of the *Tso chuan* and its relation to the Classics, see Karlgren. For the study of the *Tso chuan* as a narrative, see John C. Y. Wang, "Early Chinese Narrative"; and R. Egan.

6. For another exemplar of Confucian exegesis, especially the principles of appropriate concealment and euphemism, see the comment on the entry in the *Ku-liang chuan* (Fu, 1–4).

7. For discussions of the idea of legitimacy (*cheng-t'ung*) and related issues, see Jao; Chao Ling-yang; Chan; Bol; and Davis.

8. For informative studies of Chang's thought, see Demiéville; Nivison; and Yü Ying-shih, *Lun Tai Chen*.

9. The semiotic study of Chinese literature and thought still remains an uncharted field of investigation. For a first attempt at a Chinese theory of signs in the light of recent advances in semiotics, see Hsiao-peng Lu, "The Idea of *Hsiang*."

10. See K'ung Ying-ta, 1: 5; see also Ch'ien, 1: 8–15.

11. Roland Barthes made a similar point in "Historical Discourse":

Historical discourse presupposes a complex, twofold operation. At the first stage (speaking of course metaphorically) the referent is detached from the discourse and becomes primordial to it; this is the period of the *res gestae*, where the discourse appears as no more than *historiam rerum gestarum*; but then the very idea that history can have a meaning (*signifié*) other than referential is rejected. The referent and its expression (*signifiant*) are seen as directly related; the function of discourse is confined to the mere expression of reality; and meaning, the fundamental term of imaginary structures, becomes superfluous. *Like all discourse with pretensions to "realism," historical discourse believes it need recognize no more than two terms, referent and expression, in its semantic model. The (illusory) confusion of referent and meaning* [italics added] is of course characteristic of sui-referential discourse like the performatives; we can say that historical discourse is a fake performative, in which what claims to be the descriptive element is in fact merely the expression of the authoritarian nature of that particular speech-act. (154)

For an elaboration of Barthes's critique of historical discourse, see Gossman.

12. See Chin Sheng-t'an, "First Preface to the *Shui-hu chuan*," in Chu I- hsüan and Liu Yü-ch'en, *Shui-hu chuan*, 232–38.

13. See Chin Sheng-t'an's comments on Chapter 8 of the *Shui-hu chuan*, in Chu I-hsüan and Liu Yü-ch'en, *Shui-hu chuan*, 265–68.

14. See Chin's comments on Chapter 35 of the novel, in Chu I-hsüan and Liu Yü-ch'en, *Shui-hu chuan*, 300–301.

15. See Chin's comments on Chapter 49, in Chu I-hsüan and Liu Yü-ch'en, *Shui-hu chuan*, 318–19.

Chapter 4

1. See, e.g., Hu, 176.

2. These reflections by Liu Chih-chi echo a passage in the *Tso chuan*. In the ninth month, fourteenth year, of Duke Ch'eng, the commentary reads: "The discourse of the *Ch'un-ch'iu* is indistinct and yet manifest, purposeful and yet hidden (*hui*), indirect and yet logical, thorough and not roundabout, punishes the wicked and exhorts goodness." See Yang Po-chün, 870. For a penetrating discussion of this passage and related matters, see Ch'ien, 1: 161–66.

3. See Liu Chih-chi, *Shih-t'ung*, chüan 13, chapters "I-ku" and "Huoching," 473–520.

4. See his letter "Yü Ch'en Kuan-min kung-pu lun shih-hsüeh" (Discussing historiography with Ch'en Kuan-min), in Chang Hsüeh-ch'eng, *I-shu*, 14: 125–27.

5. For an illuminating discussion of the interweaving of history and fiction in Chinese narrative, see Anthony C. Yu.

6. For this comment by Pan Ku and comments by others on Ssu-ma Ch'ien, see Takigawa, 10: 5339–50.

7. For perceptive discussions of the ingenuities and terminologies of the commentators' methods of reading Ming novels, see Plaks, "Issues in Chinese Narrative Theory"; "Towards a Critical Theory of Chinese Narrative," in idem, *Chinese Narrative*, 309–52; *Four Masterworks*; "Where the Lines Meet"; and "Terminology and Central Concepts." For an analysis of the *Shih-chi* as a literary work, see Allen.

8. For the critique of the ideology of the aesthetic of verisimilitude (*vraisemblance*) in realistic poetics, see Barthes, *Mythologies*; *Communi-*

cations 11 (1968), a special issue devoted to "le vraisemblable"; and Culler, "Convention and Naturalization," in *Structuralist Poetics*, chap. 7, 131–60.

9. For a discussion of the methodological problems of Western historicism and modern Chinese historical studies, see Yü Ying-shih, "Shih-hsüeh."

10. See David Wang, esp. 69–70.

11. See also de Man, "Epistemology of Metaphor"; and Derrida, "White Mythology."

Chapter 5

1. On the "subservient position" of the biographies to the imperial annals, see Shih-hsiang Chen.

2. Generations of readers have admired Ssu-ma Ch'ien for his descriptions of extraordinary characters caught in inner psychological struggles in some of his biographies. However, for the same reason, others such as Pan Ku and Liu Hsieh have considered him as deviating from the norm of historical discourse. The following is a representative comment by Liu Hsieh: "His merits include his effort to create a factual record without evasion or omission, his comprehensiveness in covering his sources, his purity of style, his extensive observations, and his logical clarity; and his faults include his love for the strange, contrary to the spirit of the Classics, and the absence of order in his arrangement of certain materials" (Liu Hsieh, 171).

3. For a study of the Plutarchian influence on English biography, see Nadel, esp. chap. 1, "Biography as an Institution," 13–66.

4. In the same essay, Nienhauser brings up the notion of "pseudo-*chuan*" (see 153n2). Ch'en Yin-k'o started the controversy over Han Yü's relation to T'ang fiction in "Han Yü and the T'ang Novel." Y. W. Ma followed up on this issue in "Prose Writings of Han Yü and *Ch'uan-ch'i* Literature." For a further discussion of this story by Han Yü and the emergence of the "parodistic biography," see Franke. For a broader review of the question of the *chuan* in the T'ang and the Sung, see Nienhauser, "Structural Reading."

5. For a similar attitude in regard to the compilation of stories, see the preface to the late T'ang *Cho-i chi* (Records of the extraordinary and unusual), in Huang Lin and Han T'ung-wen, 55–56.

6. These and other English translations from Shen Chi-chi's "Jen Shih chuan" are by William H. Nienhauser, Jr., in Y. W. Ma and Joseph Lau, 339–45.

7. The Ming critic Hu Ying-lin, the first to use the term *ch'uan-ch'i* as a generic label, classified *ch'uan-ch'i* as one of six genres of *hsiao-shuo* (see

Hu, 374). The "fictional biography," the "parodistic biography," the *ch'uan-ch'i*, and the tale of "the fantastic" are not absolute categories but generic labels that approach the study of T'ang fiction from various angles. Sometimes the different narrative forms overlap and are difficult to separate clearly. For an interesting recent study of fiction focusing on the *pi-chi* (notebook), see Liu Yeh-ch'iu. The overlapping of *pi-chi* and both historical and fictional writings adds to an already complicated issue.

8. For a more detailed study of the structure of the historical biography, see Olbricht, which lists nine parts in the sequence of a biography. However, I will use the more flexible tripartite scheme in the analysis of the fictional biography.

9. See Y. W. Ma, "Fact and Fantasy."

10. For the significance of Chuang Tzu's butterfly dream for the problem of the subject in psychoanalytic perspective, see the brief discussion in Lacan, 76. For a more detailed discussion, see Touponce.

11. In "The Early Chinese Short Story: A Critical Theory in Outline," Patrick Hanan makes several heuristic distinctions in narrative methods between the "classical tale" and the "vernacular short story." He specifically points out the importance of the "relative weight" of a word or phrase, or the importance of "what is left unsaid" in the classical tale. "The art of reading a tale seems often to consist in recognizing 'what is left unsaid' or in perceiving some key word or phrase" (175). True as this might be, there are exceptions to Hanan's assertion that the rhetoric of the classical tale is implicit and self-effacing whereas that of the vernacular story is explicit and obtrusive and "deliberately calls attention to itself" (173). As will be evident in the following analysis, self-referentiality in literary presentation is sometimes quite deliberate and obtrusive in the T'ang tales.

12. Here one may see the distance between the aesthetics of T'ang tales and the classical aesthetic theory of the *Wen-hsin tiao-lung*. Liu Hsieh regards humor (*hsieh*), enigma (*yin*), and *hsiao-shuo* as low genres (*Wen-hsin tiao-lung*, chap. 15). In chap. 14, Liu discussed "miscellaneous writings" (*tsa-wen*). According to Ferenc Tokei (126–28), Liu considered "miscellaneous writings" inferior because they involve the *mixture of genres*.

13. Although differing from their approaches, my study is indebted to several previous studies of the T'ang tale. In "The Yang Lin Story Series: A Structural Analysis" and "Yang Lin ku-shih hsi-lieh te yüan-hsing chieh-kou," Han-liang Chang sets out to discover the structural unity, archetypes, and recurrent themes in Chinese literature through an examination of the relationship between T'ang tales and their antecedents. Similarly, Karl S. Y. Kao aims at the cohesive patterns of textual modeling in the Chinese literary tradition by analyzing examples of T'ang stories in his

"Aspects of Derivation in Chinese Narrative." James R. Hightower, following Ch'en Yin-k'o's "Tu 'Ying-ying chuan,'" treats the fictional biography as an autobiographical document and correlates the life of the author and the protagonist in his essay "Yüan Chen and 'The Story of Ying-ying.'" Glen Dudbridge, in his massively illuminating study *The Tale of Li Wa*, examines the fictional biography in terms of its continuity to the Confucian classics and earlier literary and historical writings. He sees the task of the philologist as shedding light on the rich patterns of allusion in the text. In my own approach, intertextuality is not a relation of continuity, cohesion, and unity. Rather, I see the text as a pastiche and ensemble of heterogeneous and contradictory elements and discourses that disembody the integrity of the represented subject in the biography.

14. The modern scholar Pien Hsiao-hsüan reads the "Nan-k'o t'ai-shou chuan" as a political allegory and locates it within its historical circumstances. For him, Li Kung-tso wrote in response to the contemporary phenomenon of the T'ang court's marriage of princesses to local warlords. The marriage between the protagonist Ch'un-yü Fen and the Princess of Golden Bough is a pointed satire of events in T'ang history. Both the *Old T'ang History* and the *New T'ang History* record as many as eight instances of marriage between princesses and warlords (Pien, 30–33). By marrying the princesses to the powerful and independent-minded warlords rather than to the sons of noble families, the emperors were able to pacify and exert some control over the country. However, the practice appeared contrary to the code of propriety and degrading to many people. For Pien, Li Kung-tso's story is a coded criticism of such an unorthodox practice and thus performs the function of admonition.

15. The English translation I originally followed was that of Elisabeth Te-chen Wang, a translation that happened to be available to me when I started my research. Later I was able to acquire several other translations. For the purpose of my present analysis, I have extensively revised her translation according to Wang Meng-ou's Chinese version (Wang Meng-ou, 201–8) and by consulting Christopher Levinson's retranslation of the story from German to English (Bauer and Franke, 93–107). Another complete English translation of the story may be found in *Dragon King's Daughter*, 44–56. An incomplete translation can be found in Edwards, 206–12.

16. The importance of the protagonist's *perception* in the *ch'uan-ch'i* is also highlighted by Han-liang Chang in his analysis of the story "Nan-yang shih-jen" ("The scholar from Nan-yang"); see "Towards a Structural Generic Theory."

17. For a discussion of the patterns of intertextual allusions of this story to earlier texts and especially to the Confucian classics and the Three

Histories (*Shih-chi, Han-shu,* and *Hou-Han-shu*), see Nienhauser, "'Nan-k'o t'ai-shou chuan.'"

Chapter 6

1. On the necessity of "disremembering history" and "dehistoriciza-tion" for the development of Chinese fiction, see Hsiao-peng Lu, "Fic-tional Discourse of *Pien-wen*"; and Martin W. Huang.

2. Although my approach differs, I have benefited greatly from earlier studies, especially the writings of Andrew Plaks; Hanan, "Language and Narrative Model," in *Chinese Vernacular Story,* 1–27; Anthony C. Yu; and Yeh Lang.

3. For an English translation of the table of contents, see Schafer; for a discussion of the problems and defects in the organization of the anthol-ogy, see Yeh Ch'ing-ping.

4. See Hightower, "*Wen Hsüan* and Genre Theory"; and Knechtges's introduction to Xiao, 1–70.

5. See Liu Hsieh, 126–35.

6. See Wei et al., 974–82.

7. See Liu Hsü et al., 1987–2016.

8. See Liu Chih-chi, 352–67.

9. Li Fang, Sung Pai, et al., 4995–5025.

10. See, e.g., Liu Chih-chi, "Miscellaneous Narratives" ("Tsa-shu") in *Shih-t'ung,* 352–67.

11. See also Kenneth DeWoskin's entry on *hsiao-shuo* in Nienhauser, *Indiana Companion,* 423–26; for the *Hsin T'ang-shu* list, see "Biblio-graphic Treatise, Part III," in Ou-yang Hsiu, Sung Ch'i, et al., 1539–43.

12. For another informative discussion of verisimilitude in narrative discourse, see Todorov, "An Introduction to Verisimilitude," in *Poetics of Prose,* 80–88. Note especially the statement: "Studying verisimilitude is equivalent to showing that discourses are not governed by a correspon-dence with their referent but by their own laws" (81).

13. For an informative general discussion of the interrelations of Wang Yang-ming's (1472–1529) brand of Neo-Confucianism—*hsin-hsüeh* (the study of the mind)—the inward, subjective turn in Ming literati, and the growing importance of *ch'ing* in Ming literary criticism, see Yüan and Liu. For a comparison with the historical process of "turning inward" in the Western narrative tradition, see Kahler.

14. The importance of the concept of *li* in fiction criticism in the Ming and Ch'ing is obviously related to Neo-Confucianism—*li-hsüeh* (the study of principles). Words like *li, shih, ch'ing,* or their compounds, become increasingly frequent and important. A parallel and perhaps related devel-

opment in poetry criticism can be seen in Yeh Hsieh's (1627–1703) *Yüan shih* (On the origins of poetry). For him, the three central things in a poem are its *li, shih, ch'ing.*

15. See Appendix, "Yeh Chou p'ing-tien *Shui-hu chuan* k'ao-cheng," in Yeh Lang, 280–302; and Appendix 2, "The Authenticity of the Li Chih Commentaries on the *Shui-hu chuan* and Other Novels Treated in This Volume," in Rolston, 356–63.

16. See Anthony C. Yu, esp. 14–19.

17. For an earlier and similar fascination with the dialectic of the real (*chen*), the illusory (*huan*), events (*shih*), and principles (*li*), see Yüan Yü-ling's (?–ca. 1674) preface to the *Hsi-yu chi*. In "*Hsi-yu chi* t'i-tz'u," he wrote: "Writing that is not illusory is not writing, and what is not extremely illusory is not illusory. Therefore we know that the most illusory events are the most real events, and the most illusory principles are the most real principles" (Tseng et al., 119).

18. These statements by Chih-yen Chai are reminiscent of Aristotle's distinction between history and poetry in the *Poetics*. According to him, history relates things that actually happened in the past, but poetry relates things that are likely to happen; history deals with particulars, but poetry, like philosophy, deals with universals. What is at stake here is the view that fiction may produce a picture of life more truthful, more real, and more authentic than that of history precisely because of its capacity for fictionality.

19. Scholars have pointed out that the importance accorded *ch'ing* in the novel shows the influence of T'ang Hsien-tsu (1550–1616). In the preface to *Mu-tan t'ing* (The peony pavilion), T'ang opposes *li* and *ch'ing* and considers the latter, not the former, as the primary force in life and the universe.

20. Chang Hsüeh-cheng regarded the historical romance *San-kuo yen-i* as confusing because it is 70 percent real events and 30 percent fictive. The novel is misleading since it is neither totally true nor totally false. See Chang Hsüeh-cheng, "Ping-ch'en cha-chi," *I-shu*, 396–97.

21. Chin's enthusiasm for the individuality of the characters is perhaps related to Li Chih's "individualistic" philosophy, his "theory of the child-like mind" (*t'ung-hsin shuo*). Chin is critical of Sung Chiang's complex and composite personality but falls in love with those heroes who display a natural, spontaneous, simple, and openhearted temperament (see John C. Y. Wang, *Chin Sheng-t'an*).

22. The commentator in the *Ch'ung-chen* (1628–45) edition—*Hsin-k'o hsiu-hsiang p'i-p'ing Chin P'ing Mei* draws attention to creation of distinct personalities in the novel. A marginal comment in Chapter 51 reads: "The restlessness of Chin-lien, the quietude of [Meng] Yü-lou, the

hatred of [Wu] Yüeh-niang, and the submissiveness of P'ing-erh are all drawn. Each has her own mind, her own mouth, and speaks her own words" (671).

23. For a recent, thorough discussion of this aspect of the traditional Chinese novel, see Plaks, "Terminology and Central Concepts."

Postscript

1. The list of structuralist and archetypal studies of Chinese narratives is long. Their methodological underpinnings can be seen in the following representative cases: Kao, "Archetypal Approach"; Adkins; Han-liang Chang, "Towards a Structural Generic Theory"; idem, "Yang Lin Story"; and Ptak.

2. Hsia's critical assumptions are fully revealed in the Introduction of his *Classic Chinese Novel*. "The modern reader of fiction is brought up on the practice and theory of Flaubert and James: he expects a consistent point of view, a unified impression of life as conceived and planned by a master intelligence, an individual style fully consonant with the author's emotional attitude toward his subject-matter. He abhors explicit didacticism, authorial digression, episodic construction that reveals no cohesion of design, and clumsiness of every kind that distracts his attention" (6).

3. John L. Bishop was responsible for the notion of the "limitations of Chinese fiction"; see his *Studies in Chinese Literature*, 237–45. For a critique of the application of Western critical standards to the evaluation of Chinese fiction, see Eoyang.

4. David Rolston's *How to Read the Chinese Novel* is noteworthy in preparing the ground for a good understanding of the conventions of reading narrative in late imperial China. It consists of translations of commentaries on the six great novels of the Ming and Ch'ing and a long critical introduction. The book is a major step toward the reception study and reader-response criticism of the Chinese novel.

5. The question of universalism versus relativism has been a particularly important topic for those involved in cross-cultural studies such as Asianists. For recent debates on the topic, see the "Forum on Universalism and Relativism in Asian Studies."

6. For accounts of attempts to overcome relativism in hermeneutics, pragmatism, neo-Marxism, communication theory, anthropology, science, and literary studies, see Bernstein; and Hoy.

7. See Eugene Eoyang's comment on this in "A Taste for Apricots."

Works Cited

Adkins, Curtis P. "The Hero in T'ang Ch'uan-ch'i Tales." In *Critical Essays on Chinese Fiction*, ed. Winston L. Y. Yang and Curtis P. Adkins. Hong Kong: Chinese University Press, 1980, 17–46.

Allen, Joseph Roe, III. "An Introductory Study of Narrative Structure in the *Shi ji*." *Chinese Literature: Essays, Articles, Reviews* 3 (1981): 31–66.

Althusser, Louis. *For Marx*. Trans. Ben Brewster. London: New Left Books, 1977.

———. *Lenin and Philosophy*. Trans. Ben Brewster. New York: Monthly Review Press, 1971.

Arii Hampei 有井範平, ed. *Hohyō Shiki hyōrin* 補標史記評林. Reprinted—5 vols. Taipei: Lan-t'ai shu-chü, 1968.

Aristotle. "The Art of Poetry [Poetics]." In *Classical Literary Criticism*. Trans. T. S. Dorsch. New York: Penguin Books, 1983.

Auerbach, Erich. *Mimesis*. Trans. Willard R. Trask. Princeton: Princeton University Press, 1953.

———. *Scenes from the Drama of European Literature*. New York: Meridian Books, 1959.

(Saint) Augustine. *On Christian Doctrine*. Trans. D. W. Robertson, Jr. Indianapolis: Bobbs-Merrill, 1958.

Bacon, Francis. *The Advancement of Learning*. Ed. G. W. Kitchen. Intro. Arthur Johnston. London: J. M. Dent, 1973.

———. *The New Organon*. In *Works of Francis Bacon*, 8: 59–350.

———. *Translation of the "De Argumentis" / Of the Dignity and Advancement of Learning*. In *Works of Francis Bacon*, 8: 385–520.

———. *Works of Francis Bacon*. 15 vols. Ed. James Spedding, Robert Leslie Ellis, and Douglas Denon Heath. Reprinted—St. Clair Shores, Mich.: Scholarly Press, 1976.

Bakhtin, M. M. *The Dialogic Imagination: Four Essays*. Ed. Michael Holquist. Trans. Caryl Emerson and Michael Holquist. Austin: University of Texas Press, 1981.

————. *Problems of Dostoyevsky's Poetics.* Trans. Caryl Emerson. Minneapolis: University of Minnesota Press, 1984.

Bakhtin, M. M., and P. N. Medvedev. *The Formal Method in Literary Scholarship: A Critical Introduction to a Sociological Poetics.* Trans. Albert J. Wehrle. Cambridge, Mass.: Harvard University Press, 1985.

Barthes, Roland. "Historical Discourse." In *Introduction to Structuralism,* ed. Michael Lane. New York: Basic Books, 1970, 145–55.

————. *Image—Music—Text.* Sel. and trans. Stephen Heath. New York: Hill & Wang, 1977.

————. *Mythologies.* Trans. Annette Lavers. New York: Hill & Wang, 1972.

Bauer, Wolfgang, and Herbert Franke, eds. *The Golden Casket: Chinese Novellas of Two Millennia.* Trans. Christopher Levenson from Bauer and Franke's German version of the original Chinese. New York: Harcourt, Brace, & World, 1964.

Beasley, W. G., and E. G. Pulleyblank, eds. *Historians of China and Japan.* London: Oxford University Press, 1961.

Bernstein, Richard. *Beyond Objectivism and Relativism: Science, Hermeneutics, and Praxis.* Philadelphia: University of Pennsylvania Press, 1983.

Bessière, Irène. *Le récit fantastique: la poétique de l'incertain.* Paris: Larousse, 1974.

Bishop, John L. *The Colloquial Short Story in China: A Study of the San-yen Collections.* Cambridge, Mass.: Harvard University Press, 1956.

————, ed. *Studies in Chinese Literature.* Cambridge, Mass.: Harvard University Press, 1965.

Boer, W. Den. "Graeco-Roman Historiography in Its Relation to Biblical and Modern Thinking." *History and Theory* 7 (1968): 60–75.

Bol, Peter K. Review of Chan Hok-lam's *Legitimation in Imperial China. Harvard Journal of Asiatic Studies* 47 (1987): 285–96.

Borges, Jorge Luis. *Other Inquisitions 1937–1952.* Trans. Ruth L. C. Simms. Austin: University of Texas Press: 1964.

Canary, Robert H., and Henry Kozicki, eds. *The Writing of History: Literary Form and Historical Understanding.* Madison: University of Wisconsin Press, 1978.

Castelvetro, Lodovico. "The Poetics of Aristotle Translated and Annotated." In *Literary Criticism: Plato to Dryden,* ed. Allan H. Gilbert. Detroit: Wayne State University Press: 1962, 304–57.

Chan, Hok-lam. *Legitimation in Imperial China.* Seattle: University of Washington Press, 1984.

Chang, Han-liang 張漢良. "Towards a Structural Generic Theory of

T'ang *Ch'uan-ch'i.*" In *Chinese-Western Comparative Literature: Theory and Strategy,* ed. John Deeney. Hong Kong: Chinese University Press, 1980, 25–49.

———. "Yang Lin ku-shih hsi-lieh te yüan-hsing chieh-kou" 楊林故事系列的原形結構. *Chung-wai wen-hsüeh* 中外文學 (*Chung-wai Literary Quarterly*) 3, no. 11 (1975): 166–79.

———. "The Yang Lin Story Series: A Structural Analysis." In *China and the West: Comparative Literature Studies,* eds. William Tay, Ying-hsiung Chou, and Heh-hsiang Yuan. Hong Kong: Chinese University Press, 1980, 195–216.

Chang Hsüeh-ch'eng 章學誠. *Chang Hsüeh-ch'eng i-shu* 章學誠遺書. Beijing: Wen-wu ch'u-pan she, 1985.

———. *Wen-shih t'ung-i* 文史通義. 1832. Reprinted—Beijing: Chung-hua shu-chü, 1961.

Chang Shih-chao 章士釗. *Liu-wen chih-yao* 柳文指要. 14 vols. Beijing: Chung-hua shu-chü, 1971.

Chang T'ai-yen 章太炎. *Chang-shih ts'ung-shu* 章氏叢書. Yangchou: Chiang-su kuang-li ku-chi k'o-yin-she, 1981.

Chao Ling-yang 趙令揚. *Kuan-yü li-tai cheng-t'ung wen-t'i chih cheng-lun* 關於歷代正統問題之爭論. Kowloon: Hsüeh-ching ch'u-pan-she, 1976.

Chao Yen-wei 趙彥衛. *Yün-lu man-ch'ao* 雲麓漫鈔. Shanghai: Ku-tien wen-hsüeh ch'u-pan-she, 1957.

Chatman, Seymour. *Story and Discourse: Narrative Structure in Fiction and Film.* Ithaca, N.Y.: Cornell University Press, 1978.

Chen, Shih-hsiang. "An Innovation in Chinese Biographical Writing." *Far Eastern Quarterly* 13 (1953–54): 49–62.

Chen, Xiaomei. "Genre, Convention and Society: A Reception Study of Chinese Reportage." *Yearbook of Comparative and General Literature* 34 (1985): 85–100.

Ch'en Yin-k'o [Tschen Yinkoh 陳寅恪]. "Han Yü and the T'ang Novel." Trans. James Ware. *Harvard Journal of Asiatic Studies* 1 (1936): 39–43.

———. "Tu 'Ying-ying chuan'" 讀鶯鶯傳. In *Yüan pai shih chien cheng kao* 元白詩箋證稿. Shanghai: Shang-hai ku-chi ch'u-pan-she, 1978, 106–16.

Ch'ien Chung-shu 錢鐘書. *Kuan-chui pien* 管錐編. 4 vols. Beijing: Chung-hua shu-chü, 1979.

Chu Hsi 朱熹, annot. *Lun-yü* 論語 in *Ssu-shu chi-chu* 四書集註. 6 vols. Ssu-pu pei-yao. Shanghai: Chung-hua shu-chü, 1927–1936.

Chu I-hsüan 朱一玄, and Liu Yü-ch'en 劉毓忱, eds. *"San-kuo yen-i" tzu-liao hui-pien* 三國演義資料匯編. Tientsin: Pai-hua wen-i ch'u-pan-she, 1983.

————. *"Shui-hu chuan" tzu-liao hui-pien* 水滸傳資料匯編. Tientsin: Pai-hua wen-i ch'u-pan-she, 1981.

Chuang Tzu. *The Complete Works of Chuang Tzu.* Trans. Burton Watson. New York: Columbia University Press, 1968.

Confucius. *Analects (Lun-yü).* Trans. and intro. D. C. Lau. New York: Penguin Books, 1984.

Cornford, F. M. *Thucydides Mythistoricus.* London: Edward Arnold, 1907.

Coward, Rosalind, and John Ellis. *Language and Materialism: Developments in Semiology and the Theory of the Subject.* Boston: Routledge & Kegan Paul, 1977.

Culler, Jonathan. *On Deconstruction.* Ithaca, N.Y.: Cornell University Press, 1982.

————. *The Pursuit of Signs: Semiotics, Literature, Deconstruction.* Ithaca, N.Y.: Cornell University Press, 1981.

————. *Structuralist Poetics.* Ithaca, N.Y.: Cornell University Press, 1975.

Davis, Richard L. "Historiography as Politics in Yang Wei-chen's 'Polemic on Legitimate Succession.'" *T'oung Pao* 69, nos. 1–3 (1983): 33–72.

de Groot, J. J. M. *The Religious System of China,* vol. 5, book 2. Reprinted—Taipei: Literature House, 1964.

de Man, Paul. "The Epistemology of Metaphor." In *On Metaphor,* ed. Sheldon Sacks. Chicago: University of Chicago Press, 1979, 11–28.

————. "The Rhetoric of Temporality." In *Interpretation: Theory and Practice,* ed. Charles S. Singleton. Baltimore: Johns Hopkins University Press, 1969, 173–209.

Demiéville, Paul. "Chang Hsüeh-ch'eng and His Historiography." In Beasley and Pulleyblank, 167–85.

Derrida, Jacques. *Of Grammatology.* Trans. Gayatri Chakravorty Spivak. Baltimore: Johns Hopkins University Press, 1976.

————. "White Mythology." *New Literary History* 6 (1974): 5–74.

Descartes, René. *Meditations on the First Philosophy.* Trans. John Veitch. In *The Rationalists.* Garden City, N.Y.: Doubleday, 1974.

DeWoskin, Kenneth J. "On Narrative Revolutions." *Chinese Literature: Essays, Articles, Reviews* 5 (1983): 29–45.

The Dragon King's Daughter: Ten Tang Dynasty Stories. Beijing: Foreign Languages Press, 1954.

Dudbridge, Glen. *The Tale of Li Wa.* London: Ithaca Press, 1983.

Edwards, E. D. *Chinese Prose Literature of the T'ang Period,* vol. 2. London: Arthur Probsthain, 1938.

Egan, Kieran. "Thucydides, Tragedian." In Canary and Kozicki, 63–92.

Egan, Ronald C. "Narrative in the *Tso chuan*." *Harvard Journal of Asiatic Studies* 37 (1977): 323–52.

Eoyang, Eugene. "A Taste for Apricots: Approaches to Chinese Fiction." In *Chinese Narrative: Critical and Theoretical Essays*, ed. Andrew H. Plaks. Princeton: Princeton University Press, 1977, 53–69.

Feng Meng-lung 馮夢龍. *Ch'ing-shih* 情史. Changsha: Yüeh-lu shu-she, 1986.

———. *Ku-chin hsiao-shuo* 古今小說. Annot. Hsü Cheng-yang 許正揚. Beijing: Jen-min wen-hsüeh ch'u-pan-she, 1958.

Fleischman, Suzanne. "On the Representation of History and Fiction in the Middle Ages." *History and Theory* 22 (1983): 278–310.

"Forum on Universalism and Relativism in Asian Studies." *Journal of Asian Studies* 50 (1991): 29–83.

Foucault, Michel. *The Archaeology of Knowledge*. Trans. A. M. Sheridan Smith. 1969. New York: Pantheon Books, 1972.

———. *The Order of Things: An Archaeology of the Human Sciences*. 1966. New York: Vintage Books, 1973.

Fowler, Alastair. *Kinds of Literature*. Cambridge, Mass.: Harvard University Press, 1982.

Franke, Herbert. "Literary Parody in Traditional Chinese Literature: Descriptive Pseudo-Biographies." *Oriens Extremus* 21 (1974): 23–31.

Frye, Northrop. *Anatomy of Criticism*. Princeton: Princeton University Press, 1957.

Fu Li-p'u 傅隸樸. *Ch'un-ch'iu san-chuan pi-i* 春秋三傳比義. 2 vols. Taipei: Shang-wu yin-shu-kuan, 1983.

Gallie, W. B. *Philosophy and the Historical Understanding*. New York: Schocken Books, 1964.

Geertz, Clifford. *Local Knowledge*. New York: Basic Books, 1983.

Genette, Gérard. *Figures of Literary Discourse*. Trans. Alan Sheridan. New York: Columbia University Press, 1982.

———. *Narrative Discourse*. Trans. Jane E. Lewin. Ithaca, N.Y.: Cornell University Press, 1980.

———. "Vraisemblance et motivation." *Communications* 11 (1968): 5–21.

Gossman, Lionel. "History and Literature: Reproduction or Signification." In Canary and Kozicki, 3–39.

Greenblatt, Stephen. *The Power of Forms in the English Renaissance*. Norman, Okla.: Pilgrim Books, 1982.

Greimas, Algirdas Julien. "The Veridiction Contract." *New Literary History* 20 (1989): 651–60.

Guillén, Claudio. *Literature as System*. Princeton: Princeton University Press, 1971.

Han Yu-shan. *Elements of Chinese Historiography*. Hollywood, Calif.: W. M. Hawley, 1955.

Hanan, Patrick. *The Chinese Vernacular Story*. Cambridge, Mass.: Harvard University Press, 1981.

————. "The Early Chinese Short Story: A Critical Theory in Outline." *Harvard Journal of Asiatic Studies* 27 (1967): 168–207.

Hartman, Charles. "*Alieniloquium*: Liu Tsung-yüan's Other Voice." *Chinese Literature: Essays, Articles, Reviews* 4 (1982): 23–73.

Hegel, G. W. F. *Reason in History*. Trans. Robert S. Hartman. Indianapolis: Bobbs-Merrill, 1953.

Hightower, J. R. "The *Wen Hsüan* and Genre Theory." *Harvard Journal of Asiatic Studies* 20 (1957): 512–33.

————. "Yüan Chen and 'The Story of Ying-ying.'" *Harvard Journal of Asiatic Studies* 33 (1973): 90–123.

Hoy, David Couzens. *The Critical Circle: Literature, History, and Philosophical Hermeneutics*. Berkeley: University of California Press, 1978.

Hsia, C. T. *The Classic Chinese Novel*. Midland ed. Bloomington: Indiana University Press, 1980.

Hsieh Chao-che 謝肇淛. *Wu tsa tsu* 五雜組. 1608. Reprinted—Taipei: Hsin-hsing shu-chü, 1971.

Hsin-k'o hsiu-hsiang p'i-p'ing Chin P'ing Mei 新刻綉像批評金瓶梅. 2 vols. Annot. Ch'i Yen 齊煙 and Ju Mei 汝梅. Hong Kong: San-lien shu-tien, 1991.

Hsü Kuan-san 許冠三. *Liu Chih-chi te shih-lu shih-hsüeh* 劉知幾的實錄史學. Hong Kong: Chung-wen ta-hsüeh ch'u-pan-she, 1983.

Hsüan-chung chi 玄中記. Pi-chi hsiao-shuo ta-kuan 筆記小說大觀, Series 19, 1. Taipei: Hsin-hsing shu-chü, 1977.

Hu Ying-lin 胡應麟. *Shao-shih shan-fang pi-ts'ung* 少室山房筆叢. Beijing: Chung-hua shu-chü, 1958.

Huang Lin 黃霖, ed. "*Chin P'ing Mei*" *tzu-liao hui-pien* 金瓶梅資料匯編. Beijing: Chung-hua shu-chü, 1987.

Huang Lin 黃霖 and Han T'ung-wen 韓同文, eds. *Chung-kuo li-tai hsiao-shuo lun-chu-hsüan* 中國歷代小說論著選, vol. 1. Nan-ch'ang: Chiang-hsi jen-min ch'u-pan-she, 1982.

Huang, Martin Weizong. "Dehistoricization and Intertextualization: The Anxiety of Precedents in the Evolution of the Traditional Chinese Novel." *Chinese Literature: Essays, Articles, Reviews* 12 (1990): 45–68.

Huang Tsung-hsi 黃宗羲, ed. *Ming-wen-hai* 明文海. Reprinted—5 vols. Beijing: Chung-hua shu-chü, 1987.

I Su 一粟, ed. *Hung-lou meng chüan* 紅樓夢卷. Beijing: Chung-hua shu-chü, 1963.

Jackson, Rosemary. *Fantasy: The Literature of Subversion*. London: Methuen, 1981.

Jameson, Fredric. *The Political Unconscious*. Ithaca, N.Y.: Cornell University Press, 1981.

Jao, Tsung-hsi 饒宗頤. *Chung-kuo shih-hsüeh shang chih cheng-t'ung lun* 中國史學上之正統論. Hong Kong: Lung-men, 1977.

Jauss, Hans Robert. "Chanson de geste et roman courtois." In *Chanson de geste und höfischer Roman*. Heidelberger Kolloquium. Heidelberg: C. Winter, 1963, 61–77.

————. "Paradigmawechsel in der Literaturwissenschaft." *Linguistische Berichte* 1, no. 3 (1969): 44–56.

————. *Towards an Aesthetic of Reception*. Trans. Timothy Bahti. Minneapolis: University of Minnesota Press, 1982.

Juan Chih-sheng 阮芝生. *Ts'ung Kung-yang hsüeh lun "Ch'un-ch'iu" te hsing-chih* 從公羊學論春秋的性質 Taipei: T'ai-wan ta-hsüeh wen-hsüeh yüan, 1969.

Kahler, Erich. *The Inward Turn of Narrative*. Princeton: Princeton University Press, 1973.

Kao, Karl K. S. "An Archetypal Approach to *Hsi-yu Chi*." *Tamkang Review* 5, no. 2 (Oct. 1974): 63–97.

————. "Aspects of Derivation in Chinese Narrative." *Chinese Literature: Essays, Articles, Reviews* 7 (1985): 1–36.

————, ed. *Classical Chinese Tales of the Supernatural and the Fantastic*. Bloomington: Indiana University Press, 1985.

Karlgren, Bernhard. *On the Authenticity and Nature of the "Tso Chuan."* Taipei: Ch'eng-wen, 1968.

Knechtges, David R. "Dream Adventure Stories in Europe and T'ang China." *Tamkang Review* 4 (1973): 101–19.

Kuhn, Thomas S. *The Structure of Scientific Revolutions*. 2d ed. enl. Chicago: University of Chicago Press, 1970.

K'ung Shang-jen 孔尚任. *T'ao-hua shan* 桃花扇. Annot. Wang Chi-ssu 王季思 and Su Huan-chung 蘇寰中. Beijing: Jen-min wen-hsüeh ch'u-pan-she, 1958.

K'ung Ying-ta 孔穎達. *Chou-i cheng-i* 周易正義. Ssu-pu pei-yao, vols. 67–70. Shanghai: Chung-hua shu-chü, 1927–36.

Lacan, Jacques. *The Four Fundamental Concepts of Psychoanalysis*. Trans. Alan Sheridan. New York: Norton, 1981.

Lai Yen-yüan 賴炎元. *Ch'un-ch'iu fan-lu chin-chu chin-i* 春秋繁露今注今譯. Taipei: Shang-wu yin-shu kuan, 1984.

Legge, James. *Ch'un Ts'ew (The Spring and Autumn Annals)*. Chinese

Classics, vol. 5. 1872. Reprinted—Hong Kong: Hong Kong University Press, 1960.

Leitch, Thomas M. *What Stories Are: Narrative Theory and Interpretation.* University Park: Pennsylvania State University Press, 1986.

Lévy, André. *Etudes sur le conte et le roman chinois.* Paris: Ecole française d'Extrême-Orient, 1971.

Li Chao 李肇. *T'ang kuo-shih pu* 唐國史補. Pai-pu ts'ung-shu chi-ch'eng, Series 46, case 12, vol. 1. Taipei: I-wen yin-shu-kuan, 1965.

Li Fang 李昉 et al., eds. *T'ai-p'ing kuang-chi* 太平廣記. Beijing: Jen-min wen-hsüeh ch'u-pan-she, 1959.

Li Fang 李昉, Sung Pai 宋白, et al. eds. *Wen-yüan ying-hua* 文苑英華. 13 vols. Taipei: Hua-lien ch'u-pan-she, 1965.

Liao, Chaoyang. "Three Readings in the *Jinpingmei cihua.*" *Chinese Literature: Essays, Articles, Reviews* 6 (1984): 77–99.

Liu Chih-chi 劉知幾. *Shih-t'ung chien-chu* 史通箋注. Ed. and annot. Chang Chen-p'ei 章振珮. Kueiyang: Kuei-chou jen-min ch'u-pan-she, 1985.

Liu Hsieh. *The Literary Mind and the Carving of Dragons (Wen-hsin tiao-lung).* Trans. and annot. Vincent Yu-chung Shih. Hong Kong: Chinese University Press, 1983.

Liu Hsü 劉昫 et al. *Chiu T'ang-shu* 舊唐書. Beijing: Chung-hua shu-chü, 1975.

Liu, James J. Y. *Chinese Theories of Literature.* Chicago: University of Chicago Press, 1975.

Liu Pao-nan 劉寶楠. *Lun-yü cheng-i* 論語正義. 6 vols. Ssu-pu pei-yao. Shanghai: Chung-hua shu-chü, 1927–36.

Liu Tsung-yüan 柳宗元. *Liu Ho-tung chi* 柳河東集. Beijing: Chung-hua shu-chü, 1961.

Liu Yeh-ch'iu 劉叶秋. *Li-tai pi-chi kai-shu* 歷代筆記概述. Beijing: Chung-hua shu-chü, 1980.

Livy. *The Early History of Rome.* Books 1–5 of *The History of Rome from Its Foundation.* Trans. Aubrey de Sélincourt. Baltimore: Penguin Books, 1960.

Locke, John. *An Essay Concerning Human Understanding.* Abridged and ed. John W. Yolton. London: Dent, 1977.

Lu, Sheldon Hsiao-peng. "The Fictional Discourse of *Pien-wen*: The Relation of Chinese Fiction to Historiography," *Chinese Literature: Essays, Articles, Reviews* 9 (1987): 49–70.

———. "The Idea of *Hsiang* in the *I Ching*: Prolegomena to Chinese Semiotics." *Chinese Comparatist* 2 (1988): 18–26.

Lu Hsün. *A Brief History of Chinese Fiction.* Trans. Hsien-yi Yang & Gladys Yang. Beijing: Foreign Languages Press, 1976.

Lyotard, Jean-François. *The Postmodern Condition: A Report on Knowledge.* Trans. Geoff Bennington and Brian Massumi. Minneapolis: University of Minnesota Press, 1984.

Ma, Tai-loi. "Novels Prohibited in the Literary Inquisition of Emperor Ch'ien-lung." In *Critical Essays on Chinese Fiction,* ed. Winston L. Y. Yang and Curtis P. Adkins. Hong Kong: Chinese University Press, 1980, 201–12.

Ma T'ung-po 馬通伯. *Han Ch'ang-li wen-chi chiao-chu* 韓昌黎文集校注. Beijing: Chung-hua shu-chü, 1957.

Ma, Y. W. "Fact and Fantasy in T'ang Tales." *Chinese Literature: Essays, Articles, Reviews* 2 (1980): 167–81.

———. "Prose Writings of Han Yü and *Ch'uan-ch'i* Literature." *Journal of Oriental Studies* 7 (1969): 195–223.

Ma, Y. W., and Joseph S. M. Lau, eds. *Traditional Chinese Stories: Themes and Variations.* New York: Columbia University Press, 1978.

Maddox, Donald. "Veridiction, Verifiction, Verifactions: Reflections on Methodology." *New Literary History* 20 (1989): 661–77.

Mair, Victor H. "The Narrative Revolution in Chinese Literature: Ontological Presuppositions." *Chinese Literature: Essays, Articles, Reviews* 5 (1983): 1–27.

McKeon, Michael. *The Origins of the English Novel, 1600–1740.* Baltimore: Johns Hopkins University Press, 1987.

Miller, Lucien. *Masks of Fiction in "Dream of the Red Chamber": Myth, Mimesis, and Persona.* Tuscon: University of Arizona Press, 1975.

Miner, Earl. "On the Genesis and Development of Literary Systems, Part I." *Critical Inquiry* 5 (1978–79): 339–53; "Part II." 553–68.

Mink, Louis O. "History and Fiction as Modes of Comprehension." In *New Directions in Literary History,* ed. Ralph Cohen. Baltimore: Johns Hopkins University Press, 1974, 107–24.

Monschein, Ylva. *Der Zauber der Fuchsfee: Enstehung und Wandel eines "Femme-fatale"-Motivs in der chinesischen Literatur.* Frankfurt a.M.: Haag & Herchen, 1987.

Montrose, Louis A. "Professing the Renaissance: The Poetics and Politics of Culture." In *The New Historicism,* ed. H. Aram Veeser. New York: Routledge, 1989, 15–36.

Morohashi Tetsuji 諸橋轍次. *Dai Kan-Wa jiten* 大漢和字典. 13 vols. Tokyo: Daishūkan, 1955.

Nadel, Ira Bruce. *Biography: Fiction, Fact and Form.* London: Macmillan, 1984.

Nai Te-weng 耐得翁. *Tu-cheng chi-sheng* 都城紀勝. In *Hsi-hu lao-jen fan-*

sheng lu san-chung 西湖老人繁勝錄三種, by Hsi-hu lao-jen 西湖老人 et al. Taipei: Wen-hai ch'u-pan-she, 1981, 61–94.

Nienhauser, William H., Jr. [Ni Hao-shih 倪豪士]. "An Allegorical Reading of Han Yü's 'Mao-Ying Chuan' (Biography of Fur Point)." *Oriens Extremus* 23 (1976): 153–74.

———. "'Nan-k'o t'ai-shou chuan' te yü-yen, yung-tien, ho wai-yen i-i" 南柯太守傳的寓言, 用典, 和外延意義. *Chung-wai wen-hsüeh* 中外文學 (*Chung-wai Literary Quarterly*) 17, no. 6 (1988): 54–79.

———. "A Structural Reading of the *Chuan* in the *Wen-yüan ying-hua*." *Journal of Asian Studies* 36 (1977): 443–56.

———, comp. & ed. *Indiana Companion to Traditional Chinese Literature*. Bloomington: Indiana University Press, 1986.

Nivison, David S. *The Life and Thought of Chang Hsüeh-ch'eng (1738–1801)*. Stanford: Stanford University Press, 1966.

Olbricht, Peter. "Die Biographie in China." *Saeculum* 8 (1957): 224–35.

Ouyang Hsiu 歐陽修, Sung Ch'i 宋祁, et al. *Hsin T'ang-shu* 新唐書. Beijing: Chung-hua shu-chü, 1975.

Pai Chü-i 白居易. *Pai Chü-i chi* 白居易集, vol. 1. Annot. Ku Hsüeh-chieh 顧學頡. Beijing: Chung-hua shu-chü, 1979.

Pai Shou-i 白壽彝. *Chung-kuo shih-hsüeh shih* 中國史學史. Shanghai: Shang-hai jen-min ch'u-pan-she, 1986.

Pan Ku 班固. *Han shu* 漢書. 12 vols. Beijing: Chung-hua shu-chü, 1962.

Pien Hsiao-hsüan 卞孝萱. *T'ang-tai wen-shih lun-ts'ung* 唐代文史論叢. Taiyuan: Shan-hsi jen-min ch'u-pan-she, 1986.

Plaks, Andrew H. "Allegory in *Hsi-yu chi* and *Hung-lou meng*." In Plaks, *Chinese Narrative*, 163–202.

———. *Archetype and Allegory in the "Dream of the Red Chamber."* Princeton: Princeton University Press, 1976.

———. *The Four Masterworks of the Ming Novel*. Princeton: Princeton University Press, 1987.

———. "Issues in Chinese Narrative Theory in the Perspective of the Western Tradition." *PTL* 2 (1977): 339–66.

———. "Terminology and Central Concepts." In Rolston, 75–123.

———. "Where the Lines Meet: Parallelism in Chinese and Western Literatures." *Chinese Literature: Essays, Articles, Reviews* 10 (1988): 43–60.

———, ed. *Chinese Narrative: Critical and Theoretical Essays*. Princeton: Princeton University Press, 1977.

Plato. *Republic*. In *Dialogues of Plato*. 4 vols. Trans. B. Jowett. 4th ed. London: Oxford University Press, 1953, 2: 1–499.

———. *Sophist*. In *Dialogues of Plato* (see previous entry), 3: 321–428.

Press, Gerald A. "History and the Development of the Idea of History in Antiquity." *History and Theory* 16 (1977): 280–96.

Pritchard, Earl H. "Traditional Chinese Historiography and Local Histories." In *The Uses of History*, ed. Hayden White. Detroit: Wayne State University Press, 1968, 187–219.

Průšek, Jaroslav. "History and Epics in China and in the West." In *Chinese History and Literature*. Dordrecht, Holland: D. Reidel, 1970, 17–34.

———. "Reality and Art in Chinese Literature." In *The Lyrical and the Epic*, ed. Leo Ou-fan Lee. Bloomington: Indiana University Press, 1980, 86–101.

Ptak, Roderich. "*Hsi-yang chi*: An Interpretation and Some Comparisons with *Hsi-yu chi*." *Chinese Literature: Essays, Articles, Reviews* 7 (1985): 117–41.

Rabkin, Eric S. *The Fantastic in Literature*. Princeton: Princeton University Press, 1976.

Ricoeur, Paul. *Time and Narrative*. 3 vols. Trans. Kathleen McLaughlin Blamey and David Pellauer. Chicago: University of Chicago Press, 1984–88.

Rolston, David, ed. *How to Read the Chinese Novel*. Princeton: Princeton University Press, 1990.

Rosenmeyer, Thomas G. "Ancient Literary Genres: A Mirage?" *Yearbook of Comparative and General Literature* 34 (1985): 74–84.

Russ, Joanna. "Speculations: The Subjunctivity of Science Fiction." *Extrapolation* 15 (1973): 51–59.

Russell, D. A. *Criticism in Antiquity*. London: Duckworth, 1981.

Sargent, Stuart H., trans. "Liu Chih-chi. *Understanding History*: 'The Narration of Events.'" In *The Translation of Things Past*, ed. George Kao. Hong Kong: Chinese University of Hong Kong Press, 1982, 27–33.

Schafer, Edward H. "The Table of Contents of the *T'ai-p'ing kuang-chi*." *Chinese Literature: Essays, Articles, Reviews* 2 (1980): 258–63.

Scholes, Robert, and Robert Kellogg. *The Nature of Narrative*. London: Oxford University Press, 1966.

Shui-hu chuan hui-p'ing pen 水滸傳會評本. 2 vols. Ed. and annot. Ch'en Hsi-chung 陳曦鍾, Hou Chung-i 侯忠義, and Lu Yü-ch'uan 魯玉川. Beijing: Pei-ching ta-hsüeh ch'u-pan-she, 1987.

Smith, Barbara Herrnstein. *On the Margins of Discourse: The Relation of Literature to Language*. Chicago: University of Chicago Press, 1978.

Spiegel, Gabrielle M. "Political Utility in Medieval Historiography: A Sketch." *History and Theory* 14 (1975): 314–25.

Struve, Lynn A. "History and the Peach Blossom Fan." *Chinese Literature: Essays, Articles, Reviews* 2 (1980): 55–72.

Takigawa Kametarō 瀧川龜太郎. *Shiki kaichū kōshō* 史記會注考證. 10 vols. Reprinted—Beijing: Wen-hsüeh ku-chi k'an-hsing-she, 1955.

Thucydides. *History of the Peloponnesian War.* Trans. Rex Warner. Intro. and notes M. I. Finley. New York: Penguin Books, 1982.

Todorov, Tzvetan. *The Fantastic: A Structural Approach to a Literary Genre.* Trans. Richard Howard. Cleveland: Press of Case Western Reserve University, 1973.

———. *The Poetics of Prose.* Trans. Richard Howard. Ithaca, N.Y.: Cornell University Press, 1977.

Tokei, Ferenc. *Genre Theory in China in the 3rd–6th Centuries: Liu Hsieh's Theory on Poetic Genres.* Budapest: Akadémiai Kiadó, 1971.

Touponce, William F. "The Way of the Subject: Jacques Lacan's Use of Chuang Tzu's Butterfly Dream." *Tamkang Review* 11 (1981): 249–65.

Ts'ao Hsüeh-ch'in [Cao Xueqin] 曹雪芹. *Ch'ien-lung chia-hsü Chih-yen chai ch'ung-p'ing Shih-t'ou chi* 乾隆甲戌脂硯齋重評石頭記. 2 vols. Taipei: Hu Shih & Shang-wu yin-shu kuan, 1961.

———. *The Story of the Stone,* vol. 1. Trans. David Hawkes. Bloomington: Indiana University Press, 1979.

Tseng Tsu-yin 曾祖蔭, Huang Ch'ing-ch'üan 黃清泉, Chou Wei-min 周偉民, Wang Hsien-p'ei 王先霈, eds. & annots. *Chung-kuo li-tai hsiao-shuo hsü-pa hsüan-chu* 中國歷代小說序跋選注. Hupei: Ch'ang-chiang wen-i ch'u-pan-she, 1982.

Tso-ch'iu Ming. *The Tso Chuan: Selections from China's Oldest Narrative History.* Trans. Burton Watson. New York: Columbia University Press, 1989.

Tuan Yü-ts'ai 段玉裁. *Shuo-wen chieh-tzu chu* 說文解字注. Taipei: I-wen yin-shu-kuan, 1965.

Twitchett, Denis. *The Writing of Official History Under the T'ang.* Cambridge, Eng.: Cambridge University Press, 1992.

Unger, Rudolf. "The Problem of Historical Objectivity: A Sketch of Its Development to the Time of Hegel [1923]." *History and Theory* 11 (1971): 60–86.

Wang, David Der-wei. "Fictional History / Historical Fiction." *Studies in Language and Literature* 1 (1985): 64–76.

Wang, Elizabeth Te-chen, trans. *Ladies of the Tang.* Taipei: Heritage Press, 1961.

Wang Fu-chih 王夫之. *Chou-i wai-chuan* 周易外傳. Beijing: Chung-hua shu-chü, 1977.

Wang Jing. "The Poetics of Chinese Narrative: An Analysis of Andrew

Plaks' *Archetype and Allegory in the 'Dream of the Red Chamber.'*" *Comparative Literature Studies* 26 (1989): 252–70.

Wang, John Ching-yu. *Chin Sheng-t'an.* New York: Twayne, 1972.

——. "Early Chinese Narrative: The *Tso-chuan* as Example." In Plaks, *Chinese Narrative*, 3–20.

Wang Kuo-wei 王國維. *Kuan-t'ang chi-lin* 觀堂集林. 4 vols. Beijing: Chung-hua shu-chü, 1959.

Wang Li-ch'i 王利器. *Yüan Ming Ch'ing san-tai chin-hui hsiao-shuo hsi-ch'ü shih-liao* 元明清三代禁燬小說戲曲史料. Shanghai: Ku-chi ch'u-pan-she, 1981.

Wang Meng-ou 王夢鷗. *T'ang-jen hsiao-shuo yen-chiu erh-chi* 唐人小說研究二集. Taipei: I-wen yin-shu-kuan, 1973.

Wang Pi-chiang 汪辟疆, ed. *T'ang-jen hsiao-shuo* 唐人小說. Hong Kong: Chung-hua shu-chü, 1973.

Wang Yao 王瑤. "Wen-t'i pien-hsi yü tsung-chi te ch'eng-li" 文體辨析與總集的成立. In *Chung-ku wen-hsüeh ssu-hsiang* 中古文學思想. Hong Kong: Chung-liu ch'u-pan-she, 1957, 124–52.

Watson, Burton. *Ssu-ma Ch'ien: Grand Historian of China.* New York: Columbia University Press, 1958.

Wei Cheng 魏徵 et al. "Ching-chi chih" 經籍志. In *Sui shu* 隨書. 6 vols. Beijing: Chung-hua shu-chü, 1973. 4: 903–1104.

Wellek, René, and Austin Warren. *Theory of Literature.* 3rd ed. New York: Harcourt, Brace & World, 1962.

White, Hayden. *The Content of the Form: Narrative Discourse and Historical Representation.* Baltimore: Johns Hopkins University Press, 1987.

——. *Metahistory.* Baltimore: Johns Hopkins University Press, 1973.

Wright, Arthur F., and Dennis Twitchett, eds. *Confucian Personalities.* Stanford: Stanford University Press, 1962.

Xiao Tong. *Wen xuan, or, Selections of Refined Literature,* vol. 1. Trans., annot., and intro. David R. Knechtges. Princeton: Princeton University Press, 1982.

Yang Lien-sheng. "The Organization of Chinese Official Historiography: Principles and Methods of the Standard Histories from the T'ang Through the Ming Dynasty." In Beasley and Pulleyblank, 44–59.

Yang Liu-ch'iao 楊柳橋. *Hsün-tzu ku-i* 荀子詁譯. Chi-nan, Shantung: Ch'i-lu shu-she, 1985.

Yang Po-chün 楊伯峻. *Ch'un-ch'iu Tso-chuan chu* 春秋左傳注. 4 vols. Beijing: Chung-hua shu-chü, 1981.

Yang Zhouhan and Yue Daiyun, eds. *Literatures, Histories, and Literary Histories: The Proceedings of the 2nd Sino-U.S. Comparative Literature Symposium.* Shenyang: Liaoning University Press, 1989.

Yeh Ch'ing-ping 葉慶炳. "Yu kuan *T'ai-p'ing kuang-chi* te chi-ko wen-t'i" 有關太平廣記的幾個問題. *Hsien-tai wen-hsüeh* 現代文學 44 (1971): 109–34.

Yeh Lang 葉朗. *Chung-kuo hsiao-shuo mei-hsüeh* 中國小說美學. Beijing: Bei-jing ta-hsüeh ch'u-pan-she, 1982.

Yu, Anthony C. "History, Fiction and the Reading of Chinese Narrative." *Chinese Literature: Essays, Articles, Reviews* 10 (1988): 1–19.

Yü Chia-hsi 余嘉錫. *Yü Chia-hsi lun-hsüeh tsa-chu* 余嘉錫論學雜著. 2 vols. Beijing: Chung-hua shu-chü, 1963.

Yu, Pauline. *The Reading of Imagery in the Chinese Poetic Tradition.* Princeton: Princeton University Press, 1987.

Yü P'ing-po 俞平伯. *Chih-yen chai Hung-lou meng chi-p'ing* 脂硯齋紅樓夢輯評. Shanghai: Shang-hai wen-i lien-ho ch'u-pan-she, 1955.

Yü [Yu] Ying-shih 余英時. *"Hung-lou meng" te liang-ko shih-chieh* 紅樓夢的兩個世界. Taipei: Liang-ching, 1978.

———. *Lun Tai Chen yü Chang Hsüeh-ch'eng* 論戴震與章學誠. Hong Kong: Lung-men, 1976.

———. "Shih-hsüeh, shih-chia yü shih-tai" 史學史家與時代. *Yu-shih yüeh-k'an* 幼獅月刊 (*Youth Monthly*) 39, no. 5 (1974): 2–11.

Yüan Chen-yü 袁震宇 and Liu Ming-chin 劉明今. *Ming-tai wen-hsüeh p'i-p'ing shih* 明代文學批評史. Shanghai: Ku-chi ch'u-pan-she, 1991.

Zhang Longxi. "The Myth of the Other: China in the Eyes of the West." *Critical Inquiry* 15 (1988): 108–31.

Character List

Ai (Duke of Lu) 哀

Chang Chi 張籍
Chang Chu-p'o 張竹坡
chang-fa 章法
Chang Hsüeh-ch'eng 章學誠
Chang Shang-te 張尚德
Chang Shih-chao 章士釗
Chang sheng 張生
Ch'ang-an 長安
ch'ang-ch'ing 常情
"Ch'ang-hen ko" 長恨歌
"Ch'ang-hen ko chuan" 長恨歌傳
Chao Ling-chih 趙令畤
Chao Yen-wei 趙彥衛
chapki 雜記
che 者
chen 真
chen-ch'ing 真情
"Chen-chung chi" 枕中記
chen-kuei 箴規
Chen-yüan (T'ang reign period)
　貞元
Ch'en Chen-sun 陳振孫
Ch'en Ching-chi 陳經濟
Ch'en Han 陳翰
Ch'en Hung 陳鴻
Ch'en Yin-k'o 陳寅恪
cheng 正
Cheng (character's name) 鄭
Cheng Ch'iao 鄭樵

cheng-fan fa 正犯法
"Cheng-ming" 正名
cheng-shih 正史
cheng-t'ung 正統
cheng-yüeh 正月
ch'eng 成
chi (belles lettres, collection) 集
chi (record) 記
chi-chuan 記傳
ch'i (begin) 起
ch'i (vessel) 器
ch'i-chü chu 起居註
Ch'i Liao-sheng 戚蓼生
ch'i-shih 奇事
chia (school, doctrine) 家
chia (unreal) 假
chia-hsiang 假象
chia-hsü 甲戌
Chia I 賈誼
Chia Pao-yü 賈寶玉
chia-shih 家史
"Chia-shu" 家書
chiang-shih 講史
Chiang Ta-ch'i 蔣大器
Chiao T'ing 焦挺
chieh-shih ming-i 借事明義
Chien-chung (T'ang reign period)
　建中
chien-hsiung 奸雄
chien-kuo 僭國
chih (knowledge) 知

chih (particle) 之
chih (treatise, record) 志
chih (wisdom) 智
chih-kuai 志怪
chih-kuan p'ien 職官篇
chih-li 至理
chih-pi 直筆
chih-t'ung 治統
Chih-yen Chai 脂硯齋
Chin 晉
Chin chi 晉記
Chin P'ing Mei 金瓶梅
"*Chin P'ing Mei* tu-fa" 金瓶梅
讀法
Chin P'ing Mei tz'u-hua 金瓶梅
詞話
Chin Sheng-t'an 金聖歎
Ch'in 秦
ch'in-che 親者
"Ch'in-meng lu" 秦夢錄
Ch'in Shih Huang-ti 秦始皇帝
ching 經
"Ching-chi chih" 經籍志
ching-hsüeh 經學
Ching-shih t'ung-yen 警世通言
Ch'ing (dynasty) 清
ch'ing (emotion) 情
ch'ing-chiao 情教
ch'ing-li 情理
Ch'ing-shih 情史
Ch'ing-shih kao 清史稿
Ch'ing-shih lei-lüeh 情史類略
ch'ing-shih shih 情史氏
chiu-shih p'ien 舊事篇
Chiu T'ang-shu 舊唐書
Cho-i chi 卓異記
Chou 周
Chou-li 周禮
Chu-chia chuang 祝家莊
Chu Fang 朱放
Chu Hsi 朱熹
Chu-ko Liang 諸葛亮
chu-tzu lüeh 諸子略

ch'ü-pi 曲筆
Ch'ü yüan 屈原
chuan (biography) 傳
chuan (transfer, change) 轉
chüan 卷
ch'uan (perpetuate) 傳
ch'uan-ch'i 傳奇
ch'uan-shen 傳神
Chuang Chou 莊周
Chuang Tzu 莊子
chün-shu 郡書
chün-tzu 君子
Ch'un-ch'iu (annals) 春秋
Ch'un-ch'iu (period) 春秋
Ch'un-mei 春梅
Ch'un-yü Fen 淳于芬
Chung Hsing 鍾惺
Chung-i Shui-hu chuan 忠義水滸傳
Chung-kuo hsiao-shuo mei-hsüeh
中國小說美學
ch'ung-chen 崇禎

fa 法
fang-fu 仿佛
fen 憤
feng-chih 風致
Feng Meng-lung 馮夢龍
feng-yü shih 諷諭詩
fu 賦

Han 漢
Han Hsin 韓信
Han-shu 漢書
Han-tan chi 邯鄲記
Han T'ung-wen 韓同文
Han Yü 韓愈
ho 合
Ho-chien 河間
"Ho-chien chuan" 河間傳
ho-chuan 合傳
ho-sheng 合生
Hou-Han-shu 后漢書
Hsi-men Ch'ing 西門慶

Hsi-yang chi 西洋記
Hsi-yu chi 西游記
"Hsi-yu chi t'i-tz'u" 西游記題詞
Hsia-shu 夏書
hsiang 象
Hsiang (Duke of Lu) 襄
"Hsiang-chung yüan-tz'u" 湘中
　怨辭
Hsiang Yü 項羽
hsiao-chia chen-shuo 小家珍說
Hsiao-ching 孝經
hsiao-hsiang 肖像
Hsiao-ko 考哥
hsiao-lu 小錄
hsiao-shih 小史
hsiao-shuo 小說
hsiao-tao 小道
Hsiao T'ung (Xiao Tong) 肖統
hsiao-tzu t'i-ti 孝子悌弟
hsiao-wu 肖物
hsieh 諧
Hsieh Chao-che 謝肇淛
Hsieh Hsi-ta 謝希大
Hsieh Hsiao-o 謝小娥
"Hsieh Hsiao-o chuan" 謝小娥傳
Hsieh-tzu 楔子
hsien 顯
hsien-che 賢者
Hsin-ch'ang li 新昌里
hsin-hsüeh 心學
hsin-shih 信史
Hsin T'ang-shu 新唐書
hsing 興
hsing-chuang 行狀
hsing-erh hsia 形而下
hsing-erh shang 形而上
hsing-fa p'ien 刑法篇
hsing-ko 性格
hsü 虛
Hsü Hsüan-kuai lu 續玄怪錄
Hsü Huang-liang 續黃粱
hsü-shih 敘事
hsü-shu 敘述

Hsüan-chung chi 玄中記
Hsüan-ho i-shih 宣和遺事
Hsüan-tsung (T'ang emperor) 玄宗
Hsün Hsü 荀勖
Hsün Tzu 荀子
hu (fox) 狐
hu (particle) 乎
Hu-yen Cho 虎延灼
Hu Ying-lin 胡應麟
hua 畫
hua-kung (artifice) 畫工
hua-kung (natural craftsmanship)
　化工
hua-pen 話本
hua-shen 化身
Huan (Duke of Ch'i) 桓
Huan (Duke of Lu) 桓
huan (illusory) 幻
Huang-fu Mei 皇甫枚
Huang-liang meng 黃粱夢
Huang Lin 黃霖
hui (euphemism) 諱
hui (hidden) 晦
hui (paint, draw) 繪
Hung-lou Meng 紅樓夢
Hung Mai 洪邁
huo-ching 惑經

i (meaning, significance) 意
i (principle, meaning) 義
I ching 易經
i-chu p'ien 儀註篇
i-jen 異人
i-ku 疑古
"I-meng lu" 異夢錄
i-shih 逸事
i-tuan 異端
I-wen chi 異聞集
"I-wen chih" 藝文志
i-wen yün-shih 以文運事

jen (human being) 人
Jen (surname) 任

jen (virtue) 仁
jen-ch'en 人臣
jen-ch'ing 人情
Jen Fan 任繁
jen-hsin ying-kou chih hsiang
    人心營構之象
Jen Shih 任氏
"Jen Shih chuan" 任氏傳
"Jen-wu" 人物
*Jinpingmei cihua (Chin P'ing Mei
    tz'u-hua)* 金瓶梅詞話
jo 若
ju-hua 如畫
Ju-i 如意
Jüan 阮
Jüan Chih-sheng 阮芝生
jun 閏
jun-yüeh 閏月
jun-yün 閏運
Jung-yü t'ang 容與堂

kan-pang 桿棒
Kan Pao 幹寶
Kao Chiu 高俅
k'ao-cheng 考證
keng-ch'en 庚辰
ko-wu 格物
Ku-chin hsiao-shuo 古今小說
"Ku-ching chi" 古鏡記
"Ku-chung hu" 古塚狐
Ku-liang chuan 穀梁傳
ku-shih 古史
ku-wen 古文
kuan-chien ch'u 關鍵處
Kuan Yü 關羽
K'uang 曠
k'uang 況
kuei-shen 鬼神
k'un-ch'ung 昆蟲
kung-an 公案
Kung-yang chuan 公羊傳
K'ung Shang-jen 孔尚任
k'ung-yen 空言

K'ung Ying-ta 孔穎達

Le-yu yüan 樂游園
lei 誄
lei-shu 類書
Li (Book of rites) 禮
li (principle) 理
Li Chao 李肇
Li-chi 禮記
Li Chiao-erh 李嬌兒
Li Chih 李贄
*Li Chih p'ing chung-i Shui-hu
    ch'üan-chuan* 李贄評忠義水滸
    全傳
Li Cho-wu 李卓吾
*Li Cho-wu hsien-sheng p'i-p'ing
    chung-i Shui-hu chuan* 李卓吾
    先生批評忠義水滸傳
Li Fu-yen 李復言
li-hsüeh 理學
Li Kuang 李廣
Li Kuei-chieh 李桂姐
Li K'uei 李逵
Li Kung-tso 李公佐
Li Mei 李枚
Li P'ing-erh 李瓶兒
Li Sao 離騷
"Li Wa chuan" 李娃傳
Liang-shan 梁山
Liang-shan Po 梁山泊
Liao-chai chih-i 聊齋志異
lieh-chuan 列傳
lieh-nü chuan 列女傳
Lin (surname) 林
ling-kuai 靈怪
Ling Meng-ch'u 凌夢初
"Liu Chang shih-hsüeh chih
    i-t'ung" 劉章史學之異同
Liu Ch'en-weng 劉辰翁
"Liu-chia" 六家
Liu Chih-chi 劉知幾
Liu Hsiang 劉向
Liu Hsieh 劉勰

Liu I-ch'ing 劉義慶
Liu Pang 劉邦
Liu Pao-nan 劉寶楠
Liu Sung (dynasty) 劉宋
Liu T'ang 劉唐
Liu Tsung-yuan 柳宗元
Liu-wen chih-yao 柳文指要
Lo Yeh 羅燁
Lu (ducal state) 魯
Lu Chih-shen 魯智深
Lu Ch'un 陸淳
Lu Chung-lien 魯仲連
Lu Huan 盧環
Lü weng 呂翁
Luan T'ing-yü 欒廷玉
Lun-yü cheng-i 論語正義
Lung-chou hui tsa-chü 龍舟會雜劇
lüeh-fan fa 略犯法

Ma Chih-yüan 馬致遠
Ma-wei (slope) 馬嵬
mao-i erh hsin-t'ung 貌異而心同
Mao K'un 茅坤
Mao Tsung-kang 毛宗崗
mao-t'ung erh hsin-i 貌同而心異
"Mao Ying chuan" 毛穎傳
Meng Ch'i 孟啓
meng-chiu cheng 夢咎徵
meng-hsiu cheng 夢休徵
Meng-liang lu 夢粱錄
meng-yu 夢遊
Meng Yü-lou 孟玉樓
mien-chen ni-tz'u fa 棉針泥刺法
Min (Duke of Lu) 閔
ming (commemorative record) 銘
Ming (dynasty) 明
mo-hsieh 摹寫
mo-hua 摹畫
"Mo-ni" 模擬
mo-shen 摹神
mu-chih 墓志
Mu-tan t'ing 牡丹亭

Nai Te-weng 耐得翁
Nan-k'o meng chi 南柯夢記
"Nan-k'o t'ai-shou chuan" 南柯太守傳
"Nan-yang shih-jen" 南陽士人
nei-shih 內史
"Ni Miao-chi" 尼妙寂
nien-hao 年號
nien-piao 年表
nü-shih 女史

Ou-yang Hsiu 歐陽修

pa-shih 霸史
Pai Chü-i 白居易
Pai Hsing-chien 白行簡
pai-kuan 稗官
pai-miao 白描
pai-shih 稗史
P'ai-an ching-ch'i 拍案驚奇
Pan Ku 班固
pan-ting ta chang-fa 板定大章法
P'an Chin-lien 潘金蓮
pei 碑
pei-mien p'u-fen fa 背面撲粉法
P'ei Chi 裴冀
pen-chi 本紀
pi 比
pi-chen 逼真
pi-chi 筆記
pi-hsiao 筆削
p'i-k'ung chuan-ch'u 劈空撰出
p'i-k'ung nieh-tsao 劈空捏造
pieh-chuan 別傳
Pien Hsiao-hsüan 卞孝萱
pien-nien 編年
pien-ting 繕訂
pien-wen 變文
p'ien-chi 偏記
"Ping-ch'en cha-chi" 丙辰劄記
P'ing-yüan chün 平原君
pu-lu p'ien 簿錄篇
pu-shih 補史

P'u Sung-ling 蒲松齡
p'u-tao 樸刀

San-kuo chih t'ung-su yen-i
　三國志通俗演義
"*San-kuo chih t'ung-su yen-i* hsu"
　三國志通俗演義序
"*San-kuo chih t'ung-su yen-i* yin"
　三國志通俗演義引
San-kuo yen-i 三國演義
"San-meng chi" 三夢記
Shen Chi-chi 瀋既濟
shen-ch'i 神氣
shen-ch'ing 神情
Shen Ch'un 申春
shen-hsien 神仙
shen-i 深意
Shen Lan 申蘭
Shen Ya-chih 瀋亞之
Shih (Book of poetry) 詩
shih (history) 史
shih (event) 事
shih (real) 實
Shih-chi 史記
shih-chia 世家
shih-chieh 石碣
Shih Chien 石建
Shih Chin 史進
shih-ch'ing 世情
"Shih-chuan" 史傳
shih-hsiang 實象
Shih Hsiu 石秀
shih-hsü 實絞
shih-hsüeh 史學
shih-hua 詩話
shih-ku 世故
Shih-kuan 史舘
shih-lu 實錄
Shih Nai-an 施耐庵
shih-pi 史筆
shih-shih (substantive deeds) 實事
"Shih-shih" ("Interpreting the
　word 'history'") 釋史

Shih-shuo hsin-yü 世說新語
Shih-t'ung 史通
shōsetsu 小說
shou (to hold a reception; to
　receive) 守
shou (to hunt) 狩
Shu (Book of documents) 書
shu (narrate) 述
Shu (state) 蜀
shu (treatise) 書
shu-erh pu-tso 述而不作
shu-jen 庶人
shui-hu 水滸
Shui-hu chuan 水滸傳
"*Shui-hu chuan* i-pai hui wen-tzu
　yu-lüeh" 水滸傳一百回文字優劣
shuo 說
shuo-hua 說話
Shuo-wen chieh-tzu 說文解字
sosŏl 小說
so-yen 瑣言
Sou-shen chi 搜神記
Ssu-k'u 四庫
ssu-ta ch'i-shu 四大奇書
Ssu-ma Ch'ien 司馬遷
Ssu-ma Kuang 司馬光
Sui-shu 隋書
Sun Ch'eng 孫成
Sun Hsüeh-o 孫雪娥
Sung (dynasty) 宋
Sung (surname) 宋
Sung Chiang 宋江
Sung Hui-lien 宋蕙蓮

ta chien-chia ch'u 大間架處
ta chü-cheng 大居正
ta i-t'ung 大一統
Ta-li (T'ang reign period) 大曆
ta-shih 大史
ta-ta 大達
T'ai-p'ing hsing-kuo (Sung reign
　period) 太平興國
T'ai-p'ing kuang-chi 太平廣記

T'ai-p'ing yü-lan 太平禦覽
t'ai-shih ling 太史令
T'ai-tsung (Sung emperor) 太宗
t'an-ching 談經
T'ang 唐
T'ang Hsien-tsu 湯顯祖
T'ang kuo-shih pu 唐國史補
tao/Tao 道
tao-t'ing erh t'u-shuo 道聽而途說
tao-t'ing t'u-shuo 道聽途說
tao-t'ung 道統
ti (brother) 弟
Ti (people) 狄
ti-chi 帝紀
Ti ju Wei 狄入魏
ti-li chih chi 地理之記
ti-li shu 地理書
t'i 悌
tieh-hsi p'ien 諜系篇
T'ien Ju-ch'eng 田汝成
T'ien-pao (T'ang reign period) 天寶
t'ien-ti tzu-jan chih hsiang 天地自然之象
tsa-chi 雜記
tsa-ch'ü hsi-wen 雜曲戲文
tsa-chuan 雜傳
tsa-lu 雜錄
tsa-shih 雜史
"Tsa-shu" 雜述
"Tsa-wen" 雜文
Ts'ai (surname) 蔡
"Ts'ai-chuan" 采撰
Ts'ai Pai-shih 蔡白石
ts'ao-she hui-hsien fa 草蛇灰綫法
Ts'ao Ts'ao 曹操
Tseng Tsao 曾慥
Tso-ch'iu Ming 左丘明
Tso chuan 左傳
ts'u-lu 粗魯
Tsui-weng t'an-lu 醉翁談錄
Ts'ui Hsü 崔需
tsun-che 尊者

ts'ung-t'an 叢談
Tu-ch'eng chi-sheng 都城紀勝
tu-chuan 獨傳
tu-fa 讀法
tu-i pu 都邑簿
"Tu *San-kuo chih* fa" 讀三國志法
"Tu ti-wu ts'ai-tzu shu fa" 讀第五才子書法
"Tu 'Ying-ying chuan'" 讀鶯鶯傳
Tuan Chü-chen 段居貞
Tun-huang 敦煌
Tung Chung-shu 董仲書
t'ung 統
t'ung-hsin shuo 童心說
tzu 子
Tzu-chih t'ung-chien 資治通鑒
Tzu-chih t'ung-chien kang-mu 資治通鑒綱目
tzu-pu 子部

wai-mao 外貌
wai-shih 外史
Wan-li 萬曆
Wang Chih-ku 王知古
Wang Chin 王進
Wang Fu-chih 王夫之
Wang Liu-erh 王六兒
Wang Meng-ou 王夢鷗
Wang Shih-chen 王世貞
Wang Tu 王渡
Wang Yang-ming 王陽明
Wei 魏
Wei Cheng 魏徵
wei-yen ta-i 微言大義
Wei Yin 韋崟
wen 文
Wen (Duke of Chin) 文
wen-chia chih fa-lü 文家之法律
Wen-hsin tiao-lung 文心雕龍
Wen-hsüan (*Wenxuan*) 文選
"Wen-shih" 文始
Wen-shih t'ung-i 文史通義

Wen-yüan ying-hua 文苑英華
wu (shaman) 巫
Wu (state) 吳
Wu Sung 武松
Wu Ta 武大
Wu tsa tsu 五雜俎
Wu Tzu-mu 吳自牧
Wu Yüeh-niang 吳月娘

yang 陽
Yang Hsiung 楊雄
Yang Kuei-fei 楊貴妃
Yang Lin 楊林
Yang Wei-chen 楊維楨
Yang Yen 楊炎
Yang Yü-huan (Yang Kuei-fei)
    楊玉環
yao-shu 妖術
yeh 也
Yeh Chou 葉晝
"Yeh Chou p'ing-tien *Shui-hu
    chuan* k'ao-cheng" 葉晝評點
    水滸傳考證
Yeh Hsieh 葉燮
Yeh Lang 葉朗
yeh-shih 野史
yen 贗
yen-fen 烟粉
Yin (Duke of Lu) 隱

yin (enigma) 隱
yin (feminine force) 陰
yin-wen sheng-shih 因文生事
yin-yüan 姻緣
Ying Po-chüeh 應伯爵
"Ying-t'ao ch'ing-i" 櫻桃青衣
"Ying-ying chuan" 鶯鶯傳
yu 有
Yu-ming lu 幽冥錄
"Yü Ch'en Kuan-min kung-pu lun
    shih-hsüeh" 與陳觀民工部論史學
Yü Chia-hsi 余嘉錫
yü-i 寓意
yü-shih 禦史
yü-yen 寓言
Yü Ying-shih 余英時
Yüan 元
Yüan Chen 元稹
"Yüan cheng-t'ung lun" 原正統論
yüan-nien, ch'un, wang cheng-
    yüeh 元年, 春, 王正月
Yüan shih 原詩
Yüan Wu-ya 袁無涯
Yüan Yü-ling 袁于令
Yüeh (Book of Music) 樂
yüeh-fu 樂府

zuihitsu 隨筆

Index

In this index an "f" after a number indicates a separate reference on the next page, and an "ff" indicates separate references on the next two pages. A continuous discussion over two or more pages is indicated by a span of page numbers, e.g., "57–59." *Passim* is used for a cluster of references in close but not consecutive sequence.

Library of Congress Cataloging-in-Publication Data

Lu, Hsiao-peng.
    From historicity to fictionality : the Chinese poetics
of narrative / Sheldon Hsiao-peng Lu.
            p.   cm.
    Includes bibliographical references and index.
    ISBN 0-8047-2319-2 (alk. paper) :
    1. China—Historiography.   2. Chinese fiction—History
and criticism.   3. Narration (Rhetoric).   I. Title.
DS734.7.L8   1994
895.13'08109—dc20   93-31744
                                                CIP

⊗ This book is printed on acid-free paper